Oracy Matters

Edited by

MARGARET MACLURE,
TERRY PHILLIPS *and*
ANDREW WILKINSON

ORACY MATTERS

Open University Press

English, Language, and Education series

General Editor: Anthony Adams

Lecturer in Education, University of Cambridge

This series is concerned with all aspects of language in education from the primary school to the tertiary sector. Its authors are experienced educators who examine both principles and practice of English subject teaching and language across the curriculum in the context of current educational and societal developments.

TITLES IN THE SERIES

Computers and Literacy
Daniel Chandler and Stephen Marcus (eds.)

Children Talk About Books: Seeing Themselves as Readers
Donald Fry

The English Department in a Changing World
Richard Knott

Teaching Literature for Examinations
Robert Protherough

Developing Response to Fiction
Robert Protherough

Microcomputers and the Language Arts
Brent Robinson

The Quality of Writing
Andrew Wilkinson

The Writing of Writing
Andrew Wilkinson (ed.)

Literary Theory and English Teaching
Peter Griffith

Forthcoming

The Primary Language Book
Peter Dougill and Richard Knott

Developing Response to Poetry
Patrick Dias and Michael Hayhoe

Lipservice: The Story of Talk in Schools
Pat Jones

English Teaching from A–Z
Wayne Sawyer, Anthony Adams and Ken Watson

In preparation

English Teaching: Programme and Policies
Anthony Adams and Esmor Jones

Collaboration and Writing
Morag Styles

ORACY MATTERS

The development of talking
and listening in education

EDITED BY
Margaret MacLure
Terry Phillips
Andrew Wilkinson

Open University Press
Milton Keynes · Philadelphia

Open University Press
Open University Educational Enterprises Limited
12 Cofferidge Close
Stony Stratford
Milton Keynes MK11 1BY

and

242 Cherry Street
Philadelphia, PA 19106, USA

First Published 1988

British Library Cataloguing in Publication Data

Oracy matters: the development of talking
    and listening in education. – (English
    language and education series).
    1. Schools. Students. Speech skills.
    Development
    I. MacLure, Margaret   II. Phillips, Terry
    III. Wilkinson, Andrew   IV. Series
    401'.9

    ISBN 0-335-15855-2

Library of Congress Cataloging-in-Publication Data

Oracy matters: the development of talking and listening in education
    / edited by Margaret MacLure, Terry Phillips, Andrew Wilkinson.
       p.   cm. – (English, language, and education)
    1. Children – Language – Congresses.   2. Oral communication –
Congresses.   3. Listening – Congresses.   4. Communication in
education – Congresses.   I. MacLure, Margaret.   II. Phillips, Terry.
III. Wilkinson, Andrew.   IV. Series: English, language, and
education series.
LB1139.L3068   1988   372.6 – dc19   88-5223

ISBN 0-335-15855-2 (pbk.)

Typeset by Rowland Phototypesetting Limited,
Bury St Edmunds, Suffolk
Printed in Great Britain at St Edmundsbury Press Limited,
Bury St Edmunds, Suffolk

Contents

List of contributors

Douglas Barnes, School of Education, University of Leeds.
Deborah Berrill, Trent University, Peterborough, Ontario.
Gen Ling Chang, Ontario Institute for Studies in Education, Toronto.
Jacqui Cousins, School of Education, University of Exeter.
John Dixon, Visiting Fellow, School of Education, University of East Anglia.
Derek Edwards, Department of Social Sciences, Loughborough University.
Roger Fowler, School of English and American Studies, University of East Anglia.
Graham Frater, Her Majesty's Inspectorate.
Elizabeth Grugeon, Bedford College of Higher Education.
David Halligan, Her Majesty's Inspectorate.
Martin Hughes, School of Education, University of Exeter.
Margaret MacLure, School of Education, University of East Anglia.
Janet Maybin, Open University.
Neil Mercer, Open University.
Stephen Parker, School of Education, University of East Anglia.
Willie van Peer, Department of Language and Literature, University of Tilburg, The Netherlands.
Terry Phillips, School of Education, University of East Anglia.
Harold Rosen, London University Institute of Education.
Gordon Wells, Ontario Institute for Studies in Education, Toronto.
Andrew Wilkinson, School of Education, University of East Anglia.

Acknowledgements

This book consists of a selection of papers from the International Oracy Convention, organised by the School of Education at the University of East Anglia, Norwich, UK, in 1987. We are grateful to the contributors for their prompt and willing co-operation with our editorial demands.

We should like to thank the Dean of the School, Professor G. Brown, and members of the academic and administrative staffs for their whole-hearted support. We wish to mention by name the Convention Secretary, Eileen Chapman, whose expertise in conference organisation was central to the success of the operation: Jim Bidwell, who served as the Convention Joint Secretary; Ivor Partridge, on reception; Lynda Williams, the School's Administrative Assistant; and Karen Bezants, reprographics. We are also grateful to members of the MA Language in Education course for indispensable social and administrative roles. They are Sandra Addington, Angela Bawden, Pamela Carter, Anne Benson, Vivien Lloyd, Geoff Robinson, Alison Tibbitt, and Philip Wright.

Finally, we wish to acknowledge the helpfulness and professional efficiency of the staff of the Open University Press.

Margaret MacLure
Terry Phillips
Andrew Wilkinson

General editor's introduction

The present is the second volume in this series to grow out of the biennial international symposia on the teaching of English organised at the University of East Anglia. (The previous volume was *The Writing of Writing*, edited by Andrew Wilkinson, 1986.) A detailed academic introduction to the contents of the book is provided by one of its editors, Margaret MacLure, as the first major essay, but it is particularly appropriate that the third editor should again be Professor Andrew Wilkinson, since he first coined the term 'oracy' in the 1960s on the analogy of literacy to stress the importance of the language skills of listening and talking. We have come a long way in curriculum thinking since that time as the present volume makes abundantly clear. It is now unthinkable that language work in schools in general, or in English departments in particular, should not pay due attention to this fundamental area of work, although as Pat Jones shows in his complementary volume, *Lip Service* (Open University Press, 1988), the reality of the classroom is often some distance behind the best of theory and expectation as demonstrated in these pages.

As, in British secondary schools, the new General Certificate of Secondary Education (GCSE) is being implemented for the first time this year, my own experience of wide-ranging school visits confirms the view that this is one of the elements of the new examination that has caused the most concern to teachers. The problem is how to capture for assessment purposes the volatile nature of talk, how to allow, within the structure of an individual examination assessment, for the dynamic nature of the talk within a group, the inter-action including listening as well as talking as an integral element. The biggest problem of all is how to engage in any kind of assessment procedure without, at the same time, destroying what is being assessed.

Yet, in spite of the difficulties, the fight that took place to establish oracy as a compulsory component of the new examination (and one that is ultimately to be extended to other subjects besides English) was a vital one. This book is far removed from being concerned with examinations as its main focus – it has much more significant matters to deal with in its pages. Yet, given the British educational system, the inclusion within an external examination structure, gives an accolade and status to the subject that carries downwards into the rest of the school curriculum, even into first schools.

The International Convention (which I was able to attend) was certainly not without its own controversies and it would be a pity if the quality of the individual articles which the editors have assembled here were to obscure the strength of some of the powerful exchanges in debate that some of the papers evoked. As Douglas Barnes's important paper makes clear oracy has a political face and it is one which we may well have to come to terms with more and more as we move into a period, in the United Kingdom, of centrally imposed curriculum. The report of the Kingman Committee on the teaching of language will probably be published at about the same time as this volume and some members of that committee were at the International Oracy Convention two years ago. It is to be hoped that the Committee was able to take on board the best of the important ideas that were aired at that time. What is quite certain is that no narrowly conceived 'skills' model of listening and talking competence will meet our needs. The future of oracy in the classroom, not just in English classes, but as a means and instrument of learning across the whole curriculum stands very much in the balance, and the present volume is an important contribution to what is likely to be a continuing debate.

The international nature of the Convention is underlined by the inclusion of several papers from Canada in the present volume and one, most interestingly, from the Netherlands. It is a pity that the limitations in attendance (because of the costs involved) and in space prevents a fuller reflection of the important work in this area also being undertaken in Australia and New Zealand where oracy is, if anything, even more firmly established in classroom practice than it is in the United Kingdom and North America.

The processes of 'active learning' to use MacLure's key phrase, and one that underlies the philosophy underpinning many of the contributors to these pages, is ultimately about more than learning processes themselves. It is also about empowerment. Through finding their own voice, in speech as much as in writing, pupils (or, rather, students) can discover how to take control over their own lives and how to inter-relate with the lives of others. Much work has been done in the last few years in the area of Personal and Social Education (some of it under threat in terms of the time that will be available for such areas of education under the 1988 Education Act); the place where much of this work has been taking place, and will have to take place in the future, is in those spaces in the school, the timetable and the curriculum, in which active learning through talk is not just encouraged but taken for granted. There are plenty of studies to show that in practice this is sound preparation for working life as well.

Yet there is still a need to persuade some teachers, and many students, parents and employers, of the central importance of this work. For those seeking arguments which cogently explore the issue from a consistent and sound theoretical perspective, the present volume will serve their needs. It makes a fine coping stone to a discussion that Andrew Wilkinson began some twenty years ago – and that is likely to be still continuing into the twenty that lie ahead.

Anthony Adams

Introduction. Oracy:
current trends in context

MARGARET MACLURE

Like many edited collections, this book had its origins in a conference – in this case the International Oracy Convention, held at the University of East Anglia during the rainy spring of 1987, and attended by more than three hundred people. Editorial practice in introducing collections such as these is often simply to state their provenance in this or that conference, and thereafter to treat the collection as a self-standing volume, avoiding further mention of the event which brought the contributors together in the first place. I would like to depart from that custom, and to start by reflecting on the context in which the International Oracy Convention was convened, since the issues raised in the chapters which follow are all, in their various ways, responses to that context.

Broadly stated, that context is the prominence which oracy has achieved on educational agendas over the past few years. In Britain, this is reflected in unprecedented activity at the level of policy-making, as Frater reports in this book. Similar developments have been taking place in other countries – for example, in the curriculum guidelines produced by various states in Australia and provinces in Canada.

For those involved in language education, these are exciting developments: they have validated the efforts of those who have been working over the past twenty years or more to assert the centrality of talk in education, and reinvigorated the search for ways of giving children a spoken 'voice' in the classroom. At the same time, though, there is a certain amount of consternation: now that oracy has apparently been given the go-ahead, what are we to do about it? Although the oracy movement has been gathering momentum for two decades, its apparently rapid acceleration over the past few years has emphasised not just how much has been gained, but how much is still to be decided and discovered: about the nature of children's spoken language development during the years of schooling; about the role that education might play in that process; about the relationship between talk and learning; and about the aims and aspirations of education for 'oracy'.

This state of affairs has left teachers in a vulnerable position. They are being enjoined in curriculum documents to shoulder new responsibilities for developing children's spoken as well as written abilities. They are being exhorted to re-examine their practice to accommodate new and negotiable forms of learning through talk. In Britain, they are coming to terms with a new examination system at sixteen-plus which requires them to carry out continuous assessment of students' oral communication, and to renegotiate the relationship between assessment and curriculum according to complex and still provisional guidelines from examining bodies. In undertaking all this they often find themselves acting, too, as unwilling brokers between the various interest groups of the ever-widening constituency to which teachers are held accountable. They may, for instance, have to confront the continuing expectations of a writing-based education, from parents, employers or governors; and they must reconcile the vision of a more open-ended education, based on talk, with a wider framework which is tending towards greater centralisation of the curriculum, clear statements of objectives, and strict accountability for definable educational 'products'.

The present climate as regards oracy could be characterised, therefore, as an exhilarating mixture of excitement and uncertainty. It seemed timely to convene a forum which would bring together as many people as possible with an educational interest in spoken language, to share ideas and work through problems and issues. This book offers only a partial reflection, of course, of the scope and diversity of the Convention itself – not only because of unavoidable restrictions on the number of contributions which could be included, but also because many of the sessions, as befits the theme of oracy, took the form of workshops at which everyone present worked collaboratively, at the invitation of the presenters, to examine language materials and explore ideas. The dynamics of sessions such as these could not easily be transformed into the single authorial 'voice' of a written presentation.

Nevertheless, the collection as a whole reflects many of the preoccupations which were voiced over the four days of the Convention, as well as a flavour of the diversity of these preoccupations. Indeed this diversity is itself a topic to be explored – as Mercer *et al.* point out in this book, it is by no means clear that there is a common project underlying the wide range of activities and initiatives that are taking place under the rubric of 'oracy'. It would, of course, be surprising to find an absolute commonality of aims, since divergent perspectives will be found even in longer-established fields of enquiry. But several of the contributors to the Convention voiced the feeling that, in the case of oracy, some of these differences had yet to be fully articulated, and that there was a need to clarify the educational implications of different perspectives.

One theme which recurs across the chapters in this book is the distinction between oracy as a medium of learning in all subjects, and oracy as a subject in its own right – as a further aspect of language competence which teachers now have an obligation to promote, alongside the traditionally recognised skills of reading and writing. In the remainder of this introductory chapter I shall try to follow through some of the implications of these two views of oracy, drawing together issues raised by the contributors.

Oracy for learning

One current strand in work on oracy places talk at the centre of the learning process. This view, which has a long pedigree in terms of curriculum innovation, had its origins in a critique of classrooms as places where children seemed to be forced to learn with, in effect, one hand tied behind their backs. Studies of classroom interaction showed how the traditional structures of teacher-directed talk often relegated children to the role of passive consumers of knowledge, rather than active learners (see, for example, Barnes 1976; Edwards and Furlong 1978; Mehan 1979). The constraints of teacher-led talk became particularly clear when this was compared with children's pre-school experience of language, and the enormous gains in learning through talk which are made during the first five years of life (see Wells 1981; Tizard and Hughes 1984). Chapter 2 of this book, by Dixon, and Chapter 3, by Frater, chart the emergence of the strong movement in schools to replace the traditional scenario of learning-by-listening with a model of active learning through talk. In the active learning approach, children are invited to engage with their own learning through collaborative exploration of ideas; to research facts, knowledge and opinion, and relate these to their own experience; and to analyse, criticise, challenge and speculate, rather than simply listen and 'absorb'. As Parker notes in Chapter 12, in his discussion of collaborative scripting, this has been from the start a cross-curricular enterprise (though some of its most eloquent spokespersons have been English or language specialists): the opportunities are there in *all* subjects to redress the balance of power and responsibility between teacher and taught.

These general principles of active learning through talk are now well established. Several of the chapters in this book suggest that there is still much to be learned, however, about what talk-for-learning actually looks like, the conditions under which it flourishes, and the criteria that we apply when we make judgements about the educational value of children's talk. Chang and Wells (Chapter 8), in their study of active learning in one Canadian classroom, argue that the learning potential of talk is centrally linked with children's 'ownership' of the task they are engaged in, and this concern is reflected, in different terms and guises, in several of the other contributions. Phillips (Chapter 6) suggests that successful small-group talk occurs when children 'appropriate' the topic and become genuinely involved in shaping and creating knowledge for their own ends. According to Phillips, this kind of talk differs strikingly from those occasions when children are merely following an agenda or topic set by the teacher. He goes on to argue that existing criteria for judging the success of small-group talk often tend, however, to dismiss just those characteristics – such as apparent digressions and absence of explicit logical links – which in his view indicate genuine engagement in the learning process. Barnes (Chapter 4) also expresses concern about approaches to oracy in which the talk becomes tyrannised by the task and dislocated from the real-life experience and purposes of the speakers, while Halligan (Chapter 7) reminds us that children may 'own' the task in different ways, depending on the relationships that are established and negotiated amongst group members, and their individual perceptions of what is required of them. Finally, the account by Hughes and Cousins (Chapter 9) of Sunnyboy's early adventures in school shows, among other things, how one five-year-old successfully subverted the discourse expectations of the infant classroom by claiming ownership of both talk and task.

Another distinctive feature of many of the chapters is the attention given to what might be called 'informal' talk – the language of stories, anecdotes, chat, rhymes and games. At first sight this might seem surprising in a book which is concerned with learning through language, since, as Mercer *et al.* point out in Chapter 10, it is often assumed that 'educational talk' has, or should aim to have, special properties which set it apart from these seemingly mundane kinds of communication which take place outside the classroom, or in the gaps between the official business of lessons. There has been a strong tradition in educational theorising about talk which places a high value on abstraction and generalisation; on language which transcends local culture, personal experience and particular contexts to achieve a level of (apparently) disinterested, rational debate about ideas and propositions. As a result, the everyday genres of anecdotes, stories, jokes or chat – rooted as they are in personal viewpoints and immediate concerns – have often been regarded as disposable language, at least as far as the serious business of learning is concerned. The strength of the boundaries which we build around educational discourse is visible in the lengths to which we go to protect it from 'contamination' by these disorderly vernacular voices: we apologise in seminars for being anecdotal; as teachers we often fear that learning through small-group talk will be subverted if students don't stick to the point, or 'lapse' into desultory chat when our backs are turned. These fears, and the assumptions they embody about the special nature of talk-for-learning, have become institutionalised in large-scale research projects such as those by Bennett (1976) and the ORACLE team (Galton *et al.* 1980), in which teacher effectiveness and pupil progress are judged partly by the extent to which pupils keep their talk 'on task' and avoid straying from the official agenda of the lesson.

From a variety of perspectives, contributors to this book suggest that we need to rethink the boundaries which have been erected around 'educationally relevant' talk, to exclude the informal genres of everyday life from serious consideration in terms of their significance for learning. Rosen emphasises in Chapter 1 the centrality of oral narratives of all kinds, as powerful devices for making sense of experience – a point which is echoed in the observations by Hughes and Cousins about the importance of story-telling among five-year-olds, not just for its entertainment value, but as a means of reflecting on, shaping and bringing together aspects of their experience. Berrill, like Rosen, challenges (in Chapter 5) the traditional demarcations which have separated narrative off from other genres of speech, and which have overlooked the extent to which narrative tends, in Rosen's words, to get 'woven seamlessly' into many different kinds of discourse. Looking at the status of anecdotes in group discussions among sixteen-year-olds, Berrill suggests that these need not be seen, as they often have in the past, as unskilled and unwelcome intrusions into the realms of abstract argumentation. In the discussions she observed, anecdotes were used productively as a method of developing and sustaining argument itself, by building collaboratively towards generalisations which nevertheless remained grounded in the experiences of the participants.

The contributions by Grugeon (Chapter 13) and van Peer (Chapter 14) extend the educational focus on talk well beyond the official agendas of classroom learning, to look at children's rhymes and games – those oral genres which are so essentially bound up with the culture of childhood that they almost fade from our memories when we make the transition to adulthood, yet which continue to flourish virtually unnoticed by parents and teachers. Both authors suggest that, far from being trivial, these playful language activities are occasions for a great deal of learning, under conditions which are organised and continuously re-created by the children themselves. In their rhymes and games children may be reflecting upon their status *vis-à-vis* the adult world into which they are being inducted; working out for themselves the transition from an oral to a literate culture; negotiating new and shared identities; and building strategies of defence against dominant groups.

As far as oracy for learning is concerned, therefore, at least two themes emerge from the chapters in this book: first, that we need a broader conception of what learning through language looks like; and second, that it may be going on in places where we often fail to look.

Oracy as competence

The second strand which recurs in contemporary work is the idea of oracy as a further area of communicative competence which schools have an obligation to promote. Just as in the past teachers have shouldered the main responsibility for teaching children to read and write, they are now held to have a major part to play in teaching them to speak and listen. Or at least, since the picture is complicated by the fact that children can already talk before they start school, and will continue to engage in it throughout their out-of-school lives, that teachers should be able to provide an environment which actively fosters the *further* development of children's spoken language abilities.

This view of oracy as an aspect of communicative competence in its own right is, I think, the one which is most strongly promoted in the recent policy documents to which Frater refers in Chapter 3. In this view, oracy tends to be seen as primarily the concern of English teachers and language specialists; and oral *assessment* means the assessment of oral skills and competences in their own right, rather than as a vehicle or expression of learning in other curriculum subjects.

It is worth noting that this view assumes that schools *can* make a difference (in a positive way, of course) to the development of children's oral abilities. Although this now seems uncontroversial, it is in fact only recently that it has gained currency among educationalists and linguists. The dominant linguistic paradigm of the 1960s and a good part of the 1970s – that of Chomsky's transformational grammar – held that many of the major milestones on the path of spoken language development had already been passed by the time children started school around the age of five; and that the supportive or instructional part played by adults during this journey was minimal. Children were thought to deduce the rules and regularities of language under the guidance of a genetic blueprint which relied on the speech of other people only as raw data for testing out hypotheses about language.

As Dixon points out in Chapter 2, it was only with the advent of functional and interactional theories of language that linguists began to rethink the path and the duration of the journey towards linguistic maturity. Once it was recognised that children also have to learn to *use* language in all sorts of situations, for many different purposes, with many different people, it became possible to envisage the path of spoken language development as stretching over many years. Moreover, interactionists began to claim a much more central role for others, especially parents, as critical figures in children's progress as communicators.

As a result, it now seems entirely possible that teachers could make a contribution to the development of children's oral competence beyond the pre-school years, even though, as already noted, we do not have a very clear picture of what that competence involves.

At present definitions of oral competence appear to be proceeding along broadly *functional* lines. The work of the Assessment of Performance Unit (see APU 1984) proposes a model which defines a range of communicative functions or purposes such as narrating, describing and reporting, and a variety of 'audiences'. Competence in oracy is then evaluated in terms of the ability to communicate effectively on a range of tasks exemplifying the various combinations of audience and purpose. Similar functional models, with an emphasis on communicative effectiveness or appropriateness over a range of purposes, are proposed in other recent British policy documents (see MacLure 1988).

There is no doubt that this heightened attention to oracy as competence has had some beneficial effects on the language curriculum. It has begun to break down the monolithic structure of classroom discourse mentioned above, where teachers talked and children mostly listened. In many classrooms children are telling stories, sharing experiences, and trying out a much wider range of voices. Functional models also offer teachers and children a critical vocabulary for examining the diversity and complexity of oral communication, and the links between language and context.

Looked at from another perspective, however, functional models – at least in the form they tend to take in educational contexts – may have their disadvantages as ways of conceptualising oral competence. For instance they tend to compartmentalise and categorise: to propose all-or-nothing definitions of different kinds of talk, for different kinds of purposes and audiences. There is either narrative *or* argument: anecdote *or* abstract discussion; informing *or* describing. These categories are often, as in the APU's approach, associated with different tasks for each of the functions – tasks to solicit story-telling, tasks for describing, tasks for problem-solving, and so on.

Several of the contributions in this book suggest that there is a need to rethink categorisations such as these. Rosen and Berrill, for instance, both suggest that the familiar dichotomy between argument on the one hand and various forms of narrative on the other fails to capture the extent to which these are used interchangeably by speakers in real-life contexts.

Then there is the question of how far it is possible to provide, within the confines of the classroom, the full gamut of communicative experiences defined by functional models of competence in oracy. Many curriculum initiatives, as Barnes suggests, seem currently to be based on the notion that the communicative conditions of life beyond the school gate can be replicated inside the classroom, as a kind of dry run for later life or out-of-school experience. In practical terms, this often means rotating the 'variables' of context, function and audience to generate a range of oral tasks, simulations or role-play exericises. Examples would include sales encounters, public enquiries, court-room re-enactions, mini-business enterprises, job and TV interviews. Many English teachers are also attempting to recast the traditional subject matter of English literature to allow students to engage actively with texts via oral activities drawn from real-life models: for example, a debate between the Montagues and the Capulets, or a radio interview with the characters in a novel.

This search for new roles and voices has undoubtedly been a positive experience for many students, who have found a new perspective on the content of the curriculum, and a much more active role as participants in classroom talk. One of the outcomes has almost certainly been to help many students to recognise their own wisdom and experience as communicators.

At the same time, some commentators are beginning to voice reservations about some of the wider implications of attempts to make classrooms micro-environments for nurturing the communicative complexity of life on the outside. The major problem, of course, is the unavoidably make-believe nature of the activities themselves. As Barnes points out, this often results in artifical tasks which require children to take on social roles of which they have no direct experience, in order to discuss topics in which they have no real-life engagement.

In effect, this could be as likely to undermine as to support children's development as communicators, since it cuts them adrift from the foundations of communication in social action; that is, from the need and desire to communicate with others, out of first-hand experience, for real and immediate purposes. At the very least, as both Phillips and Halligan suggest, children's oral 'performance' on classroom tasks – however realistic these may seem – may tell us more about the strategies that children develop to cope with the rather specialised exigencies of 'school talk' than about their more general communicative abilities.

In summary, though we now feel optimistic that schools can make a difference to the development of competence in oracy, we are less sure about what kind of difference they can make. Perhaps the central question, implicit and explicit in many of the chapters in this book, is how to help children develop, both as communicators and as learners, without cutting language off from the world of action, experience and involvement in which it originates, and to which it returns at the end of every school day.

The organisation of this book

As the foregoing discussion suggests, the contributions to this book might be organised in several different ways. For ease of reference, they have been grouped broadly in terms of their subject matter, with the exception of Part One, *Issues and perspectives*, in which each chapter provides an overview of some aspect of the field, rather than an empirical study of a particular topic. The opening chapter by Rosen takes a critical look at contemporary research into narrative, and argues for a much wider recognition of the educational significance of this 'irrepressible genre'. Dixon (Chapter 2) looks back over the (still relatively short) history of enquiry into spoken language, identifying key figures across the disciplines whose insights have informed educational thinking about oracy, and asking where we might go next. Frater, by contrast, reflects in Chapter 3 on the history of oracy in Britain from the perspective of educational policy and curriculum development, outlining the stages in the journey towards the current context of nation-wide initiatives. Barnes, too, in Chapter 4 considers oracy in its contemporary social and educational context, though his conclusions are less optimistic in some respects than Frater's.

The three chapters by Berrill, Phillips and Halligan in Part Two, *Small-group talk*, each look at a particular aspect of unsupervised group discussion, involving children of different ages. Each chapter demonstrates how much there is still to be learned about the complexities of peer-group talk in school.

In Part Three, *The dynamics of classroom communication*, the focus is primarily, though not exclusively, upon talk between teachers and pupils. Chang and Wells (Chapter 8) explore the teacher's role in promoting active learning through talk and outline the contribution which collaborative talk might make to the development of 'literate thinking'. Hughes and Cousins (Chapter 9) continue the debate about the relationship between language at home and at school, using a case study of a five-year-old child from a travellers' community to raise questions about the nature of the language experiences children are offered in their early years at school. This section concludes with the contribution by Mercer *et al.* (Chapter 10), which examines the 'ground rules' of classroom communication and argues that these need to be more fully understood by children and educationalists alike.

In Part Four, *Spoken language and the media*, Fowler (Chapter 11) looks at the linguistic devices used to achieve the semblance of oral language in the popular and 'quality' Press, and thereby to implicate readers in the views expressed. He shows how the study of devices such as these might help children to develop a critical understanding of the role of the Press in shaping popular opinion and values. Parker's account (Chapter 12) of scripting in the classroom outlines the opportunities for learning through talk which this can provide for children at different ages. Like Fowler, he raises questions about the relationship between speech and writing, and the distinctive features of writing which masquerades as speech.

In Part Five, *Language at play: children's rhymes and games*, which concludes the book, Grugeon (Chapter 13) and van Peer (Chapter 14) examine the processes of solidarity, subversion and socialisation which are embodied in the language of children at play.

References

Assessment of Performance Unit (APU) (1984). *Language Performance in Schools*, London, Department of Education and Science.

Barnes, D. (1976). *From Communication to Curriculum*, Harmondsworth, Penguin.

Bennett, N. (1976). *Teaching Styles and Pupil Progress*, London, Open Books.

Edwards, A. and Furlong, V. J. (1978). *The Language of Teaching*, London, Heinemann.

Galton, M., Simon, B. and Croll, P. (1980). *Inside the Primary Classroom*, London, Routledge and Kegan Paul.

MacLure, M. (1988). 'Assessing Spoken Language: Testing Times for Talk' in N. Mercer (ed.), *Language and Literacy from an Educational Perspective: Vol. 2, In Schools*, Milton Keynes, Open University Press.

Mehan, H. (1979). *Learning Lessons*. Cambridge, MA, Harvard University Press.

Tizard, B. and Hughes, M. (1984). *Young Children Learning: Talking and Thinking at Home and at School*, London, Fontana.

Wells, G. (ed.) (1981). *Learning through Interaction: The Study of Language Development*, Cambridge, Cambridge University Press.

PART ONE
Issues and perspectives

1 The irrepressible genre

HAROLD ROSEN

Narrative scholarship or, if you will, *narratology* has scarcely touched educational debate or even the now well-developed field of language in education. There are some good reasons for this, apart from the well-known time lag. The number of theorctical and research studies is growing every day, but their centres of attention are unevenly distributed.

A preponderance of studies is devoted to works of written prose fiction. They tend to concentrate on those works which have achieved canonical status in Europe, the Great Novels, well-known short stories. Works belie their titles. Thus Genette's *Narrative Discourse* (1980) turns out to concentrate almost exclusively on Proust, without even a nod towards spoken narrative. Barthes's *S/Z* (1975) develops its valuable theory of narrative codes from a microscopic inspection of Balzac's novella *Sarrasine* and we can scarcely apply his central distinction (the 'readerly' as opposed to the 'writerly' text) to oral narrative. It is as though these writers have stepped straight from the world of traditional literary criticism and brought all their familiar baggage with them. Gerald Prince's *Narratology: The Form and Function of Narrative* (1982) promises much more. According to him, 'Narratology examines what all narratives have in common – narratively speaking – and what allows them to be narratively different – the traits which distinguish narrative from other signifying systems' (1982: 4–5). However, continue for a few more lines and we find him saying: 'In my presentation I focus on written narrative because it is the kind I know best. However, much of what I say is applicable to any narrative regardless of the medium of representation' (1982: 5). Does this mean that the question of differences is of no importance?

Time and time again ambitious claims are made for narrative. For Mink (1978: 234) it is 'a primary and irreducible form of human comprehension, an article in the constitution of common-sense'. For Jameson (1981: 13) it is 'the central function or *instance* of the human mind'. The best-known claim of all, perhaps, is that of Barthes (1983: 79): 'narrative is international, transhistorical, trans-cultural: it is simply there, like life itself'. These claims (there are many others) are more easily assented to than developed, or so it would appear.

We might reasonably think that if we turn to folklorists and folk-story specialists we are returning to oral narrative, for this is the realm of the story-teller rather than the story-writer. Folk story, by definition, belongs to the oral tradition. As Walter Benjamin (1970: 84) says, 'Experience which is passed from mouth to mouth is the source from which all story tellers have drawn'. Yet, when we examine Propp's famous study *The Morphology of the Folk Tale* (1968), we discover that this foundation stone of structuralist analysis is based on a printed collection; we are told that he used 'a comparatively limited corpus of fairy tales chosen from the Afanasev collection' (1968: xxi). Barbara Babcock (1984: 68), an exception to this scriptist approach, who insists on treating folk narrative as *performance*, says of written versions:

> The majority of our collections of folk narrative consist of texts which record little more than narrative content . . . such 'texts' are so removed from the performance that it becomes difficult (if not impossible) to examine the 'texture' and 'content' of the text . . . with a few exceptions we have tended to study the tale at the expense of its teller, telling and reception.

Bear in mind oral story-telling is still alive and kicking: we have urban folk-tales (see Brunvand 1983), narrative jokes and the stories of ethnic minorities.

Those who are closest to looking at folk narrative as performance are usually anthropologists and ethnographers. Gossen (1984) in his study of Sumura society and its genres of verbal behaviour shows that they divide narrative into 'Recent words: true recent narrative' and 'Ancient words: the ancient narrative' and the performance of these narratives turns on broader distinctions and overlaps in genres of verbal behaviour, i.e. 'ordinary language, language for people whose hearts are heated', and 'traditional or pure language which can be recent or ancient' (1984: 89). There are now many studies of this kind. They are discussed in an illuminating way in Bauman (1984: 11):

> Performance involves on the part of the performer an assumption of accountability to an audience for the way in which a communication is carried out above and beyond its referential content. From the point of view of the audience, the art of expression on the part of the performer is thus marked as subject to evaluation for the way it is done, for the relative skill and effectiveness of the performer's display of competence.

A performance involves the use of every available channel, play with the face, and the rest of the body and voice; it is interactive with the audience's responses. Some features of the oral story-teller's performance in traditional non-urban societies we would recognise, indeed appreciate immediately, but others require us to understand and enter into another very different culture and often to rely on translations which suffer from well-known limitations. Though oral improvised narrative runs through our talk and though traditional oral tales can still be found, we are not a pre-literate society. Moreover, we are an industrial and urban society and studies of oral narrative in our context are all too rare.

Everybody knows that we tell stories in our heads. For every one we tell to others, there are thousands which are left strictly between us and our alter egos.

We daydream in narrative and dream in narrative. Our scandalous, untold and uncensored narratives are narrated in the head. No one seems very interested in this ceaseless mental story-making except perhaps Freudians. Yet as we have seen, there are widespread claims that the real significance of narrative is that it is a fundamental way in which the mind works. Bakhtin (1981) proposed that we think in the genres learned in social interaction. If this is right, then it suggests that our experience of narrative enables us to handle our experience narratively in our minds. You might think that, of all people, cognitive scientists would be eager to probe these possibilities. They have certainly done so but they are handicapped by their experimental methods and assumptions. I have criticised them elsewhere (Rosen 1986). I would prefer on this occasion simply to note that they are wedded to certain concepts of story structure (i.e. story grammars) in spite of powerful critiques of these concepts. This leads them to set up experiments of shocking insensitivity (see, for example, Hilyard and Olson 1982) in which the sole concern is to find out how well children remember and reproduce a story. Cook-Gumpertz and Green (1984) set out to look at children's story-telling in a more 'naturalistic' setting. Before doing so they reject the cognitive science approach:

> Research on oral story-telling has . . . been concerned with the structure of story narratives . . . In experimental work, children do not have to make any story-telling contributions; that is, their task is to evaluate, reproduce, recall or sequence stories presented to them. Researchers then assess children's comprehension, not children's ability to produce or contribute to narratives spontaneously (1984: 204).

Like Bauman, Cook-Gumpertz and Green consider that children's story-telling should be examined as 'an active or performance ability'. By adopting this approach they are able to show that 'children have models of narrative that include aspects of both spoken-oral and written-literate models' (1984: 217).

I have been tracing only those tendencies in narratology which place severe limitations on their relevance to an educational study of oral narrative. But I would not like to be misunderstood. Of course there is much to be learned, reinterpreted, and applied to our own context. On the other hand, there is much which is just irrelevant. Remember that for some neither the author nor the audience exist (the text and only the text!). My negative stock-taking comes out like this.

1 There is relatively little on spontaneous, naturally occurring narrative, including narrative jokes and story-swapping.
2 There is even less on oral narrative as argument (an important matter since narrative is often counterposed to argument).
3 Little attention is given to oral narrative in modern, urban, industrialised societies like our own.
4 Our own society contains a diversity of ethnic groups, languages and cultures. Is there such a thing as inter-cultural narrative? Bilingual narrative?
5 We lack and badly need an educational theory and practice of narrative.

I shall in due course refer to work which attempts to make good some of these deficiencies, including the activities of the London Narrative Group with which I am associated. For the moment, I want to turn elsewhere. To move towards an educational theory of oral narrative we have to begin by picking up some of the barest hints scattered throughout the literature. I mean all those hints which suggest that narrative is at the heart of our mental and social processes. I want to leave the narratologists behind and go to an unlikely source and setting, John Berger's *Pig Earth* (1979). It grows out of Berger's life in a peasant village in the French Alps and is full of stories, mostly retellings of stories which the peasants have told him, for the village is full of stories. What do they mean – not separately but as a single, dynamic entity?

> All villages tell stories. Stories of the past, even the distant past. Once I was walking in the mountains with a friend of seventy. As we walked along the foot of a high cliff, he told me how a young girl had fallen to her death there, whilst haymaking on the *alpage* above. Was that before the war? I asked. In 1833, he said. And equally, stories of the very same day. Most of what happens during a day is recounted by somebody before the day ends. The stories are factual, based on observation or on a first hand account. This combination . . . is what constitutes so-called village *gossip* (1979: 8)

> Very few stories are narrated either to idealise or condemn, rather they testify to the always surprising range of the possible. Although concerned with everyday events, they are mystery stories. How is it that C—— who is so punctilious in his work, overturned the haycart? How is it that L—— is able to fleece her lover J—— of everything, and how is it that J——, who normally gives nothing away to anybody, allows himself to be fleeced? (1979: 8).

As Berger continues with his observations, he offers some propositions about these everyday narratives which seem to have relevance far outside this tiny Alpine community. He sees in the village stories, perhaps of ephemeral import-ance if taken separately, an essential social process, the creation and re-creation of a collective identity. As Booth (1984: 2) writes: 'We are the stories we tell and could tell'. For Berger (1979: 9), 'Each story allows everyone to define himself. Indeed, the function of this *gossip* which in fact is close, oral, daily history, is to allow the whole village to define itself'. He later observes (1979: 9):

> Every village's portrait of itself is constructed ... out of words, spoken and remembered: out of opinions, stories, eye-witness reports, legends, comments, hear-say. And it is a continuous portrait; work on it never stops . . . Without such a portrait – and the gossip which is its raw material – the village would have been forced to doubt its own existence.

This is to do much more than observe the inevitability of story-telling or remark its recurrence as it intertwines with the processes of daily living. It transmutes the ephemeral into an enduring monument of social being. No stories, no commu-nity. Oral stories will not be put down. They may be declared inconsequential or particularistic, banned from the seminar room, but they will flourish as soon as the thought police turn their backs because we need a means of learning what as a collectivity we really are. In the great anonymous conurbations our villages are constituted through social networks and the capillaries of oral communication systems. Written narrative might be regarded as the opium of the people inasmuch as the bulk of contemporary written narrative tends to deliver a *false* sense of coherence and therefore to lend support to dominant conservative forces. Unpoliced oral stories, de Certeau (1980) suggests, are the supreme form of the 'Oppositional practices of everyday life'.

Let us step back now and consider narrative from another perspective, one which, at first glance, looks like the opposite perspective, i.e. as a mode of thought, indeed a central, persistent, ineradicable mode. If this indeed is what it is, then oral spontaneous narrative can creep out of the humble quarters often allocated to it in our intellectual culture, in much the same way as chatty conversation had since studies have revealed the complex functions of everyday conversations, the skills required to participate in them, and their heuristic potential. To start on the task we have to remind ourselves that the composition of even the simplest oral narrative is a complex matter. The usual definitions of a minimal narrative do not help us very much. For example, 'a narrative represents at least two real or future events or situations in a time sequence, neither of which entails the other'. That's really not much help if we are trying to determine what a speaker must do in order to compose a story which is no more than a report on recent experience. Consider the following:

> R. I went to the car boot-sale after all. It was all a bit feeble. Feeble – you know, just odds and ends. Real junk. It was just tatty stuff. I was going – was gonna go straight away. And it was raining. On the way out I saw something sticking out from under some blankets – all bright colours. See that hearth rug. That was it.
> H. Lovely, I'm . . .
> R. One pound fifty!
> H. One pound fifty.
> R. Yeah. I felt so good I went back – went back and bought the two blankets (laughs).

Even for such a commonplace little narrative the recent experience must be transformed and a very active productive process must be set in motion. From the continuous and unstoppable flow of events a story must be constructed. The story-teller must seize hold of and verbalise just that sequence which serves her purposes (to present the unexpected bargain, the purchaser's coup). The story has to be dissected out of life itself. Something must be transformed into a beginning ('I went to this car boot sale'; obviously there are other possibilities); something else into an end ('I bought the other two blankets'). Personae and places must be inscribed by some means, however minimal (the bargain hunting narrator; the car boot sale) – all by means of a selective process which cuts away from the original experience all that the teller decides is irrelevant. There is much more to it than this. There must be a stance towards the events. The attention of the audience must be won and kept. As Todorov (1977: 55) says,

> There is no 'primitive narrative'. No narrative is natural; a choice and construction will always preside over its appearance; narrative is a discourse not a series of events. There exists no 'proper' narratives as opposed to 'figurative' ones . . . ; all narratives are figurative.

This is what makes oral spontaneous narrative an active meaning-making process constantly renewing the tactics and strategies learned in thousands of narrative encounters.

I have already noted that some huge claims are made for narrative by almost all serious scholars in the field. Somewhere they will pause to say something about *all* narrative – its role in social life, in communication, in language and perhaps in human thought and imagination. Narrative, they would say, is irremovably installed in the human psyche. It must be of some significance that these scholars hurry away from their pronouncements as soon as they have made them. Even Labov (1972), whose tribute to working-class oral narrators of life experiences is bold and challenging, stops short: 'they will command the total attention of an audience in a remarkable way, creating a deep and attentive silence' (1972: 396). Yes, but why?

The most ambitious attempt I know to confront steadily that kind of un-answered question is in Jerome Bruner's most recent book *Actual Minds, Possible Worlds* (1986). One chapter in particular, 'Two Modes of Thought', promises a most radical view, setting out to show that narrative is not just a discourse option, one genre among many, but one of a binary choice in mental processes. It therefore justifies close scrutiny. He sets out the two possibilities as follows:

> There are two modes of cognitive functioning, two modes of thought, each providing distinctive ways of ordering experience, of constructing reality. The two (though complementary) are irreducible to one another. Efforts to ignore one at the expense of another inevitably fail to capture the rich diversity of human thought (1986: 11).

These two modes he calls 'paradigmatic' (i.e. logico-scientific) and 'narrative'. This would seem to suggest that cultures or individuals that do not use the paradigmatic mode think entirely in narrative – but let that go. What Bruner is asserting is that one way to handle experience is to narratise it, that we can perceive the world narratively. On the other hand, we may operate paradigmatically employing 'categorization or conceptualization and the operations by which categories are established, instantiated, idealized and related one to the other to form a system' (1986: 12). This 'leads to good theory, tight analysis, logical proof, sound argument, and empirical discovery guided by reasoned hypothesis'. Narrative, on the other hand, works in another way, i.e. via the simultaneous construction of two landscapes: 'the landscape of action, where the constituents are the arguments of action/agent, intention or goal, situation, instrument, something corresponding to a "story-grammar"' and 'the landscape of consciousness: what those involved in the action know, think and feel, or do not know, think or feel'.

Very early on in Bruner's text I grew uneasy in spite of its verve. What set out to show us narrative as a mode of thought soon became an examination of narratives, parts of which drew on the familiar furniture of narratology, including the familiar but challenged concept of story grammar. More disquieting still is that Bruner soon leads us far away from universal narrative thought to what he calls 'trained and gifted writers', familiar enough terrain. Oral narrative disappears.

> one does well to study the work of trained and gifted writers if one is to understand what it is that makes good stories powerful or compelling. Anybody (at almost any age) can tell a story and it is altogether good that story grammarians, so called, are studying the minimal structure needed to create a story . . . but great fiction . . . requires the transformation of intuitions into expressions in a symbolic system (1986: 15).

Among the many objections one could make to this far from obvious procedure, I want to single out one. What began as a promise to deal with a mode of thought available to everyone is realised by an examination of 'great fiction'. No need to examine traditional story-telling (really retelling), no need to examine oral everyday narrative. Instead we have an examination of James Joyce's story *Clay* and from that we shall discover all that it is essential to know about narrative.

I suggest that we should stand that argument on its head. Study what we can all do, how we do it, why we do it and what use we make of it and we shall discover the essential features of the practice of narrative. Imagine if linguists exploring how conversation works were to take as the paradigm case the talk of people somehow judged to be great conversationalists. The loss would be incalculable. So intent is Bruner on great fiction as the key to understanding narrative that he leaves no room for the consideration of the wide range of social practices which diversify narrative.

A member of the London Narrative Group provides an interesting example (see Baynham 1986). From his full account of, as he says, creating a story-telling culture in a classroom of adult second-language learners of English, I select one moment. Following the reading of a Stephen Leacock short story, the students discussed their own experiences of embarrassment and humiliation and how people are judged by appearances. At one point Manajieh, as a contribution to the discussion of these very general points, told the story of Nasreddin at the party.

> One day Molla-Nasreddin was invited to a party, he went to the party without changing his ordinary clothes, but the receptionist stopped him to go there, and told he couldn't go while he is wearing ragged clothes but he rushed backed home and changed his clothes to the best clothes he ever had.
>
> He came back to the party everyone bowed at him, and offered him nice place to sit down. It was time for dinner, they served best food, but Molla instead of eating the food he was putting food in his sleeves.
>
> Everyone was astonished, what he was doing, probably they thought he was mad. Somebody asked him why he is feeding his clothes. He said I am here because of my clothes.

Manajieh is able to draw on an oral story-telling tradition (in her second language!) to make a contribution to non-narrative talk. By the time the whole class had worked on the story and produced a bilingual version, Manajieh had learned something about written narrative and how the final sentence might go in

English. The classroom can uncover a function of narrative which the analysis of great fiction will leave untouched. A view of narrative which does not take account of its use in argument or any kind of conversation is bound to be an impoverished view. Narrative is frequently woven seamlessly into conversation, even when it takes the form of direct-speech dialogue. As Bakhtin (1981: 280) writes: 'The word in living conversation is directly, blatantly, oriented towards a future word: it provokes an answer, anticipates it and structures itself in the answer's direction.' The oral narrative here is blatantly dialogic. Some have begun to lay bare this quality of narrative. I have in mind Erickson (1984), Polanyi (1985) and Deborah Tannen (1982). The general principle to which they all, implicitly or explicitly, subscribe in contradistinction to Bruner's view has been expressed by Smith (1981: 263):

> It . . . is important to recognize that narrative discourse is not necessarily – or even usually – marked off or segregated from other discourse. Almost any verbal utterance will be laced with more or less minimal narratives, ranging from fragmentary reports and abortive anecdotes to those more distinctly framed, conventionally marked tellings that we are inclined to call 'tales' or 'stories'.

It seems to me a pity, therefore, that Bruner took the direction he did, for in his rich text there are insights and indications of another kind. In the London Narrative Group we have been studying the retellings of stories by school pupils not simply from the point of view of what they retain from the original story but also from the point of view of what they change. We are beginning to categorise these changes. For oral story-telling this is of huge importance. It reveals the delicate tension between reproduction and invention. In the same way as the traditional story-teller, school pupils give their own inflection to a story. Remember that even accounts of one's own experience are often retellings adjusted to time, place and audience. The creative judgement of the story-teller once more comes into play. Children and students may of course struggle to be word-perfect in a retelling. Indeed, it is the experience of our group that such is the force of the school culture of rote memorising and accurate reproduction that a conscious effort has to be made to liberate them. Once emancipated from that control they repossess the story and easily find ways of retelling it so as to bend it to their own purposes. As de Certeau (1984: 23) says: 'The significance of a story that is well-known, and therefore classifiable, can be reversed by a single "circumstan-tial" detail ... "The insignificant detail" inserted into the framework that supports it makes the commonplace produce other effects.' A tiny example. A very shy little Bangladeshi girl retold an Italian folk story I had told to her class in which the hero was a bold young man in search of the land where no one dies. Uniquely in her class, she changed him into a resourceful young woman who sets out taking the whole family with her. The contrast between word-perfect regurgitation and creative retelling is a supreme example of the contrast between what Bakhtin (1981) called 'authoritative' and 'internally persuasive' discourse. On the former, Bakhtin (1981: 242) says:

> The authoritative word demands that we acknowledge it, that we make it our own; it binds us, quite independent of any power it may have to persuade us internally; we encounter it with its authority already fused to it . . . it is, so to speak, the word of the fathers.

On the latter (1981: 345):

> Internally persuasive discourse . . . is, as it is affirmed through assimilation, tightly interwoven with 'one's own word.' In the everyday rounds of our consciousness, the internally persuasive word is half ours and half someone else's. Its creativity and productiveness consist precisely in the fact that such a word awakens new and independent words.

Bakhtin develops these ideas over some half-a-dozen pages and offers us some hints at how we might look at retelling.

The same is true of Bruner (1986: 6) who, unusually, proposes a psychological view of genre.

> One gets a sense of the psychology of genre by listening to readers 'tell back' a story they have just read or spontaneously 'tell' a story about a 'happening' in their lives. Genre seems to be a way of both organizing the structure of events and organizing the telling of them – a way that can be used for one's own storytelling or, indeed, for 'placing' the stories one is reading or hearing.

This way of regarding original telling or retelling offers more promise and general relevance than concentrating on great fiction, for all narrative both organises the structure of events and organises the particular telling of them. Bruner picks up and elaborates a scheme taken from Todorov. This is a set of 'transformations' of straight affirmation through modality, intention, result, manner, aspect, status. He calls this the subjunctivisation of the text, gets a young student orally to retell James Joyce's story *Clay*, and compares the retelling with the original. The student, he concludes through his analysis, has in fine detail picked up the subjunctivisation of the original. 'The subjunctive landscape is richly constructed' in the retelling because, we gather, the original is a great work of fiction and therefore sufficiently subjunctive to catch the reader's imagination. The procedure is both elegant and complex and certainly usable for other kinds of retellings where it would illuminate the methods of every kind of story-teller. But this should not blind us to the fact that the student's oral retelling, as the text very clearly shows, is not what I would call a story-telling performance (i.e. to a real audience) but an effort to recall a story for a researcher.

Much later in his book Bruner, when dealing with what he calls his 'language of education', puts forward some propositions about culture. If he had only integrated them with his ideas about narrative, a most productive synthesis might have emerged. Culture, he says (1986: 123),

> is constantly in process of being recreated as it is interpreted and renegotiated by its members. In this view a culture is as much a *forum* for negotiating meaning and explicating action as it is a set of rules or specifications for action . . . It is the forum aspect of a culture that gives us participants a role in constantly making and remaking the culture – an active role as participants.

Therefore, he argues, schools must be part of this forum-like culture-creation and should not operate with 'the so-called uncontaminated language of fact and objectivity'. Exactly! And we all know too well how many classrooms bear not the slightest resemblance to a forum. A narrative culture needs to have a central place in that forum not merely through a recitation of time-honoured tales, nor by poring over hallowed masterpieces with all the archaeological practices borrowed from classical studies, nor by embalming stories in the oil of bogus moral values. We should learn from a quite different time-honoured practice still to be found in the secular world outside schools – the *reworking* of narratives. We can depend on pupils to refashion them to their own meanings, influenced by the mobile and diversified culture which they are both living through and making. The narratives of the classroom must not be holy relics of the past represented as both inviolable and unattainable. All stories need to be challenged, perhaps by telling others. The pupils themselves need to be story-tellers, and so do teachers.

References

Babcock, B. A. (1984). 'The Story in the Story: Metanarration in Folk Narrative' in Bauman (1984).
Bakhtin, M. M. (1981). *The Dialogic Imagination*, Austin, University of Texas Press.
Barthes, R. (1975). *S/Z*, London, Jonathan Cape.
Barthes, R. (1983). 'Introduction to the Structural Analysis of Narratives' in S. Sonntag (ed.), *Barthes*, London, Fontana.
Bauman, R. (1984). *Verbal Art as Performance*, Prospect Heights, Ill., Waveland Press.
Baynham, M. (1986). 'Bilingual Folk Stories in the ESL Classroom', *ELT Journal*, vol. 40, no. 2, April.
Beaman, K. (1984). 'Coordination and Subordination Revisited: Syntactic Complexity in Spoken and Written Discourse' in Tannen (1984).
Benjamin, W. (1973). 'The Story Teller: Reflections on the Work of Nicolai Leskov' in H. Arendt (ed.), *Illuminations*, London, Fontana.
Berger, J. (1979). *Pig Earth*, London, Writers and Readers Publishing Cooperative.
Booth, W. (1984). 'Narrative as the Mold of Character' in *A Telling Exchange*, Report of the 17th Conference on Language in Inner City Schools, University of London Institute of Education.
Bruner, J. (1986). *Actual Minds, Possible Worlds*, Cambridge, Mass., Harvard University Press.
Brunvand, J. H. (1983). *The Vanishing Hitchhiker: Urban Legends and their Meanings*, London, Pan Books.
de Certeau, M. (1980). 'On the Oppositional Practices of Everyday Life', *Social Text*, vol. 1, no. 3.
de Certeau, M. (1984). *The Practice of Everyday Life*, Berkeley, University of California Press.
Cook-Gumpertz, J. and Green, J. L. (1984). 'A Sense of Story: Influences on Children's Story-Telling Ability' in Tannen (1984).
Erickson, F. (1984). 'Rhetoric, Anecdote, and Rhapsody: Coherence Strategies in a Conversation among Black American Adolescents' in Tannen (1984).
Genette, G. (1980). *Narrative Discourse*, Oxford, Basil Blackwell.
Gossen, G. H. (1984). 'Chamula Genres of Verbal Behaviour' in Bauman (1984).

Hildyard, A. and Olson, D. (1982). 'On the Comprehension and Memory of Oral vs. Written Discourse' in Tannen (1982).

Jameson, F. (1981). *The Political Unconscious: Narrative as a Socially Symbolic Act*, London, Methuen.

Labov, W. (1972). *Language in the Inner City*, Pennsylvania, University of Pennsylvania Press.

Mink, L. O. (1978). 'Narrative Form as a Cognitive Instrument' in R. H. Canary and H. Kozicki (eds), *The Writing of History: Literary Form and Historical Understanding*, Madison, University of Wisconsin Press.

Polanyi, L. (1985), 'Conversational Storytelling' in T. A. Van Dijk (ed.), *Handbook of Discourse Analysis*, Vol. 3, San Diego, Academic Press.

Prince, G. (1982), *Narratology: The Form and Function of Narrative*, The Hague, Mouton.

Propp, V. (1968), *Morphology of the Folktale*, Austin, University of Texas Press.

Rosen, H. (1986). 'The Importance of Story', *Language Arts*, vol. 63, no. 3, March.

Smith, B. H. (1981). 'Narrative Versions, Narrative Theories' in W. J. T. Mitchell, *On Narrative*, Chicago, University of Chicago Press.

Tannen, D. (ed.) (1982). *Spoken and Written Language: Exploring Orality and Literacy*, Norwood, NJ, Ablex.

Tannen, D. (ed.) (1984). *Coherence in Spoken and Written Discourse*, Norwood, NJ, Ablex.

Todorov, T. (1977), *The Poetics of Prose*, Oxford, Basil Blackwell.

2 Oral exchange: a historical review of the developing frame

JOHN DIXON

Constraints in a period of take-off

Until around 1970 oral communication and exchange did not exist as a field of enquiry; instead there were fragmented interests pursued within a range of specialist journals – in anthropology, sociology, linguistics and the behavioural sciences; in social, comparative and developmental psychology; in psychiatry and group therapy; and in communication and management studies (to mention some of the more prominent). So far, I know of no attempts during the 1960s to synthesise this scattered work.

It was in this context, in 1965–70, that teachers I knew first began to set up observations and enquiry into classroom exchange. To understand this formative phase from a historical perspective, we need first to bear in mind the absence of any synthesis; but there were other constraints actively present within the prevailing research traditions. The most obvious today, I suppose, would be the predominance of behaviourist and wider positivist assumptions. (If it's knowledge, count two variables and find the correlation!) But there were more subtle pressures. Let me take three examples.

Bernstein, a pioneering sociolinguist of the 1960s, was being widely discussed in educational circles and received powerful backing in England from the Ministry of Education. His hypotheses about the social formation of language uses were increasingly complex and subtle. Yet his analysis of group discussions went no further than counts (of pause lengths, or later of passive verbs, adverbs and the like); the oral exchange itself was never analysed – indeed, it was never even quoted in the 1960s.

With regard to linguistic theory, there were equally serious drawbacks. The 1960s was a period when significant efforts were made to bridge the gap between university linguistics and English teaching. Thus Trim (1959) and Davies (1965) were among the first to alert teachers in the UK to some of the significant differences between speech and writing. But the analysis stopped there: 'speech' itself was not differentiated into dialogue and monologue. We are not talking here, remember, of lapses on the part of individuals: it is the prevailing traditions that concern us.

In cognitive psychology, the work of Bruner can be taken as valuably representative of the period: Bruner *et al.* (1966), for example, was widely read internationally. Its sophisticated view of cognition as 'the interaction of systems' – 'enactive, ikonic and symbolic' – suggested a dominant yet not exclusive role for language in learning. Yet while many of the laboratory experiments inevitably involved dialogue (and some of these 'protocols' were actually given in full) the opportunity to analyse verbal interaction was never taken.

It is the impact of traditions of enquiry that we have to study, then, not simply the development of conceptual frames. How could such powerful constraints be challenged and transformed? In the space available, I want to suggest a few critical turning points. (Which is not to imply that we are somehow miraculously out of the wood!)

Teachers move into the field

In the mid-1960s there were suddenly two very different kinds of incentive for British teachers to become interested in the field. First, it was officially recognised (at long last) that oral communication should form a substantial element in English courses for the eleven-to-sixteen age range; and second – as a corollary – some assessment of 'oracy' had been included in several of the new sixteen-plus examining systems. In my view, this dual interest led to conflicts of focus as efforts were made to develop a satisfactory frame.

However, in general terms, Andrew Wilkinson's (1965) position was central. So far as education was concerned, 'The spoken language in England [had] been shamefully neglected'; where it had been mentioned in official reports, the concepts had been puerile, distorted or misconceived. 'Oracy' was as fundamental to education as literacy and numeracy. It was not a 'subject' – 'it is a *condition of learning in all subjects*' (Wilkinson 1965: 58, emphasis added).

> Its encouragement is a matter of the fundamental attitudes of the school towards its pupils; of their relationships with the staff; of the degree of responsibility accorded them; of the confidence they acquire . . . Where children are given responsibility they are placed in situations where it is important for them to communicate – to discuss, to negotiate, to converse – with their fellows, with the staff, with other adults. And of necessity they are likely to develop oral skills (1965: 59).

Already, as you see, some crucial directions for enquiry had been clarified: the institutional relations and mutual attitudes of staff and pupils (within the culture of the school); the responsibilities (and thus the initiatives and roles?) that pupils are given in communication; the possibility of a range of different types (or genres?) of interaction – 'to discuss, to negotiate, to converse'; and the range of possible participants in group exchange – peers, staff, other adults. Nor was the enquiry neutral and value-free; for Wilkinson (1965: 59) as for many of us at the time, 'oracy and democracy are closely related'. The role of students was not to be passive subjects of an 'autocratic regime'; their contributions to a lesson were expected to include asking questions as well as answering them, discussing and interpreting their assignments as well as carrying them out. There would be dialogue in independent student groups as well as teacher–pupil dialogue.

In 1965 these bold directions for enquiry were still schematic. Later came *Language, the Learner, and the School* (Barnes *et al.* 1969), containing the first extensive transcripts of teacher–pupil dialogue and group discussions, thus opening up the way for a more detailed analysis. The conclusions were relatively crude – but devastating. Most of them still apply today, world-wide I should guess. First, 'classroom dialogue' was characteristically a series of exchanges between teacher and individual student. For most of the time we teachers were retaining the initiative throughout, by a strategy of asking questions and mono-polising any commentary on the answers that were given. Second, within the restricted form of dialogue that resulted, there was a 'yawning gap' between the language and conceptual frame of the teacher and that of the students.

These were the main findings of Barnes *et al.* (1969); by way of contrast, however, Barnes recorded and began to analyse some teachers who were attempting different strategies. In brief, he had begun the investigation of a crucial educational issue: how are students to be helped, in the course of classroom exchange, to accommodate to new conceptual frames? In order to answer this question, he saw that it would be necessary to treat dialogue as a progressive interplay between participants with a variety of conceptual frames; to study any shifts in students' language that suggested changes in their ways of conceptualising a problem; to look for progressive signs of movement from a more restricted to a more comprehensive and differentiated frame; and to experiment with various strategies on the teacher's part for optimising the dialectical interplay between various contributors.

Such criticisms of practice and attempts to assert new traditions made altogether new demands on theory. We had to have a theory of dialogue. But our interests were more specific. We wanted to place dialogue within institutional structures and classroom relations that liberated students from autocratic regimes. And we wanted ways of studying students' progressive constructions within a variety of dialogic genres, all of these orientated towards outcomes that would count as learning.

Efforts to extend the linguistic frame

From this point of view, what happened to theory in the early 1970s was fruitfully destructive of many constraining assumptions – and that was encouraging – but sketchy and programmatic in terms of answering such demands. Let us look at one of the highlights.

Halliday (1975) made a bold original effort to develop a theoretical frame that would account for his son Nigel's language development in infancy. In doing so, he realised (1975: 139) that:

It seems sensible to assume that neither the linguistic system itself, nor the learning of it by the child, can be adequately understood except by reference to some higher level of semiotic organisation . . . The child's task is to construct the system of meanings that represents his own model of social reality. This process takes place inside his own head; it is a cognitive process. But it takes place in contexts of social interaction, and there is no way it can take place except in these contexts. As well as being a cognitive process, the learning of the mother tongue is also an interactive process. It takes the form of the continued exchange of meanings between self and others. The act of meaning is a social act.

In a discussion with Parrett (1974: 59), Halliday said: 'I am trying to characterize human interaction; I am personally glad to see that there is a return to . . . [a] perspective in which we take account of the fact that people not only speak, but that they speak to each other'. Yes, indeed. But our formation by the traditions of university disciplines is generally more powerful than we know. The research on Nigel had actually begun with 'notes on the *child's* utterances' (Halliday 1975: 11, emphasis added), and though dialogues were noted later, you will look in vain in *Learning How to Mean* for any attempt to analyse in detail 'the continued exchange of meanings' between parent and child.

Yet how near he was: right on the brink! 'In Phase II Nigel recognises two generic structures: narrative and dialogue', Halliday claimed. And 'an interesting feature of such [narrative] sequences is how they are built up through dialogue'. Yes? 'The following is an example . . . Nigel [who has been to the zoo and handled a goat] is reviewing the incident after returning home' (Halliday 1975: 111). Now for it!

N. try eat lid
F. What tried to eat the lid?
N. try eat lid
F. What tried to eat the lid?
N. goat . . . man said no . . . goat try eat lid . . . man said no

Then, after a further interval, while being put to bed:

N. goat try eat lid . . . man said no
M. Why did the man say no?
N. goat shouldn't eat lid . . . (*shaking head*) good for it
M. The goat shouldn't eat the lid; it's not good for it.
N. goat try eat lid . . . man said no . . . goat shouldn't eat lid . . . (*shaking head*) good for it

So there, as Halliday said, was the evidence of crucial exchanges. For instance, we might note that it is the parent who signals the generic tense, the interest in agents/participants, and the need for a significant relation if two events are to constitute a narrative – and, what's more, these prompts are given in a step-by-step procedure, helping to form a fascinating cumulative outcome. Teaching indeed! And look at the child: he is learning to 'review' his piecemeal bits of progress retrospectively, and in that light to reconstruct his possible intent. There is no comment on all this by Halliday – despite the lead-up. Instead his discipline takes over, and, abstracting himself from the dynamic exchange of meanings, he focuses in a static way on examples of anaphora and given/new intonation.

Nevertheless, the positive lessons were clear:

1 Look beyond the three levels of (current) linguistic analysis.
2 Study the exchange of meanings in social interaction, as the main site for cognitive change.
3 Look out for an emerging recognition of generic structures, built up through dialogue.
4 Treat the child's meanings as a model of social reality.
5 Treat 'culture as a system of meanings, a semiotic system' and the child as 'constructing for himself a social semiotic, a model of the culture'. (*For* himself but *with* others, we might add.)

What I want to suggest is that for Halliday, as for other linguistic theoreticians, this was a period of intense speculative reconstruction, full of implications that necessarily eluded them for the moment. However, given his emerging focus on social interaction, there is a puzzling absence in Halliday's references at the time – the names of Searle and Austin.

Dialogue as social action

As a philosopher fascinated by 'ordinary language', John Austin had come to challenge some of the oldest assumptions about it.

> Besides the question that has been very much studied in the past as to what a certain utterance means, there is a further question – what was the force ... of the utterance? We may be quite clear what 'shut the door' means, but not yet at all clear ... [whether] it was an order, an entreaty, or whatnot. What we need is a new doctrine about all the possible forces of utterances (Austin 1970: 251).

Naturally,

> there are a great many devices that can be used for making clear ... what act it is we are performing when we say [Shut the door] – the tone of voice, cadence, gesture – and above all else we rely on ... the context in which the utterance is issued ... Still, in spite of these devices, there is an unfortunate amount of ambiguity ... And that is why the explicit performative verbs evolved

in languages (1970: 244) – I *order* you to shut the door, I *entreat* you ... I *advise* you to shut the door, I *warn* you ... I *argue that* it's up to you to shut the door, I *concede that* you ... and so on.

From this perspective,

> the traditional 'statement' [in philosophy and logic] is an abstraction, an ideal, and so is its traditional truth or falsity ... *The total speech act in the total speech situation is the only actual phenomenon which, in the last resort, we are engaged in elucidating* (1962: 147, emphasis added).

This was fighting stuff, especially for someone as unassertive as Austin. Moreover, it followed from such an analysis, according to Austin, that 'stating' was just one name among perhaps a thousand others for speech acts; that statements were not unique in being treatable as true or false; and that 'the familiar contrast of "normative or evaluative" [expressions] as opposed to the factual [statement] is in need . . . of elimination' (1962: 147–8).

These 'hopeful fireworks', set off in Harvard in 1955, primarily undercut the way philosophers regarded statements. But by the early 1970s it had been recognised, thanks to Searle (1969), that various categories of speech act might have a syntactic base; this opened up a damaging critique of fundamental assumptions in contemporary grammars – Chomsky's especially. It was part of the radical reconstruction characteristic of the new decade. However, so far I have been able to find no one before 1977 who took up Austin's revolutionary suggestions as a whole. That year Labov and Fanshel, as it seems to me, made the first sweeping breakthrough on this front.

They began (unlike Searle) with the 'actual phenomena', speech in situation – tape recordings of a series of therapeutic interviews, backed by further tape-recorded interviews with the therapist, in which she discussed what she had been trying to *do* as she *said* various things. On this basis Labov and Fanshel (1977: 71) attempted an analysis of

> two planes of conversational behaviour. On the one hand there is . . . 'what is said', which includes the text, paralinguistic cues, and implicit references to other texts and propositions; on the other hand, there is 'what is done', the plane of interaction that is itself a multilayered complex of speech acts.

I can only sketch here the rich significance of this analysis, and the theorising it gave rise to.

I have space for just the first utterance in the twenty-fifth session (the one that starts their investigation). Rhoda, a nineteen-year-old woman with a history of anorexia nervosa, opens the interview:

Rhoda: I don't . . . know, whether . . . I – I *think* I did – the right thing, jista-
            little . . . situation came up . . . an' I tried to uhm . . . well, try to . . . use
            what I – what I've learned here, see if it worked.
Therapist: Mhm.
Rhoda: Now, I don't know if I did the right thing (1977: 113).

We don't need to go any further to see that these forms require massive expansion, if they are to be understood. This 'thing', this 'little situation', and 'what I've learned here' are all going to need explication, whether tacitly or explicitly. So the researchers set about constructing an ideal (retrospective) expansion. However, in doing so, they discovered that the expansion process was open-ended: there were always further texts that might be brought to bear. Theoretically, this was a vital point to recognise, I believe. Moreover, the paralinguistic cues already offer the therapist important evidence to qualify what is being said. There were signs of tension: hesitations, self-interruptions, long silences, uneven tempo . . . All of these modified the force of 'I think' – which turned out to be contrasted with a more confident 'I know' shortly afterwards.

By using these cues, then, and following up the tacit or explicit references, Labov and Fanshel (1977: 119) produced the following *partial* expansion:

> I am not sure I did the right thing, but I claim that I did what you say is right, or what might actually be right, when I asked my mother to help me by coming home after she had been away from home longer than she usually is, creating some small problems for me, and I tried to use the principle that I've learned from you here that I should express my needs and emotions to relevant others and see if this principle worked.

It will be clear at once that this expansion is 'ideal' in several respects! But the most important for me here is that it constitutes a construction by the listening researchers – a construction that synthesises and integrates in ways the speaker is highly unlikely to be doing at this point in her life. Such constructions, I would claim, serve to reveal potentials within a dialogue, in ways that underlie (and can assist) not only therapy but teaching. (For an educational parallel at the time, based on group discussion of a poem, see Dixon 1974).

Labov and Fanshel moved on a step, though. Looking across the sessions, they recognised within this extract an underlying proposition, a persistent potential reference point: the notion that 'one should express one's needs and emotions to relevant others' (1977: 121). In other words, that was 'the right thing' to do. After this was recognised, it became possible to construe Rhoda's utterance as the opening of a characteristic discussion about 'whether an event just . . . reported is an instance of general propositions known to both of them though not necessarily believed by both' (1977: 122). Thus, to be fully understood, the conversation had to be 'read' at varying levels of abstraction. (Again, the relevance to education in many subjects seems obvious.)

Returning to the tapes, Labov and Fanshel next considered the interaction. Some of this was metalinguistic: for example, why did Rhoda initiate the session and present material on which the therapy could be based? 'Because she knows what her responsibilities are', said the therapist. The whole session was set within a tacit or explicit frame of needs (desires), abilities, obligations and rights, and to some degree this was socially regulated within structures of power and solidarity.

Having accepted the responsibility, Rhoda acted in a number of complex, overlapping ways: among other things, explicitly *expressing* uncertainty about what she was going to say; ambiguously *questioning* what would have been right (or what she did do); *suggesting* she did do the right thing; implicitly *indicating doubts* whether it would work anyway – and, thus, twice tacitly *challenging* the authoritative status of her therapist's assumptions (see 1977: 126).

The therapist's response to this utterance was a 'non-committal sign of reinforcement', and Rhoda continued by re-expressing her uncertainty about what she had done, this time more confidently (to judge by the paralinguistic evidence). It was in keeping with this analysis that, when the therapist finally responded verbally, among other things she asked: 'Well, what's your question?'

Standing back, we can readily see the importance of this speech-act analysis for therapy. After all, the *interactive relation* with the therapist was precisely one of those that Rhoda had to learn to use productively. Nevertheless, if we turn to education, aren't there likely to be occasions when questioning of premises, proposing evaluations, casting doubts on practicabilities, and challenging of authoritative assumptions – to go no further – need to be taken into account by teachers? Indeed, will the whole range of speech acts incorporated into discussion and argument, say, not be of interest to us in teaching?

Where does this take us? 'Conversation is not a chain of utterances,' say Labov and Fanshel (1977: 30),

> but rather a matrix of utterances and actions *bound together by a web of understandings and reactions* . . . We do not see conversation as a linguistic form. We have come to understand conversation as the means by which people deal with each other . . . *to interpret to each other the significance* of the actual and potential events that surround them and to draw the consequences . . . (emphasis added).

Among many positive ideas we could use, I would suggest these as a start:

1 Try to understand how assumed (or negotiated) rights, desires, obligations, abilities, and needs structure a social exchange.
2 Recognise that understanding has to reach well beyond the sentence or utterance, moving through provisional (because open-ended) expansions to underlying propositions that may well be tacit.
3 Read the interplay of speech acts, especially for their combined, progressive effect on interpreting the significance of events.
4 Bear in mind varying levels of abstraction in your interpretation of what is said and done.
5 Include the participants' retrospective interpretations in your evidence.
6 Do not expect a one-to-one relation of form and speech act, or of utterances and any overall expansion of what's said.

These in themselves are valuable enough – and they are only a sample. But it seems to me that Labov and Fanshel unconsciously also signalled the main theoretical question that lay ahead. While proposing formal structures for expansions and interactions, they acknowledged that these (and the details within them) arose from complex interpretative decisions. In retrospect, it seems to me that such procedures were crying out for a more explicit theory of understanding.

Towards a theory of understanding and significance

There is little doubt that the past ten years have seen a revolution in our discussions of talking/listening and reading – and thus in our notions of language in operation. Again, I am going to choose one examplar, to allow for a little detail. Mikhail Bakhtin and his group emerged very slowly from the shadows of Stalin, from the late 1950s onwards, so until this year our translations went back to their work of the 1930s. However, that was quite revolutionary enough: *Marxism and the Philosophy of Language* (Voloshinov 1973, written in 1929) offered a radical critique of 'objectivism' and 'idealisation' in the European linguistic tradition, while proposing a theory of both speech and writing as social dialogue. In the course of its rich philosophical analysis, it began to theorise 'the problem of understanding'.

The Bakhtin group were concerned precisely with the kind of process you and I are currently engaged in. Even as I frame what to say and do, I recognise the fact

> that when the listener perceives and understands the meaning (the language meaning) of speech, he simultaneously takes an active, responsive attitude toward it. He agrees or disagrees with it (completely or partially), augments it, applies it, prepares to carry it out, and so on . . . Any understanding of live speech, of a live utterance, is inherently responsive, although the degree of this activity does vary extremely (Bakhtin 1986: 68).

Bakhtin seems to be feeling his way here to a model of active listening as *inner* speech acts: let us see how that develops. Thus,

> to understand another person's utterance means to *orient oneself* with respect to it, to *find* a proper place for it in the corresponding context. [And] for each word of the utterance that we are in the process of understanding, we lay down, as it were, a set of answering words . . . *Understanding is to utterance as one line of dialogue is to the next* (Voloshinov 1973: 102 emphasis added).

If this were the case, wouldn't your current inner speech acts be a form – perhaps the form – of understanding? For I guess that in inner speech you are already laying down the piecemeal basis for a developing 'response'. If so, how does that knowledge affect me, the speaker?

> The word in living conversation is directly, blatantly, oriented towards a future answer-word; it provokes an answer, anticipates it and structures itself in the answerer's direction . . . This relationship towards the concrete listener, taking him into account . . . enters into the very internal construction of [everyday dialogue and] rhetorical discourse.

As we speak, we sense response 'as resistance or support enriching the discourse' (Bakhtin 1986: 275 and 281). On this view, then, the existence of your listening response may be mutually acknowledged, and thus affect the very formulation of what I am about to say. (And that was true even in the act of writing my script.) Bakhtin (1986: 69) knows as much.

> The speaker himself is oriented precisely toward such an actively responsive understanding. He does not expect passive understanding that, so to speak, only duplicates his own idea in someone else's mind. [Well, let's hope not!] Rather he expects response, agreement, sympathy, objection, execution (of his requests), and so forth . . . Moreover, any speaker is himself a respondent to a greater or lesser degree. He is not, after all, the first speaker, the one who disturbs the eternal silence of the universe. And he *presupposes* not only the existence of the language system he is using, but also *the existence of preceding utterances* – his own and others' – with which his given utterance enters into one kind of relation or another (builds on them, polemicizes with them, or simply presumes that they are already known to the listener). Any utterance is a link in a very complexly organised chain of other utterances.

What follows from this view of active listening? In general terms

> The linguistic significance of a given utterance is understood against the background of language, but its actual meaning is understood in the background of other concrete utterances on the same theme, a background made up of contrary opinions, points of view and value judgements . . . present to the speaker . . . [and] in the consciousness of the listener (1973: 281).

But your background is not necessarily the same as mine, is it? 'Thus each of the distinguishable significative elements . . . and the entire utterance as a whole, are translated in our minds into another, active and responsive, context. Any true understanding is dialogic in nature' (1973: 102)

More precisely, it follows that

> for a person speaking his native tongue, a word presents itself not as an item of vocabulary [a dictionary entry] but as a word that has been used in a wide variety of utterances by co-speaker A, co-speaker B, co-speaker C and so on, and has been variously used in the speaker's own utterances (1973: 70).

'A word is territory shared by both . . . the speaker and his interlocutor' (1973: 86). Each participant 'assimilates the word to be understood into [his] own conceptual system, filled with specific objects and emotional expressions'. And sometimes, we hope,

> the speaker strives to get a reading on his own word, and on his own conceptual system that determines this word, within the alien conceptual system of the understanding receiver; he enters into dialogical relationships . . . [and] constructs his own utterance on alien territory, against [the other's], the listener's, apperceptive background (Bakhtin 1981: 282).

Well, here we are (readers included) and this time I do not need to transcribe evidence for you to examine – you are engaged in producing your own, one way or the other.

You will readily see that I have not been content simply to reproduce Bakhtin (or Wilkinson, or Barnes and the rest). I have selected from Bakhtin what may illumine my own problems, and in so doing have assimilated his utterances to my own conceptual frame, no doubt. But my act of selection is also critical: I have (largely) omitted any passages I find obscure or not congruent with his later ideas (in my view), and I am bound to say I now think he (and I) need to shake off this umbrella word 'response' and recognise the variety of processes he has speculatively described. So I want to resist, extend, test against some empirical material . . . and a lot more. But I also need to reread, to question the translator, and find if I have more to learn as I check my own reconstructed ideas against the frame of alien possibilities I am sure to find there in his thinking. So it goes on.

What can we learn from Bakhtin and others, then, about understanding?

1 We can now see the 'speaker' (or writer) as the next *contributor* to a network of *dialogic acts*. ('Speaker' is incidentally shown to be a kind of abstraction.)
2 A dialogic act can be seen as a production which is also, sometimes consciously, an 'interpretant' response to some preceding utterance(s). It indicates what this contributor finds significant.
3 Thus, in agreement with Peirce and Welby-Gregory (1977), I can now see the *significance* of my current utterance as an (open-ended) series of dialogic interpretants produced by myself and others in a network.
4 From this perspective, 'making meanings' together can be seen as producing dialogic interpretants of each other's utterances *for* each other (whether consciously or not): 'Goat shouldn't eat lid . . . (*shaking head*) good for it' leads to 'The goat shouldn't eat the lid; it's not good for it'!
5 Thus our interpretant expresses (or betrays) the nature of our *interest* in what the other contributor has said and done, and our *evaluation* of it.

We are back to Nigel, and to a history of exchanges that organise socially 'shared experiences', or to Rhoda, who negotiates with the therapist a joint (social) significance of her continuing life story, week by week. And we can now go on, I hope, to answer with more confidence some of those pioneering questions that seemed so difficult to handle twenty years ago.

References

Austin, J. L. (1962). *How to Do Things with Words*, Oxford, Oxford University Press.
Austin, J. L. (1970). *Philosophical Papers*, 2nd edn, Oxford, Oxford University Press.
Bakhtin, M. M. (1981). *The Dialogic Imagination*, Austin, University of Texas Press.
Bakhtin, M. M. (1986). *Speech Genres and Other Late Essays*, Austin, University of Texas Press.
Barnes, D., Britton, J. and Rosen, H. (1969). *Language, the Learner, and the School*, London, Penguin Books.
Bruner, J. S., Olver, R. R. and Greenfield, P. M. (1966). *Studies in Cognitive Growth*, New York, John Wiley & Sons.
Davies, A. (1965). 'Linguistics and the Teaching of Spoken English' in Wilkinson (1965).
Dixon, J. L. (1974). 'Processes of Formulation in Group Discussion', *Educational Review*, vol. 26, no. 3.
Halliday, M. A. K. (1975). *Learning How to Mean*, London, Edward Arnold.
Labov, W. and Fanshel, D. (1977). *Therapeutic Discourse*, New York, Academic Press.
Parrett, M. (1974). *Discussing Language*, The Hague, Mouton.
Peirce, C. S. S. and Welby-Gregory, V. (1977). *Semiotics and Significs*, ed. C. S. Hardwick, Bloomington, Indiana University Press.
Searle, J. R. (1969). *Speech Acts, An Essay in the Philosophy of Language*, Cambridge, Cambridge University Press.
Trim, J. L. M. (1959). 'Speech Education' in R. Quirk (ed.), *The Teaching of English*, London, Martin Secker.
Voloshinov, V. N. (1973). *Marxism and the Philosophy of Language*, New York, Seminar Press (reportedly by Bakhtin or joint work).
Wilkinson, A. M. (1965). *Spoken English*, Educational Review Occasional Publications no. 2, University of Birmingham School of Education.

3 Oracy in England – a new tide: an HMI overview*

GRAHAM FRATER

Introduction

We stand, in 1987, at a point where the flywheel of curriculum development is moving with sufficient momentum to be generating real changes in the classroom. That it has taken more than twenty years from Wilkinson's early signalling of the importance of the spoken word (and its neglect!) for shifts in process and procedure actually to occur in fairly widespread form, is a point which all of us with responsibilities for research, teacher training, and administration, with advisory roles, or with managerial and political responsibility need to understand. It is clear that there is a sharp disjunction between structural or organisational change and process or behavioural change at classroom level. In the same period, that is from the early 1960s to the present, the educational scene in England has witnessed enormous structural changes. When Wilkinson was first playing with the word 'oracy', English secondary education was largely selective and primary schools were dominated by the eleven-plus selection tests which all pupils underwent in order to identify the 20 per cent or so who were destined for the grammar schools. At that time the GCE O-level examination was on a far smaller scale than the present and CSE, which by 1987 had risen to over 600,000 candidates, had hardly begun. Since then we have seen massive structural changes in the system. At secondary level, comprehensive schools, of which there were no more than a handful in 1962, are now the norm. The same period has also seen a huge-scale administrative change: in 1974 local government reorganisation led to the overnight disappearance of many administering education authorities and the emergence of new ones; boundaries, administrative and advisory staffs, procedures and patterns of primary and secondary schooling were all rescrambled one April morning. And, at present, we are undergoing a change in our examination structure at the age of sixteen whereby the GCE and CSE examinations, which have lasted for about thirty-six and twenty-four years, respectively, are in the process of being combined in a new examination, the

* Crown Copyright

General Certificate of Secondary Education (GCSE), which, in curricular terms, will be a good deal more than the sum of its parts. What all this demonstrates is that, for all the upheavals, it is far simpler and speedier to change nomenclature, to shift the counters on the administrative chequer board and even to make substantial changes in the conditions under which teachers operate than it is to bring about the deep-rooted changes in thinking, attitudes and behaviour which are implied by curriculum development and which carry the prospect of giving pupils the chance of developing new competences, new attitudes and raised standards to match the increasing and complex demands of life beyond the school gate.

Oracy: the first phase

I do not intend to offer a potted history of the early oracy movement. Instead, I should like, briefly, to reflect on some of the early developments as they seemed to me then as a young teacher, and as they seem to me now when we can see something of the inheritance.

First, the abiding debt we owe to Wilkinson and his early colleagues in the 1960s is the recognition of the importance of the spoken word for the school curriculum. What now seems obvious was far less clear to most teachers then: the curriculum was delivered in an essentially prescriptive mode, writing had the almost exclusive prestige and, as recordings of many of the public figures of the time make clear, Received Pronunciation (RP) was too often the stiflingly respectable measure and model of appropriate speech. In particular, the role of talk in learning, its importance in the shaping of thought, the internalising of concepts, the development of argument, and of its interplay with the other language modes, was little understood. A sea change has not occurred and much remains to be done at classroom level, but the case for oracy is now clear and organisational support – of which more later – is now in place. The tide is running.

In some measure, the early oracy initiatives were blessed with good luck: they coincided with the introduction of CSE and secured a foothold in that examination which had been designed for the 'average' pupil. One notes, however, that oracy was largely excluded from the older and more prestigious GCE O-level examination in English and will have been so excluded throughout its life span of thirty-six years. The new GCSE will require oral assessment of all candidates. By formal and informal means, there is little doubt that our examination system, particularly at the age of sixteen, has been our prime determinant of the content and delivery of the secondary school curriculum. It is a two-edged sword and most of the pitfalls I hinted at in my opening remarks have been associated with oral assessment in examinations. However, before I illustrate those problems, it is important that I should nail up the achievement: the public examination system in England (first CSE and now GCSE) has secured an irreducible place for the spoken word in the English curriculum.

In brief, oral assessment in public examinations hitherto has not been undertaken consistently by all examination boards, nor is consistency of approach guaranteed between examining groups in the new GCSE. At the heart of the problem of assessment in the spoken word in our public examinations lie the competing interests of: validity; reliability; and 'backwash' into classroom practice. The tension is between the needs of the boards very properly to present scrupulous, honest, reliable and consistent assessments and those of the schools both generally to educate their pupils and to prepare them for the formal tests they must inevitably face. I have little hesitation in saying that test preparation has won, the backwash has been generally unhelpful, and that the defensible *principle* of compulsory oral assessment has often been diminished by the *practices* which have gained currency as a consequence.

At this point, I ought perhaps to illustrate and suggest a solution. In general, oral assessments have been of four kinds, not all of which have operated within or across any one examining board or group: listening tests; reading aloud; short talks; and individual interviews with teachers and/or external examiners. The characteristics these forms share are their formality, their artificiality, the performance pressure they bring to bear, and their remoteness from language use within the learning process. The backwash from concentrating upon test rehearsal of this kind is to foreground *product* as distinct from *process*, and to expose rather than to remedy weakness because the variety of language experience which might promote growth has been sacrificed to the diet of the test forms rehearsed.

Perhaps the best illustration of this process is the listening comprehension test whose early development in England Andrew Wilkinson was closely involved with. Many of its weaknesses derive from ignoring advice which he gave to the CSE boards in 1963 through the then Ministry of Education and reiterated in his pioneering *Spoken English* (1965). In the twenty or so years of CSE, typical listening tests, where employed, have *not* taken samples of real utterance as their core material; they have *not* been 'different in kind' from what is 'commonly presented in written form' (Wilkinson 1965: 104). Thus to the manifest weaknesses of the traditional reading comprehension tests has been added the massive inappropriateness of treating written code as if it were spoken and still testing it in written form whilst relying almost entirely upon memory. It follows that the distinct features of speech which make for its ready assimilation have seldom been present in tests which have masqueraded as listening comprehension.

But in addition to these pitfalls, there has been the generally poor quality of the test materials themselves: many were poorly recorded; they were often embarrassingly performed and ineptly scripted (by chief examiners themselves?); and they have frequently carried social assumptions which set the mind reeling. My criticism of the tests is not intended to detract from the importance of listening, but to point up the generally wrong direction taken by assessment.

Thankfully, the effect of the new GCSE has been to eliminate most of these listening tests, though one examining group plans to retain them in modified form. Its concession to criticism has been to offer candidates a copy of the tape transcript – at least this has the virtue of eliminating the memory test and permitting questions to be asked on aspects of delivery; but it also blurs the identity of the test, as between reading and listening. Sadly, in unmodified form, listening tests are gaining a new market in the growing movement to offer tests of basic skills to pupils whose abilities are thought to be limited.

Before I leave public examinations entirely I must return briefly to the pitfalls of formality to which the other forms of test I described earlier are equally open. The danger in the new GCSE is that, though a wide range of demands will rightly be made, the apparatus of assessment may become overwhelming. For instance, schools offering individual interviews are already talking of one and two whole weeks which must be redirected from teaching to assessment. Even ten minutes each for a class of thirty pupils would require a minimum of 300 minutes which is well over a week's typical allocation of English teaching time and it would have the additional knock-on costs of administration time, of cover for the teachers undertaking the assessments and of timetable disruption for the school as a whole. Moreover, a ten-minute interview will not tell you much. If this is how it is approached and works out in practice, the 'opportunity cost' looks very high.

There is a possible solution which, so far, has not been widely entertained: it lies in making oral assessment genuinely continuous, in training teachers appropriately – probably on the model of the APU assessors (e.g. APU 1984), and then in trusting them without further moderation or validation. We have a model and a precedent for such an approach in the assessment role accorded to West German teachers in the *Abitur* examinations. Such an approach, using a simple agreed scale and criteria, would remove much of the artificiality of our oral assessment inheritance, would be far more flexible than anything we have hitherto envisaged, could be made clear to pupils and, being always open to modification, could eliminate some of the conflicts of interest between teaching and assessment which many teachers of English feel with regard to coursework at present.

Other developments

The public examination system, then, guaranteed a place for the spoken word and this now extends to all pupils in the secondary school system, but it has not been an unalloyed benefit. However, the impetus, of which oral examining was a part, was unstoppable and outside the formal examination apparatus, other important work was also happening.

One of the most valuable of these other strands of development was the work of Harold Rosen at London University. It first impinged on my own awareness as a West Riding teacher with the *Talkshop* publications (e.g., Rosen 1977). They valued the richness of our oral tradition; they tapped the same vein that Charles Parker, A. L. Lloyd and others had drawn on for the BBC radio ballads in the 1940s and 1950s and which, with different intentions, the great Leeds Dialect Survey had also revealed. What Rosen did for me was to put flesh on the arguments of Labov (see Labov 1972) by accumulating an archive of British recordings and transcripts which, *inter alia*, demonstrated to young teachers like myself the subtleties, complexity and rich vitality to be found and encouraged in the speech of *all* our pupils. It is a lesson of long-standing importance which is still needed, especially if the assessment and testing of pupil performance is not to be in narrow and simplistic terms which would have damaging consequences for the quality of education.

And then, in 1975, came the Bullock Report (DES 1975). Chapter 10 on oral language is still as vitally relevant today as it was twelve years ago – its diagnosis as accurate and its suggestions just as applicable. In magisterial terms, this Johnsonian compendium sounded out the key principles:

> language competence grows incrementally, through an interaction of writing, talk, reading, and experience, the body of resulting work forming an organic whole (DES 1975: 7).

> The point to be emphasised is that the child's language should be accepted (1975: 143).

> The teacher's role should be one of planned intervention, and his purposes and the means of fulfilling them must be clear in his mind' (1975: 145).

> A good deal of the oral work we saw . . . suffered from a lack of contact with reality in the sense that it did not carry this conviction of real purpose. Its air of contrivance was apparent to the children themselves and since their language was answering no real need beyond that of elaborate exercise it had an artificial restraint about it (1975: 146).

And so on. What Bullock did was to confirm the importance of oracy in the curriculum.

In the primary sector, Joan Tough (e.g., Tough 1973) put flesh upon the Bullock principles by the cascade of action-research groups she established in which teachers both scrutinised their own practice and the development of their pupils. It generated enormous enthusiasm, as I saw at first hand in the North as adviser and, later, as HMI.

At this point I should like to sweep forward in time and draw your attention to some of the more recent strands of development. The first, though not in strict temporal sequence, is *teacher opinion*. Two HMI publications (DES 1984; 1986) did not pass without controversy. The first of these offered for discussion a series of suggestions on aims, objectives, principles and assessment for the English curriculum for the ages five to sixteen. The second recorded reactions (chiefly from the profession), plotted areas of agreement and disagreement, and showed that HMI were ready to respond to the points made. However, for all the heat generated, that exercise revealed virtual unanimity on the matter of oracy. If the responses are representative, as I believe them to be, it is no exaggeration to say that the teaching profession in England is agreed upon 'the importance of the spoken word in the curriculum and the need for a strengthened emphasis upon it in the work of schools' (DES 1986: 31.12). But, despite this widespread accord, there were very few suggestions for its development and there were many expressions of uncertainty, perhaps strengthened by GCSE and its assessment requirements, about how this enhancement might be brought about in schools.

Some of the ways in which oracy may be advanced have been suggested by the Wiltshire Oracy Project, funded by the DES but planned and implemented by that local authority within the Low Attaining Pupils Project (LAPP). Wiltshire has been another pathfinder; its officers and elected members took a brave decision to put all their eggs in the oracy basket when bidding for government funding – it could so easily have failed to attract a grant. But they won and the work has been particularly important. The project is on a small scale (essentially four schools) but its approach has been *cross-curricular* and *collaborative*. These two strands, combined with lively project leadership, have ensured that the project has had its roots deep in classroom practice and that teacher confidence, goodwill and enthusiasm have been at a level which have permitted locally *a general reappraisal of teaching methods and classroom interaction*. It has been a project in which individual teachers have had an identifiable stake, but also one in which a corporate philosophy can be recognised as growing in the schools concerned. These are most important achievements; additional lessons have highlighted, once again, the value of in-service training, and indicated the virtue of developing an assessment mechanism, of doing so gradually and, at the same time, of exercising a measure of tentativeness about assessment. Many further lessons of a practical and procedural nature have also been learnt. What Wiltshire has done has been widely influential and many local authorities have read the documents, have visited Wiltshire and have taken the message home.

This leads me to what is perhaps the best news I have to deliver and it complements what I have already noted about widespread teacher support for oracy. Beginning in 1987, we have another government-funded initiative: oracy is to receive central funding under the Education Support Grants (ESG) mechanism. The sum is modest and only six local education authorities (LEAs) will, in fact, receive grants. But the good news lies in the number and quality of the LEA grant submissions made. Sixty-two authorities made bids, about 30 per cent of which were of outstanding quality and most of which were clearly viable. What I read from this is that not merely has the message about the spoken word taken root on a wide scale, but that a variety of thoughtful, resourceful and sometimes ingenious approaches to its development are emerging nationwide. I see this not only as a flowering of some of the seeds sown by the pioneers over twenty years ago, but as a substantial tribute to my colleagues in the LEA advisory services and the National Association of Advisers in English in particular.

There is further good news: the Schools Curriculum Development Council (SCDC) has now announced that there will be a National Oracy Project, as was recommended by HMI in DES (1986). This means that, in addition to and linked with the ESG apparatus, we have a further funded structure to support the development of the spoken word in the school curriculum. Better still, neither the ESG nor the National Project will be taking the process of individual assessment, in the examination system, as its starting point: neither is required to short-circuit *process* in the interests of *assessment product*. Moreover, the ESG proposals set a positive precedent for the national project: after schemes like those it will be unacceptable for applicants to submit narrowly circumscribed agendas to the national project. In addition, I have no doubt that economy of effort will dictate that many of the excellent schemes for which room could not be found in the ESG oracy scheme will be reworked for the national project and, in view of their quality, I welcome such a move.

The Assessment of Performance Unit

The APU was established as a direct result of the Bullock Report (DES 1975). The Unit was charged with monitoring the corporate (*not individual*) perform-ance of pupils in the nation's schools. Its language assessments did not, at first, embrace the spoken word, but when it made its late entry, it proved that the wait had been worthwhile. The unit began by reappraising all the current research before devising its own assessment frameworks and procedures. Thus, at a single stroke, it broke away from the flimsy but long-standing structure of precedent upon which public examinations had depended. Its assessments, founded upon important and clearly articulated principles and concepts, held that talk is purposeful; that assessment should reflect the variety and complexity of spoken language; that talk is relevant throughout the curriculum; that the spoken word is essentially reciprocal in nature; and that spoken language is sensitive to context (APU 1984). Moreover, the tasks they devised were interesting and enjoyable to undergo.

With interesting and ingenious tasks and a highly effective and efficiently trained team of assessors, the APU offers important lessons for the rest of the assessment movement. However, the implied challenge has not been widely taken up. I will not discuss the APU findings and conclusions in any detail, but the following have vital implications both for the curriculum as a whole and, equally, for individual teachers' perceptions of their pupils. Thus, the APU has found that most eleven-year-olds are capable in some measure of modifying their speaking and listening strategies appropriately in accordance with the com-municative purpose of the task; girls and boys perform equally well in oracy; performance varies according to the communicative purpose being assessed.

Oracy in the classroom: some findings from inspection

We have seen that the LEA advisers, the professional standard-bearers of English, not only stand behind the development of the spoken word, but have resourceful and detailed plans for its enhancement in schools. The response to the debate addressed by DES (1984) showed that the teachers themselves are also behind an extension of oracy, but that they are less clear about ways forward. If we turn to the results of inspection, we can confirm this picture at classroom level, and other strands are also revealed.

Across the language modes, my colleagues and I are able to record tentative progress in the delivery of the English curriculum at classroom level: some of the same good ideas are reaching receptive class teachers across the country and are being put into practice effectively. At classroom level the momentum is less strong than among the 300 or so subject leaders to be found together in the advisory services, in teacher training and directing the national subject associations, but evidence can be found. An increase in oral activity may be on the way and we are finding oral work which is both purposeful and *about* something; we are finding evidence of group-work and we are finding examples of skilful and effective practice.

We also find differences between primary and secondary practice in oracy. In primary schools, my colleagues are impressed by the many opportunities provided for talk and listening; books, writing and practical work have all been noted as stimulating and focusing talk particularly effectively. We also found that the disposition of furniture could play a significant part in the effectiveness, or otherwise, of the spoken word. In addition, we have noted that, as children move up the age ladder within the primary school, there seems to be some decline of activity in the spoken word. The general picture, as you might expect, is varied – it includes liveliness and resourcefulness as well as neglect and unimaginative approaches to talk.

In secondary schools, my colleagues have recently given particular attention to the spoken word. The prevailing picture still suggests that it is generally undervalued in the teaching of English and that both activity and response in oracy decline sharply in the fourth and fifth years once examination courses begin, though this may be changing with the onset of GCSE. Unsurprisingly, tasks and assignments specifically related to examinations in the spoken word were found to result in stilted exchanges. Significant factors in the establishment of effective oral work appear to be the experience of the teachers concerned; the appropriate structuring of the work; and the suitability of the teacher's communication with pupils. An important message seems to be that talk which is related to tasks, to getting something done with others, is far more effective than oral activities which are specifically carried out with a view to the improvement or the assessment of the spoken word. Nevertheless, things may well be stirring, though quantification is hardly possible. Reports across the country record instances of good practice which have positive features in common: the variation of group sizes; clear purposes; simulation activities; good links with reading activities; and so on. Drama, in particular, was noted as prompting confident talk when it was effectively planned, but improvisation work, when it fell into social stereotyping, was felt to be unhelpful. As with the primary sector, there is both a growing interest in and a manifest need for in-service training in the spoken word; it is likely to be a long-term need.

If we remain in the secondary school, but move away from subject English to language across the curriculum, the general picture of the spoken word shows fewer signs of movement. High points are certainly to be found across the subject range with particularly lively examples emerging from some lessons in science, CDT and home economics, when problem-solving is required. In history, too, examples of lively practice could be found as, for instance, when in a fourth-year history lesson pupils were involved in group discussions preparing briefing papers to give the positions of the PLO, Israel and the superpowers in the politics of the Middle East. More widely, however, lessons were too often over-directed with little challenge to pupils to think for themselves or express themselves clearly. Oral work was too often made to comprise mainly monosyllabic and factual answers to questions which required no other response. And it was also generally true that pupils spent more time in the classroom reading, and especially writing, than talking or listening to each other. Pupils often seemed to be articulate, but it was clear that they were given insufficient opportunities to develop their oral skills further. Schools' statements of aims often mentioned the importance of oral communication, but few have reached the stage of developing a policy for implementing such aims. Taken together, the findings of short inspections suggest that standards of oral work were satisfactory or better in 41 per cent of the schools inspected in the first three years, and this figure fell to 38 per cent in the fourth and fifth years. At sixth-form level the picture was rather better, especially for the more able pupils among whom discussion featured more frequently as part of the working pattern than in the main school – in 60 per cent of the schools with sixth forms the spoken word was regularly used as a means of reinforcing or extending understanding on A-level courses and in 50 per cent of those schools the same was true for pupils not studying A level. However, the general picture was that, taking the curriculum as a whole, too few schools provided sufficient opportunities for the development of talking and listening, and most need to establish and implement policies which encourage all teachers to increase the scope for spoken-word activities and development.

Some conclusions

When we talk of oracy in the classroom we are talking of substantial behavioural change and perhaps the clearest message of the last twenty-five years is that, by comparison with these matters of process and methodology, structural and organisational changes, for all the traumas they have cost, have been ludicrously easy to achieve.

Nevertheless, the momentum for change has been created; the flywheel is running. We have support and dissemination structures in place through the Education Support Grants and the National Oracy Project. The LEA advisory services generally have both the expertise and, in many cases, detailed schemes for the enhancement of oracy. From the APU we know in performance terms where we stand. Among teachers it is plain that there is strong support for the enhancement of the spoken word and clear appreciation of its importance in the learning process. The filaments of good practice are permeating the educational soil, but they have not yet mushroomed. They are more likely to be found in the primary sector and in secondary English departments than in the secondary sector as a whole, but growth is occurring. It will continue to need cultivation; it will continue to need fertiliser and protection from frost, but the widespread recognition of the importance of the spoken word does bode well for the future.

References

APU (1984). *Language Performance in Schools. 1982 Primary Survey Report*, London, DES.

DES (1975). *A Language for Life*, Report of the Committee of Enquiry chaired by Sir Alan Bullock, London, HMSO.

DES (1984). *English from 5 to 16, Curriculum Matters 1. An HMI Series*, London, HMSO.

DES (1986). *English from 5 to 16, The Response to Curriculum Matters 1*, London, HMSO.

Labov, W. (1972). 'The Logic of Non-Standard English' in *Language in Education*, London, Routledge and Kegan Paul for the Open University, pp. 198–212.

Rosen, H. (1977). *Talkshop 2*, London University Institute of Education.

Tough, J. (1973). *Focus on Meaning*, London, Allen & Unwin.

Wilkinson, A. M. (1965). *Spoken English*. Educational Review Occasional Publications, no. 2. University of Birmingham School of Education.

4 The politics of oracy

DOUGLAS BARNES

Any curriculum presents to its students a picture of the world, with implicit priorities which push some elements of experience and action into prominence and obscure others. It is my purpose in this chapter to enquire what values are implicit in the programme for oracy that has been espoused not only by many educators but by the present British government, and then to suggest some of the characteristics of an acceptable programme for oracy.

It is not true that the subject English has no content. Language has to be used about something, and an examination of the topics written about in English lessons is highly informative (Barnes *et al.* 1984). English in secondary schools in England embodies a view of experience in which the individual is the measure of all things: intense personal experience is highly valued, and dealt with in a manner which is self-conscious, romantic and introspective. It is a morality of face-to-face relationships, as if we played no part in the lives of those we never meet. If such a pre-emptive selection from experience – or perhaps reinterpretation of experience – can be found in the teaching of written language, what interpretation of experience would a programme of oracy as presently conceived transmit to students? Of course, the word 'oracy' has no content of itself: it is we who ascribe one to it. No doubt North American courses in speech and drama, with their traditional interest in rhetoric, express quite other priorities and values from those to be found in Britain.

What, then, are the tacit cultural messages of oracy? What pictures of people's activities, goals and relationships are implicit in current proposals for education in spoken language? Such cultural messages propose tacit priorities for young people to pursue in their future lives, and model for them a politico-cultural style. It behoves those of us who advocate oracy as part of the curriculum to take responsibility for what we propose.

When Her Majesty's Inspectors of Schools (1979) reported on aspects of secondary education, they treated speech as a means of teaching and learning and at no point considered the possibility of making it a goal of teaching in itself. Only five years later (DES 1984), however, they listed explicit goals for oracy teaching at seven, eleven and fifteen years of age. What had happened to cause such a change?

I have no wish to revive here the debate about DES (1984), but will merely point out that no mention is made of contextualising speech in real-life purposes. We talk because we have something to say. Or, to put it differently, in our everyday lives what we say, like what we write, comes out of our commitments to people, to activities and purposes, to the ongoing projects and relationships that constitute the texture of our lives. Even chat is a celebration of shared experiences and concerns. Yet in DES (1984) speech hangs unsupported in mid-air. There seems something flawed in such a view of spoken language.

While working two years ago with a group of teachers in a small local study of the teaching and assessment of spoken language, my wife and I noticed that many of these enthusiasts were far from having a clear view of what they were doing. Should an oracy programme content itself with setting up a variety of language activities, or is there some overt instruction to be done? If the latter, at what point should the teacher intervene? We had noted the same phenomenon during observation of Communications Studies in Further Education (FE) colleges (Barnes, 1982), where the teaching of spoken communication has been accepted for some years. The lecturers set up simulated speech events, but then found themselves at a loss to know what aspects of the students' speech they could usefully comment on. (It may have been coincidence that almost every time we saw work in spoken communication in a college it turned out to be a simulated job interview.)

When we speak we operate intuitively an extremely complex set of choices and skills; do we know at what points an increase in conscious awareness of those choices and skills would improve performance, whatever 'improve' might mean? Some of these choices are at least potentially conscious, and these entail others which run off more automatically without reflection. I suggest the following levels of choice.

(A) Context: 1. Awareness of situation and relationships
                2. Purpose(s)
(B) Message: 1. Constituents of the message ('gist units', see Scardamalia *et al.* 1982)
                2. Role choices (on which style, polite forms, etc., depend)
(C) Speech act: 1. Elicit, command, state, etc.
                2. Organisation of information within the utterance
(D) Forms I: 1. Syntax
                2. Intonation
                3. Choice of words
(E) Forms II: Sound production (delivery, phonology, etc.)

Thus if a person with a foreign accent asks me in the street the way to the university, my construal of his identity and needs (Level A) leads me to make choices in the overall content, style and organisation of the message (Level B), and to realise these choices by engaging in a sequence of speech acts (Level C). The choices made at the level of speech acts are then automatically encoded at the levels of form. These choices are not made sequentially, but simultaneously within a hierarchy of control: choices at the 'higher' levels tend to entail choices 'lower' in the hierarchy.

My purpose in offering this analysis is to indicate that in teaching oracy the teacher may intervene at any of these points, so that we need to consider the likely effects on pupils' speech behaviour of intervention at various levels. (In outlining some considerations I shall begin with the 'lower' levels.)

1 It would be possible to highlight the students' vocal quality and style of delivery, their intonation patterns, and also some of their phonological choices. (This was the level at which traditional 'elocution' teaching operated, but few regret its passing.) Of course, such intervention can never be neutral: even so common a concept as 'clarity' can only be applied by treating the usage of one social group as standard for all.

2 There can be discussion of the lexical and syntactical forms used. There are undoubted difficulties here: for example, we do not think to ourselves 'How felicitous a subordinate clause of result would be as the conclusion of my present utterance', and there would be little value in urging pupils to do so. Many teachers think of language development in terms of vocabulary, an approach which misrepresents the nature of meaning by separating our understanding of words from our general understanding of how the world is (Greene 1986). Teaching focused upon words rather than upon the intention to mean is likely to harm not help. Though we often stress the importance of choosing language which is appropriate to the situation, purpose and to the interlocutors, it is not obvious that this is to be achieved by highlighting words and structures rather than situations and purposes.

3 In monologue and to a lesser extent in dialogue it would be possible to persuade students to plan and order the content of what they say. It is well established that in the assessment of writing in public examinations the choice and arrangement of content carry the greatest load: perhaps in oracy too the criteria used in assessment will move teaching towards an emphasis on the content and organisation of the message. We should consider whether this is what we want.

4 The fourth possible focus of intervention might be called 'interactiveness', and it would constitute only one aspect of what I have included in the level of 'Context'. In monologue, interactiveness would include sensitivity to audience needs; in small-group discussion it would also include responsiveness to others' ideas, encouragement, persuasiveness, self-control, and the ability to deal with overassertiveness. It might also include some quasi-cognitive abilities, such as interrelating apparently diverse perspectives, or producing evidence to support assertions, or summarising a discussion. (I shall argue later that, though valuable, this alone is not enough.)

5 Our knowledge of language is not separate from our understanding of the

world to which that language refers and in which it is used. Thus the level of 'Context' must include an understanding of uses and users of language in the context of our society, and perhaps of other societies. Some aspects of sociolinguistics would be relevant but so would a wider awareness of people and their behaviour, built upon pupils' first-hand experience of the world. Intervention at this level is likely to be the more effective in that when we talk we are conscious of people and purposes, rather than of words and structures.

Thus in lending support to the teaching of oracy we need to be clear at which of these levels we are proposing that teachers should intervene, and about the implications of making this choice or that. In the study which I have already mentioned we found that most teachers set up situations for speech but made minimal interventions. Those which did occur were of two kinds, either rather random comments about the appropriateness of voice or language forms to the (usually imaginary) situation, or a considerably more systematic programme of intervention at the level of 'interactiveness'. This will perhaps be the dominant pattern in any future oracy courses in this country, accompanied by more desultory attention to the other levels: the other aspects of speech are so difficult to reflect upon and control. Teachers should be aware of the different levels at which they can intervene, and of the implications of choosing to do so at one or another.

It is at the level of content, situation and purpose that greater reflective awareness is most likely to influence pupils' language behaviour, so it is to these levels that the teaching of oracy should initially be addressed. We should not be teaching an abstracted oracy, but setting up occasions for students to engage through speech with important aspects of the social and physical world. That is, we should look critically at any tendency to isolate spoken language from the topics and contexts in which it is used. Even some of the best oracy teaching which we saw appeared to have as its implicit model a vision of a decision-making committee concerned with a matter of not very urgent concern to the participants: the central message of the activities related to self-discipline and acceptance of the group's goals rather than to understanding or engaging with the world's concerns. If this does prove to be the dominant pattern it will be important to consider its implications as a tacit message to the students about their future roles in society.

I do not propose at this point to consider these implications but to compare oracy as a cultural phenomenon with a new element in secondary education which has made remarkably rapid progress in establishing itself in secondary schools. This new element is usually called 'Personal and Social Education' (PSE, or sometimes PSD), though it is related to 'Social and Life Skills' courses which can also be found in schools and in colleges of further education. Since the beginning of the 1980s PSE has not only spread rapidly across secondary schools and FE colleges but has proved to be one of the areas of change extended by the funds provided by the government's Manpower Services Commission as part of the Technical and Vocational Educational Initiative (TVEI). There appear to be some interesting similarities between oracy and PSE, both of which are strongly supported by the present government via the DES.

PSE as taught in secondary schools at present is amorphous and changing, at times including such matters as careers or sex education, or even information technology. At the centre of PSE courses is always a concern to influence at some depth the attitudes and behaviour of the students. There is commonly a marked stress on learning in small groups, especially through discussion, and this is often accompanied by a rhetoric of self-discovery and learning to collaborate with others. Most PSE courses are less concerned with understanding the world than with providing experiences that might change the students' behaviour by changing their view of themselves and their relation with other people whom they interact with face to face. In current jargon, they are concerned with 'process' rather than 'product' though in another sense they turn the student him or herself into the product.

Williams (1981) writes that 'Personal and social education is . . . primarily concerned with the development of understanding – of society, of human relationships, of our own and other people's behaviour – and [with] . . . a sympathetic concern for other people.' In practice a concern to help students to understand society is rather infrequent in such courses, which are more often concerned with the students' immediate relationships. Williams rejects any suggestion that PSE is concerned with 'education for obedience' and identifies it rather with 'a capacity to look critically at values and beliefs'. It would be interesting to have empirical evidence of how far this is carried out in practice; we have not found this to be the case in our evaluation of TVEI (Barnes *et al.* 1987).

The Centre for Counselling and Career Development (CCDU), which trains teachers for work in PSE courses, lays special stress on what is called 'education towards self-empowerment': the approach is acknowledged to be an individual-istic one, via the teaching of what are called 'life skills'. These include: 'How to take stock of my life'; 'How to manage negative emotions'; 'How to live with other people'; and 'How to work in a group' (Hopson and Scally 1981). The stress falls mainly upon the individual's reflection upon his or her strategies for living, and there is also some reference to more public matters such as 'How to use community resources', though these play only a small part.

What then does PSE have in common with the teaching of oracy as commonly practised? Both speak for the value of enhancing the individual student's competence to deal with his or her life. Both stress small-group collaboration, including sensitivity to others' perspectives, joint decision-making, persuasion rather than conflict. Both are likely to treat communication as made up of decontextualised skills which are not dependent upon any particular topic or context, but are closely linked with the values of self-control and sensitivity to others. In many ways these are admirable values, very like those advocated by liberal-minded English teachers in the 1960s when spoken language came to the forefront as an educational issue. Yet now they are being advocated from a quite different quarter. They are almost identical, for example, with aspects of the pre-vocational programmes which are recommended by government-sponsored bodies such as the Further Education Unit of the DES or by the Manpower Services Commission.

It is not easy to represent briefly the policy shown in the many documents which have come from the FEU since their highly influential *A Basis for Choice* (DES 1979). Typical aims for pre-employment courses include: 'To bring about an ability to develop satisfactory personal relationships with others', including the sub-aims 'Experience directly and vicariously a variety of personal encounters and a range of responses to them' and 'Identify and practise alternative responses' (e.g., 'being aggressive, conciliatory, submissive, understanding, distant'). Another aim, labelled 'Communication', included 'Speak audibly and give clear verbal explanations of processes/opinions/events to a variety of audiences', and 'Make a disciplined contribution to group discussion'. Six years later, in 1985, the FEU published a set of aims for the 'core' element in courses for fourteen- to sixteen-year-old students set up under TVEI, including 'an ability to be sensitive to and tolerant of the needs of others, and to develop satisfactory personal relationships' and 'the necessary skills for coping with everyday situations together with the ability to collaborate with others and to contribute to their well-being' (DES 1985). Most of these aims are acceptable and some are admirable. My purpose in quoting them is not to reject them but to place oracy in a context of which they are part. The official support for oracy should in my view be seen in the same context as the powerful advocacy and funding of pre-vocational education and of PSE. The aims of the three are not identical, certainly, but when they are seen side by side their support by the government seems not to be a chance collocation but part of a coherent programme for education which is also a politico-social policy for the country as a whole. When we lend our support for oracy, what wider programme are we also lending tacit support to? My purpose in this chapter is essentially to ask that question.

The situation is a piquant one. A brief inspection of the pages of the *Daily Mail* will show that the Old Right is still advocating 'back to basics', tighter discipline, conformity to standard English, and more spelling tests. The Radical Right, which Mrs Thatcher's government represents, however, is asking that students be prepared for the world of work (and for the world of unemployment) in a different way. This 'new vocationalism', as we have seen, includes a marked stress on interpersonal relationships, on negotiation rather than conflict, on individual responsibility and initiative, and yet at the same time on collaborative work in small groups. It is not easy to say whose interests the Radical Right speaks for: certain sections of commerce and industry are certainly amongst them. What does this apparently liberal programme have to offer to industrial interests? A full answer to this question would necessitate discussion of the values of entrepreneurship, changing work patterns, and the role of education in social control, but I shall have time only to touch on these.

Certainly the emphasis on group discussion and on self-empowerment is very different from the cruder forms of conformism: the new priorities can be interpreted as a shift from an emphasis on external control to internal self-discipline. If the students internalise and make the required values their own then there is little need for external controls. It has been suggested that with rising youth unemployment, young people are no longer being socialised in the workplace so that the government is now requiring schools to undertake to socialise them in the values of work (Davies 1981; Bates *et al.* 1984; Wellington 1986). Many secondary schools, particularly those taking part in TVEI, have set up mini-enterprises, and these are said to be very successful since students who would otherwise have rejected schooling have often shown unsuspected skills. Such a stress on the development and validation of entrepreneurship by schools fits well with the Conservative government's policies outside education.

This has been accompanied during Mrs Thatcher's administrations by an extension of accountability. For example, it is the government's stated intention to extend assessment to students of all abilities, and for this to include their attitudes and behaviour, as well as the traditional academic achievements. This has been typically associated with unit accreditation, the extension of counselling, and the use of assessment profiles by teachers. What all this extra evaluation amounts to is not only an extension of control to new sections of the population, but deeper penetration into the individual's values and behaviour. No longer will school success rest solely upon academic achievement; appropriate attitudes will be required. It is not difficult to see what these changes offer to hard-pressed teachers: they will have ready ways of putting pressure upon some of the most uncooperative of their charges. But what do they offer to industrialists and other employers?

There is strong evidence from both the FEU and from the Manpower Services Commission that employers want something different from what schools have previously provided, and it seems likely that this is because extensive changes are expected in patterns of work. Why should employers value awareness of others' perspectives, the ability to work together, effective communication, the ability to take responsibility, when in the past the most valued characteristics have been accuracy, obedience and punctuality? Three hesitant answers can be offered. It has been suggested that in future a larger proportion of the population will be employed in service industries, in which the need to please the client face-to-face is of central importance (for various views, see Clark 1982; Stonier 1983; and Cohen 1984). Moreover, for many years both industrial and commercial concerns have been willing to send their managers on expensive privately-run courses, which use group problem-solving methods to change their attitudes and skills in working and communicating with others. Although industry and commerce are built on competition, in the running of their concerns they need to employ people who can collaborate and show sensitivity to others' needs. Moreover, some of the most economically successful producers, both in Europe and in the Far East, base their success on rapid response to changes in market demand: to change products so rapidly requires not only design and technical resources, but attitudes and flexibility in the workforce that will make radical changes possible without prolonged negotiation with unions. The director of the MSC, Geoffrey Holland, has said in a speech to the Institute of Personnel Management (*Times Educational Supplement*, 31 October 1986) that it is not technology that makes for economic success but people. It is ironical if, because of these projected changes in work patterns, industry is making 'liberal' proposals for collaborative practices in secondary schools, since in preparing students for examinations schools can hardly avoid promulgating the values of individualism and competition.

It will be clear from what I have just said that there seem to me to be marked similarities between certain aspects of pre-vocational education, and oracy as it might be developed in secondary schools as a focus of teaching and testing. These include the separation of language skills from the context in which they will be used and from the purposes of the learner. I have no doubt that spoken language should play a much greater role in education than it has formerly done, at least in England. But is 'oracy', as it is often conceived, the best way of representing speech in the curriculum? What I have in mind is the possibility that oracy will separate speech as language skills from speech as acting upon the world. Or, to put it differently, I am concerned that oracy will be decontextual- ised. Inevitably oracy teaching *will* have a content; we should prevent it from taking on the inert repertoire of uncontroversial controversies that we have seen in the past, corporal punishment, town and country, school uniform, and so on. New textbooks for pre-vocational courses are no better. Activities based on pretended documents from an imaginary firm, or on sets of imaginary letters, or on pretences such as 'You are a magistrate . . .' (Irving and Smith 1986) are only meretricious gestures towards the real world; the whole is as artificial as any traditional English exercise.

The emphasis should shift from language to the critical understanding of issues and purposes, and to engagement with the world outside school. I am disposed to agree with the government's concern to move education closer to the real world of action, though my real world would have wider boundaries than just employment. Using language in the world is not just a matter of skills but of understanding that world in all its complexity and variety, and knowing how to influence it. Courses in PSE typically separate the communication from the understanding and it seems to me all too likely that oracy will do the same.

Normally when we talk it is in the pursuit of purposes generated by our current engagement with our lives, and we moderate and adjust these in response to what other people say and do. Sometimes our purpose is simply to share experience through chat or anecdote, but this, too, is an outcome of our day-to-day social commitments. For this reason I see little value in developing oracy skills out of context. Spoken language should be developed in a context of living issues, of critical inquiry into how the world is, not of neutralised pseudo-topics invented solely to give a semblance of content to talk for talk's sake. This implies that the context for speech should be the whole curriculum. The purpose should be to learn to understand and influence the world through speech, not to develop decontextualised speech skills which may prove to be a chimera.

One difficulty of a programme of this kind is that it requires students to undertake a range of speech roles that are hard to find in traditional classrooms. Typical teaching exchanges give the students little opportunity to argue for their rights, to persuade a reluctant superior, to canvass someone else's opinions, to cross-question, to present a case, to plan with others an attack on a problem, or to explain a matter on which they have expert knowledge. All of these do happen in schools, but usually in contexts seen as 'control' not 'learning'. I suspect that one of the reasons why speech has so long been absent from the curriculum is that to develop it in a manner which validly matched speech in adult life would offer a major threat to the conduct of schooling as we know it.

What is needed is not a new mini-subject, oracy, but a changed pattern of teaching across the curriculum; we had this insight some years ago, as the HMI survey shows. Have we now lost it? The changed pattern would stress the uses of spoken language (and written, too) as a tool for enquiry, discussion, and engagement in a range of activities directed towards increasing students' critical understanding of the world they live in and their ability to take an active role in it. This would involve radical changes not just in communication in schools but in the locus of control over what counts as knowledge. Moreover, particularly for older students, there would have to be changes in the relationship between school and the world outside. It cannot be ignored that the classroom offers at best an extremely limited range of speech roles and activities, and that a diet of simulations is no substitute for real experience. Thus students will have to go outside school to gather information, pursue projects, engage in outside activities, including those in work contexts, as well as coming back into school to reflect, synthesise, and create. This will imply new teaching strategies to support these activities of inquiry, synthesis, and action, as well as other strategies to help students become more aware of their speech behaviour. If oracy can become a tool for students to use for critical understanding and action, then I am in favour of it.

References

Barnes, D. (1982). 'Finding a Context for Talk', *Spoken English*, vol. 15, no. 2, May.

Barnes, Douglas, Barnes, Dorothy and Clark, S. (1984). *Versions of English*, London, Heinemann.

Barnes, D. *et al.* (1987). *The TVEI Curriculum, 14–16. An Interim Report Based on Case Studies in Twelve Schools*, Sheffield, Manpower Services Commission.

Bates, I. *et al.* (1984). *Schooling and the Dole? The New Vocationalism*, London, Macmillan.

Clark, G. (1982). 'Recent Developments in Working Patterns' *Employment Gazette*, July.

Cohen, P. (1984). 'Against the New Vocationalism' in Bates *et al.* (1984).

Davies, B. (1981). *The State We're In*, Leicester, National Youth Bureau.

DES Further Education Unit (1979). *A Basis for Choice*, London, DES.

DES Further Education Unit (1985). *Supporting TVEI*, London, DES.

Greene, J. (1986). *Language Understanding: A Cognitive Approach*, Milton Keynes, Open University Press.

Her Majesty's Inspectorate (1979). *Aspects of Secondary Education in England*, London, HMSO.

Her Majesty's Inspectorate (1984). *English from 5 to 16*, London, HMSO.

Hopson, B. and Scally, M. (1981). *Lifeskills Teaching*, New York, McGraw-Hill.

Irving, J. and Smith, N. (1986). *Core Skills in Communication*, Basingstoke, Macmillan.

Scardamalia, M., Bereiter, C. and Goelman, H. (1982). 'The Role of Production Factors in Writing Ability' in M. Nystrand (ed.), *What Writers Know*, New York, Academic Press.

Stonier, T. (1983). *The Wealth of Information*, London, Thames Methuen.

Wellington, J. J. (1986). 'The Rise of Prevocational Education and the Needs of Employers', *The Vocational Aspect of Education*, vol. 38, no. 99, April.

Williams, T. (1981). 'Aims and Objectives in Personal and Social Education', unpublished: quoted by K. David, *Personal and Social Education in Secondary Schools*, London, Longman, 1983.

PART TWO

Small-group talk

5 Anecdote and the development of oral argument in sixteen-year-olds

DEBORAH P. BERRILL

Can sixteen-year-old students conduct reasoned argument? Few studies have looked at students' abilities to use language in an argumentative fashion. And those studies which have addressed themselves to students' abilities in this area of reasoned language usage have concluded that too many sixteen-year-olds are not successful, either in oral or in written argument (Pringle and Freedman 1985; Barnes *et al* 1986).

Oral argument is at best only very loosely defined. In fact, at present, for any definition at all we have to look at the characteristics of written argument, which in itself is somewhat problematic. However, as a starting point, argument seems to involve moving from the particular to the general and making connections between the resulting generalisations which are logical or rational (Dixon and Stratta 1986). As well, part of the form of argument seems to necessitate making logical choices between two or more alternatives (Wilkinson 1986).

Anecdote, on the other hand, has characteristics of a very different and sometimes opposite nature. Anecdote is the relating of a personal, concrete story from a single point of view. Rather than being rooted in logical order, anecdote, as narrative, is supported by sequential order, by chronology (Rosen 1982; Wilkinson 1986). And often it seems that anecdote introduces irrelevancies into what is an otherwise focused and even logical discussion.

Why, then, have I found that sixteen-year-olds incorporate anecdote into their discussions when they are supposed to be doing oral argument? Is this yet another indication of how poor they are at argument? Not necessarily. In fact, the use of anecdote may help participants in a discussion to build a reasoned argument based on valid evidence.

In this study, I asked sixteen-year-olds who were divided into groups of four to discuss the question 'Should parents control the lives of their teenage children?' The groups were friendship-based as much as possible and each individual in the group knew that she or he would write an essay on the topic after a maximum of two seventy-minute class periods of small-group discussion. Groups held their discussions in rooms separate from the classroom and were left alone, with a tape-recorder, for the duration of their talk.

Anyone briefly monitoring the talk that followed would have heard conversations like the following, between Iona, Rachel, Sharon and Kim.

> *I:* I mean, if I moan – if I moan, my mum tell me, you know, you should think yourself lucky 'cos when I was your age I had to walk five miles to school – and all that rubbish.
> *R:* Yeah.
> *S:* My mum never says that.
> *I:* Oh my mum does. She say, 'Oh, you ought to think yourself lucky' – Does yours?
> *S:* ⎫
> *K:* Yeah. ⎭
> *I:* – 'I had to walk five miles and catch a train and then from the train I had to get a bus just to get to school' and that.
> *K:* And my mum go on about 'cos there was nine kids she had to look after all –
> *S:*   [Yeah.
> *R:*   [Yeah.
> *K:* – 'cos she was the oldest – right, and all that.
> *S:* I didn't get none of that.
> *I:* Think yourself lucky.
>   [*Laughter*]

Although this conversation might initially sound like irrelevant swapping of personal information, closer analysis reveals that other things are going on. If we add the additional context to this conversation, we see that it is preceded by the following statements:

> *S:* They had – they had their – Their teenage life was different to ours, wasn't it. I mean probably half of them grew up in the war . . . No –
> *K:* No – No, it was after that.
> *I:* Yes. [*Laughter*]
> *S:* They had a different life to us, didn't they, they didn't have money like us, weren't many jobs – I've got two different ones.
> *K:* Yeah.
> *I:* Plus I think their parents were stricter weren't they?
> *K:* Yeah.
> *I:* Their parents were stricter and they follow that.
> *S:* 'Cos they had to be strict about everything didn't they, 'cos – everything that happened.

Here, then, personal information and anecdote follow the generalisation about parents being raised in a stricter environment than today's teenagers. Rather than being irrelevant, the personal information and anecdotes serve as a means of validating the generalisation. The students provide anecdotes here which generally support the idea that their parents operated under greater constraints as teenagers than they presently do.

We know that stories frequently appear in clusters of two or more, or in short strings (Ryave 1978), and it seems that the recounting of other personal information is manifested in a similar fashion. In the above conversation, three of the four group members add their own personal information to the string. In so doing, they may well be establishing how common their particular experience is and how valid the generalisation is when it is tested against particular situations. The discussion which results from this particular topic, which demands sorting through one's personal experience to answer an abstract question, would support Rosen's (1982: 12) point that 'abstractions and generalizations are, at however great a remove, rooted in a tissue of experience'.

Generalisation through anecdote

In addition to validating an initial generalisation, personal experience and anecdote strings are sometimes followed by new generalisations. The above chunk of conversation is followed by Sharon saying: 'That's probably why I've had such an easy – so much freedom. My mum don't want to interfere.' Sharon's personal experience does not corroborate the operant generalisation that the students' parents lived under stricter or more constrained rules than the students presently do. A new generalisation is not stated here but a new implied generalisation, which has something to do with a parallel between the way one is raised and the way one raises one's own children, is given application in Sharon's utterance. At this point the new generalisation is not pursued further nor made more explicit.

How common is this sequence of a string of anecdotes or personal information followed by a generalisation which arises from the anecdote? Let us look at another example from the same conversation.

> *K:* Yeah, that's another thing; if you dye your hair or something they think it's really drastic and they don't want to be seen with you or something.
> *S:* My mum, she was in the latest fashion, she had a big *beehive* and everything –
> *K:* Yeah, my mum too.
> *S* And my dad was a teddy, ted boy.
> *I:* Yeah, my dad was a teddy boy, my mum had the pony tail, high pony tail.
> *K:* My mum had a [*beehive.*
> *S:*   [*beehive.* [*Laughter*]
> *K:* This big thing on top of their head. Moths and everything used to live in it.
> *S:* Aaoooo.
> *S:* [*To another group*] Don't shout!
> [*Small pause*]
> *S:* Yeah, carry on.
> *K:* Uhh, they find it hard to accept today's fashion and everything –
> *S:* Yeah.
> *K:* And say like you go [out –
> *S:*   [Just, just –
> *K:* No hang on a minute. Say you go out to choose some clothes –
> *S:*   [No, listen –
> *R:* They don't *all* find it difficult, do they?
> *?:* No, my mum – ⎫
> *?:* My mum don't, she don't. ⎬
> *?:* Some things – ⎭
> *K:* Some things.

R: No my mum's [all right.
I: [It depends what you wear, I s'pose, don't it.
S: Yeah.
K: Yeah.

Kim, one of the participants who relates an anecdote, offers a tentative generalisation ('Uhh, they find it hard to accept today's fashion and everything –') which is a new synthesis emerging from the string of beehive and teddy boy anecdotes. However, Rachel, who was not a contributor to the string, queries the validity of the generalisation ('They don't *all* find it difficult, do they?'). Her query and qualification of the generalisation is followed by Iona's qualification ('It depends what you wear, I s'pose, don't it.'). These qualifications prompt yet another string of personal information and anecdotes which further explores the issue. The conversation continues as follows:

I: If you went home with pink hair your mum would hit the roof, wouldn't she?
R: No, not really, [she don't, she don't say nothing about it.
S: [At first –
S: At first, first my parents when I was about thirteen, they wouldn't let me have my hair highlighted, permed or nothing.
I: Well I'm still not allowed to have mine highlighted.
S: No, I wasn't until I was old enough to take – 'cos if I was about thirteen having my hair permed and it turned drastic I would start crying, wouldn't I. [*Laughter*]
R: Did you cry this time, Sharon? [*Laughter*]
I: [Oh, that wasn't very nice.
S: Now I'm old enough to realise if, if I have my hair done and I don't like it, it would be my fault.
I: No, what my mum says is –
S: Old enough to –
K: [Accept – responsibility.
R: [take the consequences.
I: [responsibility.

The initial generalisation ('they find it hard to accept today's fashion') was tested and qualified ('They don't *all* find it difficult' and 'It depends what you wear, I s'pose, don't it') and the personal information and anecdote which follow the qualifiers result in a new generalisation ('Old enough to – Accept responsibility') which is confirmed by the whole group. Anecdote here is hardly irrelevant. The students use their combined personal experience to evaluate the generalisations which are generated. If a single person contributes information which is contrary to the experience of the rest of the group, the group treats the new information very seriously and uses the new information to qualify the generalisation. If as Dixon and Stratta (1986) contend, the quality of argument includes how scrupulous the individual is in generalising, that is in qualifying the generalisation, then we see in the above conversation a process of oral argument which is certainly of good quality.

Not all strings of anecdote or personal information end with formulation: however, we do know that sixteen-year-olds can and sometimes do end such strings with generalisation or new abstract synthesis. I will later explore reasons why more anecdote does not end in this way.

Logical extension through anecdote and personal information

The conversation between these four girls could now go in several directions; but what does happen is that, having accepted the generalisation that a teenager should have more control of her own life when she is old enough to accept responsibility, the students follow through the *logical* consequences of this generalisation. Implicit here is their agreement that *they* are old enough to accept responsibility for and/or the consequences of their actions. However, they discover that the parental point of view does not hold when the position is logically extended to practical application. Again, this is discovered through anecdote and personal information.

I: What my mum says is if I'm old enough to pay for it and keep having it redone and I pay for it myself then she don't mind but if she's got to keep paying out for me –
S: Would your mum like it if you come plastered – went to school with eye liner up to there?
R: No.
S: Makeup right up there to go to school?
I: She won't even let me come to school without a blouse that hasn't got any collar on.
K: Oh, my mum don't care about that, as long as I go to school she don't care – what I wear but –
S: No, because I'm the one whose gonna get done for it, not her.
K: Yeah, it's my fault if I get done for it.
I: Yeah, and yet my mum, she come into school and she sees what everybody else is wearing so she should let me wear –
R: That's the same with mine but mine doesn't.
I: No, mine don't either. You would have thought that as they saw what everybody else is [wearing –
R: [Yeah.
I: They'd be a little less –
S: But if you come to school with – wearing, I don't know, the wrong uniform – your parents phone up –
S: Your parents ain't gonna – you – you, um, sort of – they say, 'Oh that's Mrs – *Bailey's* daughter,' they're gonna say something like –
?: Oh look at the
?: That's gonna
?: She's –
S: That's gonna go reflect on your mother, isn't it –

Here, the students pursue the problem that although they are willing to accept responsibility for their actions, their parents still refuse to give them that responsibility. In their attempt to find reasons behind the parental behaviour, reasons from an alternate point of view which might resolve why the control is exerted, the students explore the issue of why parents seem unwilling to allow their children to accept responsibility for their choice of dress. Their solution is that a child's behaviour reflects back on her parent ('That's gonna go reflect on your mother, isn't it –'), with the implicit generalisation that misconduct of a child somehow reflects misconduct of the parent. Personal information and anecdote are used here to establish an alternative point of view, the exploration of which is one of the characteristics of argument.

In this conversation there is a dynamic interaction between anecdote and generalisation. Anecdote and personal information have been used (1) to generate generalisations through validation of combined particular, concrete information; (2) to test the validity of generalisations by applying the generalisations to particular experience; (3) to qualify generalisations when needed; (4) to extend generalisations logically through application to new material; and (5) to explore alternative points of view. Rather than being irrelevant tangents, these anecdotes and personal experiences have served the development of the argument quite directly, giving the students solid evidence on which to base their decisions and make their choices.

The cyclical nature of oral argument

However, as noted earlier, anecdote and personal information are not always followed by formulations of the nature we see here, which provide an explanation, summary or synthesis of the conversation or which give the gist of what has just been said (Garfinkel and Sacks 1970). Let us go back to the first string of anecdotes where the group members were relating stories of their parents' childhoods.

Although Sharon provides a coda to the conversation ('That's probably why I've had such an easy – so much freedom. My mum don't want to interfere.'), there is not yet group consensus. Subsequent talk shifts the topic and the generalisation is left incomplete, just dropped as it were. The relation of how a parent was raised and how that parent subsequently raises children is left unresolved and unformulated. However, later in the conversation, after intervening talk about smoking, about beehives, teddy boys and fashion, about accepting responsibility for one's own actions and about how one's actions reflect on one's parents, the topic of parental background is revived.

K: Whereas other parents [– would be.
S: [Mmmm.
R: It's only what they think though, i'n't it, their opinions –
I: It has – a lot of it has come from what background they come from.
K: Yeah.
S: Yeah, my mum had an easy background and everything.
K: My mum didn't.
I: My mum and dad didn't.
I: Yet my mum and dad are stricter than your mum and dad are.
K: Yeah. – Not much more though.
I: They are.
K: Oh, I don't know – [*Small laugh*]
I: I reckon they are – 'cos, as I say, your mum don't care if you come to school

looking how you are but my mum hit the roof when I tried to come to school with a blouse that hadn't got any collar on it. She hit the roof because of that. She – she make me sit at home and revise, and she sometimes even goes through my homework after I've done it.

S: Yeah, and everything, they make you revise and study.

K: Yeah, if they think you're not sitting up in your bedroom for three hours that you haven't revised – or you [haven't done your homework.

I: [Yeah.

R: [Yeah.

R: You could just have been sitting up there for three hours anyway doing nothing, couldn't you.

I: Yeah – I try to. [*Laughter*]

S: Shh –
    [*Pause*]

I: So, what else was after that? – They try to stop teenagers making the same mistakes they made, e.g., smoking and homework.

Sharon fills in more of the implied generalisation (that there is a parallel between how one was raised and how one raises one's own children) when she says: 'Yeah, my mum had an easy background and everything.' It is Iona, though, who further explores the still vague generalisation when she says: 'Yet my mum and dad are stricter than your mum and dad are.' However, once again the generalisation is left without being explicitly formulated and the topic shifts to parental control over homework. There seem to be strong social reasons here for a shift from the present topic which has the danger of slipping into opinion-based personal disagreement about whose parents are stricter: Sharon focuses instead on the homework issue which Iona has raised and in so doing takes the discussion in a new direction which includes the whole group in consensus and which elicits further personal information from Kim. The topic shift may account for some of the reasons that formulation does not occur here. However, what else is interesting is that a new generalisation *is* formulated which synthesises the personal information given here about homework with preceding information about smoking. This happens when Iona says: 'So, what else was after that? – They try to stop teenagers making the same mistakes they made, e.g., smoking and homework.' So, although one generalisation is left undeveloped for a second time, the group nevertheless abstracts and synthesises from personal information and anecdote.

It is not until the next day that this implied generalisation is explicitly formulated. After a self-initiated summary of the previous day's discussion, the participants begin talking about parental control over teenage drug use. Eight minutes later, after a full day's lapse and much intervening talk of all sorts, the conversation returns to the unresolved discussion of the day before. We enter the conversation as the students are addressing the topic of what parents would do in relation to teenagers and drug abuse.

R: But there's – no, I can't see any parent doing that.

S: I know quite a few who would.

K: Yeah, I know quite a few who would.

R: Well, go on then –
K: Anyway –
R: But why would they?
S: 'Cos they had such an easy childhood themselves.
K: Yeah.
R: So it's *their* childhood what bases *this* – i'n't it.
S: Mmm, it is.
R: So the way they bring up their children is the way they were brought up?
S: Yeah, basically.
R: Based on, right.
K: Yeah.
I: So they must think that their childhood was right otherwise they thought that
    their parents were sort of being hard on [them –
R: [True, true.
I: – and they sort of say things like, 'Oh when I have children I'm not going to do
    that', but they *do* – sort of thing.
    [*Small pause*]
I: Parents, as they get older, they know better don't they?
R: Yeah.
K: Yeah, and they're, um, they're trying to stop you making the same mistakes that
    they made, well they found out for themselves and, in a way, that would be better
    for *you* if you found out yourself, you know, the mistakes and everything.
I: Yeah, but looking at it from the teenagers' point of view, the teenagers can't see
    that, can they. They just think their parents are being right misery-guts if they
    tell them what to do.
K: Yeah, in some ways. I mean if they sort of sit down and talk to you about
    something – sort of helping you and giving you advice but then if they sort of –
I: If they just tell you, say, 'Don't do this, don't do that', then of course the kid is
    going to rebel against it but if, I think, the parents sit down and actually talk to
    them and tell them *why* they shouldn't –
K: Yeah, but a lot of teenagers haven't got that close relationship with their parents
    so they can sit down and talk.

Although we are not looking at anecdote here, we certainly seem to be looking
at formulations which are strongly dependent on the strings of personal information and anecdote from the preceding day. Once again, Sharon refers to the 'easy
childhood' of some parents, remaining consistent with her position when it was
first brought forward the day before. It is Rachel, who did not contribute to the
earlier strings of information and anecdote, who provides the explicit synthesis
('So it's *their* childhood what bases *this* – i'n't it.') and then rewords the
generalisation: 'So the way they bring up their children is the way they were
brought up?' This repetitious rephrasing both emphasises the importance of the
generalisation and calls for a group response, which she receives. In a conversation which lasted approximately an hour and a half and which stretched over two
days, the group has explored its combined personal experience to come up with a
generalisation which was then tested, further explored and qualified to
accommodate the differing experiences of everyone in the group.
    In addition the students continue their logical argument, probing to discover
why parents exhibit this behaviour. In so doing, they implicitly refer back to other
anecdote, synthesising the generalisation that parents are 'trying to stop you from

making the same mistakes that they made' with their new synthesis of parents bringing up their children the way they were brought up. At this point they also explicitly include an alternative point of view, one of the apparently essential characteristics of argument, when Iona says: 'Yeah, but looking at it from the teenagers' point of view, the teenagers can't see that, can they. They just think their parents are being right misery-guts if they tell them what to do.' Also, they speculate about how to avoid the confrontation and rebellion assumed in the initial question of parental control.

Anyone briefly monitoring this conversation at various of the points presented here might easily have missed the importance of personal information and anecdote in the development of the argument. Either the personal information could have seemed irrelevant to the larger development of generalisation or, on the second day where logical reasoning is occurring, the underlying presence of shared anecdote and personal information as the evidence for that reasoning would not have been apparent.

It seems worthwhile to note that it may have been the opportunity to speak at length on this topic which enabled the students to come up with one of their most important generalisations. Teachers often feel so pressured by time constraints that students do not get a chance to engage in discussion of this duration. This example shows the importance of such time and further strengthens Wells and Chang's (1986: 129–30) demand for students to have the opportunity 'to speak at length on a topic on which . . . they have acquired expertise'.

The importance of strings of anecdotes to development of argument

This study has shown that sixteen-year-olds do use anecdotes and other personal information to develop oral argument. It may be important that the anecdote and personal information we have looked at have occurred in strings, with an initial anecdote serving as an offering for others to follow with their own contributions. The combined experience may serve as a way to see how individual personal experience fits into a larger scheme of things. If we accept Dixon and Stratta's (1986: 19) contention that 'learning how to find and evaluate further "public" evidence becomes an important part of the dynamic process [of argument]', then again we see the development of argument being fostered through small-group work which incorporates strings of anecdotes. The recounting of a single anecdote may not result in the personal information serving the development of argument in the same way as does a string of anecdotes: for if only a single story is told, the commonness of the experience cannot be explicitly tested and any generalisation is bound to be more of an assertion based on a single point of view rather than a more complete or precise generalisation based on several points of view.

The sorts of anecdote and personal information that we have looked at also differ from village-gossip anecdote where stories are probably told for much different purposes. Within the larger context of a reasoned argument, successive stories may add additional support to an implicit generalisation, they may add weight to the significance of the preceding account, or they may reorder the strengths and constraints of the preceding speakers' designs (Ryave 1978: 130). In the context of reasoned argument, anecdote or personal information is laid out for wider verification and comment which then feeds back into the logical argument.

Also, anecdote and personal information provide a way for one to feel for oneself what an original argument means: it is a way of making abstract argument more concrete. This certainly follows the educational tradition which emphasises the crucial nature of personal reinterpretation of the world and of meaning-making through the active use of one's own language. As students use their own stories and information rather than the teacher's information, the question of whose knowledge is being used, whose argument is being developed, is no longer an issue: it is solidly the students'.

Conclusions

Can sixteen-year-olds conduct reasoned oral argument? Certainly this study shows sixteen-year-olds can and do do the following: (1) pursue a question from different points of view; (2) evaluate the personal evidence at their disposal for making their choices; (3) use these evaluations to qualify the generalisations they make; and (4) synthesise earlier generalisations into more complex abstractions, building their choice of position from a foundation of evidence. Whether or not by this we mean 'oral argument' is still open to debate.

Initially I referred to the lack of a model of oral argument. For this study, Dixon and Stratta's discussion–argument continuum has proven helpful in the attempt to understand what oral argument is. An earlier study which examined argumentative talk of sixteen-year-olds found it to have features of 'sharp retort, flat contradiction, rejection by counter-statement and abuse, and steam-rollering use of repetition'. Also, although useful elements of the topic were 'laid out' by the speakers, 'in the heat of the argument, very little [was] done with them and certainly they [were] not manifestly put together to arrive at any solution, any resolution of the conflicting opinions' (Barnes 1986: 117–18). If in the development of argument we are looking for the development of *reasoned* exploration of alternative viewpoints with logical choices being made between those viewpoints, then well-developed oral argument may have features that we have in the past attributed more to exploratory discussion than to the type of impassioned argument noted above.

Although the group in this study used anecdote effectively in building an argument, we know that anecdote in oral argument is not always associated with the kind of formulation or generalisation that we have seen here. Why is much anecdote not associated with formulation of some kind? What conditions promote or hinder synthesis after anecdote? Labov and Fanshel (1977: 109) point out that 'one of the most difficult problems to solve in delivering a narrative is how to finish it'. We have seen that with a string of anecdotes we should not necessarily be in a hurry for the 'ending' or formulation of a story as the group may not have enough evidence on which to base a formulation. However, we still hope for an eventual formulation, and that may also never appear, keeping the development of argument to a minimum.

Formulation and resolution may be absent in some discussions because the group cannot come to a consensus. But it may also be absent because the group does not understand the importance of reflecting back on its own talk. Schiffrin (1980) points out various ways that individuals do focus on their own talk, ways that help them organise and evaluate what has been said. Likewise, Heritage and Watson (1979; 1984) describe how some conversationalists are especially orientated to the process of reflecting back on their own talk. We might expect these people to be especially valuable participants in oral argument.

But not all conversationalists take time to focus on their own talk. Barnes and Todd (1977) suggest the value of making students aware of what they are doing and how they are using talk when they are in small-group situations. Incorporating reflective tasks into argumentative talk may well help students to understand the relevance of their own personal experience to developing abstract argument. Dixon and Stratta (1986) see this sort of increasingly reflective and self-critical awareness of one's own assumptions and perspectives as one of the important facets of the development of argument. The question of where in a conversation a group should pause and reflect back on what has been said is not an easy one to answer: however, the fact that such reflection is important to the development of oral argument seems indisputable.

We do know that anecdote and argument are different from each other, each arranging experience in its own way, chronologically or logically. However, sharing personal information and anecdote may be a powerful method for people to reconstruct and evaluate their worlds in ways that can be ultimately logical and reasoned. We should not underestimate the potential of sixteen-year-olds to build reasoned oral argument.

References

Barnes, Douglas and Todd, Frankie (1977). *Communication and Learning in Small Groups*, London, Routledge and Kegan Paul.

Barnes, Douglas, Britton, James and Torbe, Mike (1986). *Language, the Learner and the School*, 3rd edn, Harmondsworth, Penguin.

Dixon, John and Stratta, Leslie (1986). 'Argument and the Teaching of English: A Critical Analysis' in A. M. Wilkinson (ed.), *The Writing of Writing*, Milton Keynes, Open University Press.

Garfinkel, Harold and Sacks, Harvey (1970). 'On Formal Structures of Practical Actions' in J. C. McKinney and E. A. Tiryakian (eds), *Theoretical Sociology*, New York, Appleton Century Crofts.

Heritage, J. C. and Watson, D. R. (1979). 'Formulations as Conversational Objects' in G. Psathas (ed.), *Everyday Language: Studies in Ethnomethodology*, New York, Irvington Publishers, Inc.

Heritage, J. C. and Watson, D.R. (1984). *Structures of Social Action: Studies in Conversation Analysis*. Cambridge, Cambridge University Press.

Labov, W. and Fanshel, D. (1977). *Therapeutic Discourse*, New York, Academic Press.

Pringle, Ian and Freedman, Adele (1985). *A Comparative Study of Writing Abilities in Two Modes at the Grade 5, 8, and 12 Levels*, Toronto, Ontario Ministry of Education.

Rosen, Harold (1982). *Stories and Meanings*. Sheffield: National Association for the Teaching of English.

Ryave, Alan L. (1978). 'On the Achievement of a Series of Stories' in Jim Schenkein (ed.), *Studies in the Organization of Conversational Interaction*, New York, Academic Press.

Schiffrin, Deborah (1980). 'Meta-Talk: Organizational and Evaluative Brackets in Discourse', in *Sociological Inquiry, Language and Social Interaction*, Special Issue, vol. 50, no. 1.

Wells, Gordon and Chang, Gen Ling (1986). 'From Speech to Writing: Some Evidence on the Relationship between Oracy and Literacy' in A. M. Wilkinson (ed.), *The Writing of Writing*, Milton Keynes, Open University Press.

Wilkinson, A. M. (1986). 'Argument as a Primary Act of Mind', *Educational Review*, vol. 38, no. 2, Special Issue no. 18, 'Aspects of English Composition'.

6 On a related matter: why 'successful' small-group talk depends upon not keeping to the point

TERRY PHILLIPS

'Successful' talk? All definitions of 'success', whether they come from individual or institutional sources, are embedded in particular and partial views of the world; consequently all definitions of 'success' demand to be examined. Some definitions, however, carry internal contradictions which initiate the wider discourse. In England and Wales, the 'official' definition of what constitutes 'successful' classroom discussion, and more precisely 'successful' argument (DES 1984; DES 1986), contains many such contradictions. According to this composite of objectives (and what is that but a definition?), 'success' is confidently equated not only with the ability to be courteous, accurate, and factual (DES 1984: 6–7), the ability to 'engage in co-operative discussion in order to clarify or explore a matter or to *produce an agreed outcome*', and the ability to 'listen with concentration to extensive exposition or discussion, *noting down the salient points*' (DES 1984: 9–10, emphasis not in original); but also with the ability to 'put a point of view *and sustain it* in discussion', and the ability to 'follow a speaker's *line of argument*' (DES 1984: 6–7). In this definition we have a particular perception of 'success'; we also have a view which argues with itself. And, as with all things that are inherently problematic, attempts to resolve the contradictions from within the original parameters only highlight those contradictions and continue the discourse. For this reason, it is no easier to understand what constitutes 'successful' argument when we are informed subsequently that there is a strong case for 'a widening of the spoken word objectives to embrace more fully such issues as the presentation of and response to argument, reasoning, and the use of and validity of evidence' (DES 1986: 13). The original definition remains essentially unstable, and continues to argue with itself in a way that reveals that it has grown out of popular orthodoxies rather than research in classrooms.

The best information about what makes successful task-focused talk – which is the kind of talk referred to when 'discussion' and 'argument' are spoken of in the context of a discourse about curriculum and learning – comes from the language users themselves. It comes in the form of behaviour; that is, in the form of what they *do* whilst 'doing talking'. It comes through the principled study of language in use. This chapter reports research which has begun that study.

Determining what the task is when the topic is 'official'

I want to examine conversations from classrooms where, in the course of a normal week, the children talk in small groups about a 'school' topic. I have chosen to focus on 'school' topics, by which I mean non-spontaneously arising topics that are in some way related to the official business of schools, because I recognise a situation in which teachers have only limited control over what is taught. The resourceful teacher finds it possible to offer space for the children in her class to discuss issues that they themselves introduce, issues directly related to experiences they all have in common but which come from individual, out-of-school occasions, or which arise from corporate, on-the-premises experiences. And because of that resourceful teacher's determination to create such spaces, her children are able to explore together their feelings, and shape their understanding of things that have immediate meaning for them. But the same teacher will find that she often has to ask the children to talk about topics which arise through planned work, and are not their own. It follows that in the majority of classrooms, during a typical week, children will take part in both types of discussion. It also follows that the older the children get, and the more differentiated the school curriculum becomes, the more the balance will tip in favour of discussions about school topics. It is imperative, therefore, that we investigate discussions which take place when the departure points are the wholly unpromising but seemingly inevitable ones that derive from an imposed agenda. The task-focused small-group discussions of ten- to twelve-year-olds are ideal for such an investigation: ten-, eleven-, and twelve-year-olds meet the 'school' topic many times during the school week. If we can describe the variety of approaches they adopt to handling the problems created, we may discover what 'successful' small-group talk is really like, and perhaps by implication, what the contradictions are in current definitions.

Let us begin by looking at a group of ten-year-old girls who were asked to decide what they would put on the timetable if they were free to plan the school day. This is a topic which might be expected to be of some intrinsic interest to the group, but it is a 'school' topic nevertheless because it was introduced in order to involve the children in discussion *per se*.

1. *D:* we could have craft all day
2. *?:* yeah
3. *A:* no ⟨ * * ⟩ different. just reading 'n' sitting down ⟨ sewing ⟩
4. *C:* clay . n' cooking ['n' art . 'n':n:n
5. *D:*   [yeah cookin'
6. *?:* h:h:h
7. *?:* erm . . .
   (*2 seconds*)

8. *B:* um . I'd like maths
9. *A:* no
10. *C:* oh [no
11. *D:*   [o:h n:o
12. *E:* <u>no</u>
13. *D:* [English
14. *C:* [no working
15. *D:* English
16. *E:* yeah
17. *C:* no work at all (*1 sec*) erm (*1 sec*)
18. *B:* I can't think of anything
         (*laughter and pause*)
19. *C:* I'd like art 'n' painting
20. *D:* mmm (*1 sec*)
20. *B:* no
21. *A:* <u>yeah</u>

What do we hear happening? Each child offers a personal preference for inclusion on the timetable, thus we have proposals for reading, craft, clay and sewing (both apparently different from craft), maths, English, art, and painting. As each item is mentioned it is either accepted without comment or rejected out of hand. The unpopularity of maths is established by a series of children saying 'no', cooking is affirmed by repetition of the word itself. Where there are differences of opinion, as there are over art and painting, these are allowed to remain unresolved, despite there being several pauses in which an attempt at resolution could have been slotted in if any of the group had wanted to do so. At this point in the discussion the children seem to feel that it is important to make succinct statements of their preference and reach an agreed outcome as quickly as possible. But, as the extract below shows, the pattern changes subtly as the discussion continues.

1. *B:* nine till half past two . the tele
2. *?:* yeah the tele
3. *B:* some tele . some on readin'. some on games (*2 secs*)
4. *D:* um . definitely not [French
5. *A:*   [I wouldn't mind doing PE . . . no I wouldn't mind
         doing PE
6. *B:* I would
7. *?:* I [wouldn't
8. *?:*   [it's boring
9. *A:* I wouldn't mind playin' ⟨ * * * * ⟩
10. *D:* no . rounders is more like it

Although the conversational pattern remains predominantly the same as before, with personal preferences offered without grounds or elaboration, and accepted or rejected in a similar vein, there is evidence of the occasional, undeveloped attempt to deviate from this pattern. B, for instance, includes several items in a single turn, the beginning perhaps of a summary or formulation. And at turn 8 someone provides a throwaway justification for rejecting PE as an option. These are small things but they do serve to demonstrate that the speakers are not simply conducting the discussion according to a preset protocol, but are actively engaged in constructing its form as they interact. This makes it all the more significant that what eventuate for the most part are polar (i.e. yes/no) responses to proposals, and a process of agreement by means of a series of endorsements which add no further content to the point (as, for example, in turns 1–3) rather than by argument about the pros and cons of a proposal.[1]

A structural account of the complete discussion would describe it as a series of syntactically independent (i.e. not cohesively associated) exchanges that reach rapid closure as each response becomes progressively more elliptical (cf. Berry 1981, on propositional ellipticity in exchanges). For this group of ten-year-olds 'doing discussion' consists of creating such structures in order to produce a list.

The 'listing' event

Having detected a pattern in one discussion, it should be easier to see it in others. In moving to a second and third discussion with a similar starting point to the one described above, however, I must sound a note of caution. No two discussions are exactly the same, and it is the differences between them which tell us most about the discussion process. Such small but significant details focus attention on how each group constructs its conversation.

The children in the first of these other groups – a mixed-sex group of eleven-year-olds – are this time discussing what would make a suitable schedule for a week's TV organised *by* children *for* children. They are aware that they will be required to consult the schedule at some future point in their work, but do not know precisely why. They are also aware, of course, that they will not be able to affect the TV companies' output one iota. This is another 'school' topic.

```
 1. A:  we can 'ave Playschool on Friday afternoon . .
        [ first . that'll amuse =
 2. ?:  [ oh
    A:  = the little 'uns . they'll be able to watch that
 3. B:  right
 4. C:  alright then
 5. D:  yeah
 6. A:  then we can 'ave the . erm . [ Dallas
 7. C:                              [ Grange Hill
 8. A:  no . [ Horizon
 9. C:       [ Grange Hill
10. D:  what
11. B:  no not Horiz: [ on . how about . how about =
12. D:                [ not a bloomin' party political broadcast
    B:  = Top of the Pops
13. A:  yeah
14. C:  go on then
        (A writes 'Top of the Pops')
```

This time one of the children tells the others why she feels her proposal should be accepted. D suggests that 'Playschool' should be included to 'amuse' the youngest viewers (1), and that 'Horizon' should be rejected because it has the qualities of a party political broadcast (12). She does not make fully explicit what this means, but like the members of the group we share the same cultural background and understand that she thinks it is wordy, takes itself too seriously, has a preaching tone, and is generally about things that 'ordinary' people are not interested in. So, on this occasion it cannot be claimed that suggestions are put forward entirely on the grounds of personal preference. It is significant, therefore, that the *general* pattern of the discussion remains the same as that for the 'timetable' discussion. Where disagreement occurs (as it does even over the 'Horizon' proposal) the children move on quickly to a new suggestion, demonstrating by this action their priority is something other than arguing each dispute through to a satisfactory resolution. The point of the lesson, as far as the children can tell, is to draw up a list. Keeping to the point requires that the group find as many things as possible to agree upon; it is beside the point to 'waste' time hammering out disagreements.

From another classroom comes a third group. The topic is about what soldiers would take with them on a battle mission to the desert. The discussion is part of a project on historical battles, and involves a group of ten-year-old boys for whom war is currently a major preoccupation.

1. *G:* they don't have tin cups
2. *S:* they do
3. *J:* [they *do*
4. *G:* [they don't have plates
5. *J:* they do
6. *S:* they do have metal ones
7. *G:* yeah metal ones 're not plates
   . they're called erm
8. *S:* (*irritated tone*) I'll just put plates
9. *J:* mm (*long pause*) same thing
10. *S:* yeah still eat out of them
11. *G:* you gotta call them by their proper name though.

The pattern we have seen before is repeated once again, with one speaker making a proposal and the others responding to its polarity, its yes/no-ness. When G says that soldiers don't have tin cups or tin plates, S and J counter by refuting the truth of his statements. What makes this encounter different is that G is not merely wanting to provide an item for the list, but is concerned that the others should use the correct names for army utensils. However, although this matter is clearly of great importance to him it is apparently not to the other members of the group. They have taken part in numerous discussions like this one and seem to have come to regard the point, or purpose, to be the finalisation of a list; for them it is not part of the point of the discussion to refine terminological – or even categorical – accuracy. But, there is, however, a second and possibly more important difference in this discussion, for what these children are doing in the course of compiling their list is asserting what they take to be *facts*. It is worth noting, then, that their conversational style is no different from the one others adopt when proffering opinions. Could it be that the speakers see facts and opinions in the same class as far as task-focused small-group talk is concerned, and that for the purpose of such events both are deemed to be 'collectables', and as such of equivalent status?

Each of the small-group discussions I have described could be said to be 'successful' according to one half of the set of criteria which were discussed in the early part of this chapter. Speakers are polite (they do not shout at, or insult, one another), and on the whole they do not interrupt each other. Nor do they begin 'irrelevant' discussions, or loop back to previously mentioned points. They keep very much to the task by creating a series of short exchanges each of which embraces a single sub-topic. On the other hand, the members of the group fail to meet the other half of the criteria in which it is suggested they should follow the line of an argument and sustain a point of view. In these discussions, as in all the others they engage in, they have to decide which set of criteria to 'go' for. This they will do interactively, that is, whilst 'doing discussion'.

It can be seen from those extracts we have examined so far that small-group talk in school is about more than the official task. Each discussion is an *event*, in which the speakers explore the possibilities of small-group talk itself. The groups I have described are taking part in a particular type of event, a 'drawing-up-a-list' event. As they do so, they construct that *type* of event as one during which facts and opinions are asserted forcefully, acceptance of those facts or opinions is given uncritically, opposition to the facts or opinions is made in the form of unelaborated counter-statements, and progress from talk about one assertion to talk about the next is accomplished as rapidly as possible. To return, then, to the issue of the 'success' of the discussion *qua* discussion, it would not seem sensible to consider any of the examples as better or worse discussions than any others we might hear. In so far as they use a style of small-group talk from which a list, or a set of facts, eventuates, not only do the groups achieve what they set out to do, but they achieve it in a demonstrably effective way. In that sense they are highly 'successful'.

The interactive construction of knowledge as 'facts'

Small-group discussions do not happen in a vacuum, the children who take part in them come with a history of expectations about talking and learning built up through other classroom conversations. One-to-one conversations with the teacher, class discussions, earlier group discussions, all these contribute to those expectations. The discussion of the moment does not merely reflect those expectations, however, it reconstructs them (Foucault 1972). As speakers take part in a conversation they 'shape again' their understanding of conversation itself. And if conversations re-create the possibilities of conversation, each classroom discussion about a 'school' topic will redefine the status and purpose of 'school' knowledge, and probably, by implication, all other forms of knowledge. What this means for our groups, it seems, is that they expect to deal with a body of knowledge which is already parcelled into securely wrapped packages: they do not expect to have to reveal how the knowledge got into the package, or to discuss whether it is in the right package in the first place. Each time they hold a discussion which eventuates as a 'drawing-up-a-list' event, they re-establish or reconstruct the perceptions by which they are able to continue to look upon discussion as an activity in which assertion and counter-assertion of inert facts is the name of the game. And so it goes on throughout their schooling.

Schools are places where meanings about learning are constructed, but the most pervasive meanings are constructed through the most regularly occurring events. It is, therefore, perhaps not entirely coincidental that in several significant ways the discourse structures our small groups use are close to those they will have experienced during transmission-type class lessons (cf. Barnes 1975; Sinclair and Coulthard 1975; Willes 1983; Edwards and Westgate 1986). A single issue is dealt with within a single exchange, the opening of each new exchange is clearly marked by the function of the opening move, and the closure of an exchange is normally marked by an acceptance which is also an evaluation. As with class discussions, long turns are the exception, short turns the rule. In both the transmission-type class discussion and the 'listing'-type group discussion, the speakers signal to each other, and confirm by continuing to 'do' together, that they perceive meaning-making as a process of tabling items on an agenda for approval or disapproval. And in both cases, knowledge is 'created' non-negotiable; a thing either 'is' or it 'isn't' so. I would suggest that from this perspective the small-group discussions we have studied can be regarded as 'unsuccessful'. They are perfectly acceptable argumentative discussions of their kind but, when taking part in them, children become orientated to knowledge in a way which is likely to limit their potential for creative thinking. Is that, maybe, why there are contradictions in official attempts to produce criteria for successful discussion? Do the tensions exist, perhaps, because the compilers are unsure about which view of knowledge they prefer?

Criteria and values, the things which matter

Before turning to a quite different kind of discussion in the final part of this chapter, I want to look in detail at one more discussion of the 'drawing-up-a-list' type. The discussion I have chosen appears at first hearing to be in the same style throughout, but it actually undergoes a number of significant shifts as it progresses. These shifts reflect the speakers' attempts to deviate from the 'official' point of the discussion (as their talk reveals they perceived it) at the outset. The group are trying to decide what animals, if any, it would be 'legitimate' to use for medical research that might provide a cure for lethal human diseases. Earlier class discussion had been about the more traditional roles of animals in human communities, and had arisen out of a project on energy. The topic is slightly bizarre – one might have suspected that there were prior questions to ask (of which more below) – but it is not untypical of the sorts of topic which emerge as 'school' topics. From the extracts I have chosen it can be seen that the members of the mixed-sex group of eleven- and twelve-year-olds progress beyond mere listing.

 1. *C:*   they should use sewer rats =
 2. *K:*   they should use sewer rats an'
     C: = an' not rabbits an' dogs [an'
 3. *?:*   [no just rats
             [an' mice
 4. *Ju:* [<u>and</u> [mice   (*leans forward*)
 5. *Ja:*   [and dogs
 6. *D:*   yeah . dog [pets
 7. *K:*   [any other pets
 8. *S:*   an' horses
 9. *K:*   no . not horses . but there should be rats
10. *Ju:* yeah rats . rats [an' like all
11. *K:*   [an' wh : ite mice
12. *C:*   we should use it on . old rats . [old rats that have =
13. *K:*   [yeah. old rats
     C: = you know . not the young . young [animals
14. *S:*   [diseased animals
15. *C:*   yeah
                     (*Break in transcript*)
16. *S:*   or they should do it on animals what've got thousands more of
17. *C:*   [yeah
18. *K:*   [yeah an' nothing that's extinct . say like an elephant or something . if they
             use that and then they know it's gonna be extinct
19. *S:*   yeah like they use the ivory off the tusks =
20. *C:*   [that's not
     S: [= they have to kill the elephants first
21. *C:*   [yeah but [that ain't experiments really is it
22. *D:*   [yes
23. *S:*   yeah but it's still cruel though

In the early part of the discussion (turns 1–11) the children are creating a list as the others were; however, it soon begins to emerge (12–15) that the choices of animal victim for inclusion are principled ones. Experiments should only be carried out, they suggest, on expendable creatures such as the old and infirm ones. This attention to the grounds for including or excluding a proposed animal continues for the rest of the discussion, until C warns that they are 'off the point' (21), and S makes explicit the fact that for her at least there is a moral consideration which links the apparently irrelevant comments about elephants, to the 'point' of the discussion (23). In effect, she is saying 'it's not the point with which we started, but it is on a related matter'.

The group members have begun to make the discussion their own by 'digressing' to talk about the suffering that animal experimentation can cause. The move from straight 'listing' to 'listing and evaluating' is mirrored by the move from short, syntactically independent exchanges, to exchanges which are much longer and contain jointly produced propositions. The first eight turns, for example, really make up a single proposition about creatures that are fair game for the vivisectionist (cohesively tied with 'and', 'just', and 'other', words that invite the hearer to seek associations, comparisons, and contrasts). Turns 18 and 19 make up another (with 'like' acting as a cohesive device because it stands for 'for instance'). In each of these cases one child's proposal is extended by the next speaker who brings forward a further example without beginning a new proposition (cf. Halliday 1985, on propositional extension). In the former case the proposition could, in theory, continue to be extended in the same way until it became impossible for any group member to remember what was in it. Unlike the children in the earlier discussion groups, these children are not anxious to close each exchange without first raising (if not actually discussing in much detail) related matters. They are ready, therefore, to progress from considering the specific off-the-point issue of the pain that will be caused to the animals used for experiment, to the general related issue of whether it is morally right to experiment on animals anyway. (The question we ourselves might have wanted to ask at the outset, too.)

1. *K:*   erm . the people that go in for ⟨hurting 'em⟩ they should be punished for it
2. *C:*   they shouldn't punish them they should use them as guinea pigs
3. *D:*   yeah
4. *Ja:* (*to some-one passing*) [oii
5. *Ju:*   [Shaun put that
   ⟨***⟩
6. *K:*   they should use us as guinea pigs [really shouldn't they
7. *C:*   [not us
8. *K:*   no not us . but the [people that do it =
9. *Ja:*   [let's use them as guinea pigs . . wouldn't be able to do it then would they
10. *K:* = the people that do experiments . because the animals haven't done anything wrong have they but the people who're in prison they've done a lot wrong
11. *C:* yeah but it still saves people's lives doing it though

As the children feel freer to discuss what matters to them, and begin to question the values implicit in the task itself, the group begins to loop back to issues that an individual has attempted to 'tick off' as closed. Whereas at the start of the discussion the group seemed to feel obliged to move immediately to the next point once the current one had been marked as closed by someone using a content-free acceptance particle ('yes', 'yeah', 'mm', etc.), by this stage K has made the matter under discussion sufficiently his own to want to break the listing pattern. He continues with the point raised by C, despite the fact that D has already indicated that the matter is closed for her (3), and Ju has marked closure even more clearly by instructing Shaun to write the point down. It may be that it is in response to these attempts at closure that K feels obliged to make fully explicit his reasoning (and in the process to contribute the longest utterance of the discourse so far). He, like most other speakers, uses logical explicitness in response to a particular problem that arises interactionally, and not because it is necessary for the production of 'successful' argument *per se*.

The language of logic

I hope that by now I have established that it is possible to have talk which keeps to the point and successfully accomplishes the perceived task (of drawing up a list, or of listing and evaluating) but which must be deemed educationally 'unsuccessful' if one's view of education encompasses active engagement with knowledge and the creation of increased opportunities for coming to know. Before leaving this part of my argument altogether, however, I must comment a little further on 'the language of logic' used by ten- to twelve-year-olds, and consider the implications for learning of the presence or absence of such connective particles as 'so' and 'because' (or 'cos, as it more commonly is in speech). The point is illustrated by returning to the discussion by the children who are making up a TV schedule. At various junctures they provide criteria for their choice of programme but by no means all of these are marked by the use of logical connectives.

```
 1. A:  Grange Hill . and then we can 'ave . for the adults [. . .Horizon [ 'cos
 2. C:                                                       [ not racing
 3. D:                                                                   [ Horizon .
         ooh < not that sorta [ broadcast
 4. C:  yeah but we gotta 'ave . 'ave somethin' for the adults
 5. A:  they 'ave to 'ave one programme though in't they (grins)
 6. D:  give . start with < Doctor Who >
 7. A:  no not [ < Doctor Who >
 8. D:          [ The Dick Emery Show
 9. A:  no 'cos that's all funny . that's
         all [ funny
10. ?:      [ yeah
11. C:      [ no 'cos that's gonna [ be on every night
12. A:                             [ that's all
         comedians . sorta . like comedy
13. C:  yeah . 's too much shows
```

Without using 'the language of logic' A lets the others know (1) that he has selected his programme because it is suitable for adults and because a TV schedule should provide for different groups of people. It is true that A's criteria are not particularly good criteria because the task was to draw up a schedule specifically for *children*, but this would be the case whatever degree of explicitness there was in his statement. Besides, it is not uncommon for a speaker who uses one way of 'making arguable' at one point, to use another at some other point (see the vivisection discussion above). If successful argument was dependent upon speakers' use of logical explicitness, then it would be possible to demonstrate that interlocutors react differently to utterances with them in (e.g., turns 9 and 11) from the way they react to those without them (e.g., turn 1). This cannot be done, of course. What can be shown, though, is that when speakers provide evidence of reasoning – whether they make it fully explicit or not – they alter the nature of the discussion, turning it into genuine argument, i.e. into talk about a world which is 'arguable'. In the execution of the business of that world people make choices, and in one way or another indicate to each other that they *have* made them. What counts is whether individual speakers offer proposals in an arguable form, and not what particular linguistic forms they use to do so.

Creating knowledge negotiable

In argument of the kind examined so far, speakers re-create knowledge as a sort of commodity, to be collected and stored. Knowledge is outside of them, in a territory Boomer (1985) has termed 'elsewhere'. If the topic is not one in which they have an immediate investment, some of the more determined groups may nevertheless deviate from the original point of the discussion to argue about an aspect which they can make their own. The criteria for categorisation, and values, are two of these. In these discussions children achieve 'success' by appropriating the task, and questioning its assumptions, whilst still proceeding to an agreed outcome in a series of relatively tidy steps. But what of arguments in which the speakers make no attempt to keep to the point in the first place; arguments which would fail to meet the 'success' criteria applied to the 'listing' and the 'listing-and-evaluating' discussions, but would fulfil the criteria that would remain if the first set was extrapolated from the HMI list reported at the beginning of the chapter? What are *their* characteristics, and how do *they* reflect and re-create knowledge and knowing? There is neither space nor need to record the linguistic features in detail (but see Phillips 1985; and in preparation) but, in outline, these arguments are characterised by long exchanges without a clear indication of closure; by utterances full of uncertainties, hesitations, substitutions, non-equivalences, and tentative modalisations; and by sub-topics which are picked up, dropped, and returned to as the moment demands. Most of these features indicate that a speaker is actively engaged in the thinking process as he or she speaks. Substitutions, for instance, can be explained only in these terms: repetitions at points of overlap are quite common as place-holding devices (McLaughlin 1984), but substitutions such as the one below would be inefficient as a way of achieving place-holding and must therefore be heard as evidence of the speaker taking the opportunity of overlap to substitute a word closer in meaning to his or her original intention. The following extract, incidentally, is not part of any discussion mentioned so far, although the group of ten-year-old girls come from the same class as the others who were talking about animal experimentation.

1. *E:* yeah um . you gotta good thing about it
   [is it sa. it could save =
2. *R:* [you'd have no animals left if you keep putting them [⟨ in the experiments⟩
3. *Z:*   [I know
   E: = it could help somebody you care about

Utterances in which a speaker either abandons what he or she was going to say, or explicitly cancels it, provide further examples of ongoing thinking. The following examples come from an eleven-year-olds' discussion of 'how to purify water':

E: = an' then you have different pipes taking it to different tanks . one tank for clean and the other tank for the dirty . . . no that ain't a very good idea is it

A: yeah but (*3 secs*) oh yeah you've gotta catch it in't yer

And non-equivalence particles (Schourup 1986), or 'imprecision' particles (Phillips 1985) reveal that the speaker is still seeking to formulate the precise idea about which he or she is talking:

C: no well if they . if they . if they had something like a filter an' all the water go through and the fish they go into sort of another bag

The presence of all these features not only reflects the fact that the speakers are still thinking, and are coming to terms with what they know as they interact in the group with each other's ideas, but they also come together to create a discussion in which knowledge *has been constructed* as a negotiable. It is no longer treated as a commodity, but a living and growing entity which is part of the speakers' own experience.

One of the most notable features of this style of argument is the exchange structure, which is extremely complex. It is not possible to describe in simple terms the structure of a discussion in which one exchange flows into another and is therefore not really a new exchange at all. Unlike in the earlier conversations, speakers often respond by expanding the propositional content in their responses, and the next speaker responds, in turn, to the additional component of the first response. It is also difficult to describe the structure of an exchange which begins with a speculation or a hypothesis, for one of the purposes of such a contribution is to invite the holding off of responses until a later moment when full consideration has been given to it (Phillips 1983). The exchange may 'close' forty turns away, or simply remain 'unclosed'. These non-linear exchange patterns make it appear that speakers are wandering off the point, and are not making logical connections between contiguous parts of the argument. In fact what is happening is that the speakers are making their connections across a much wider span, and are holding several ideas or hypotheses in mind at once until such moments as they may naturally merge to create a new idea or offer proof of the hypothesis. Each 'point' is arrived at at a much later moment in the discussion than in the other forms of argument, and knowledge itself therefore remains arguable for longer.

Schools are places where children discover what knowledge is. In school children can become explorers, experimenters, and hypothesisers coming at knowledge from the inside, or they can become marketeers trading in knowledge 'goods' which come from a central store in which they have no stake. They can take part in constructing knowledge as a vast consensus, with which all politely agree even when they feel in their bones they want to object (and may indeed, in some cases, have voiced that objection in a token manner), or they can become seekers of difference, celebrators of divergence, and creators of 'new' knowledge. But the way in which they habitually discuss together will play a key part in deciding which of these they eventually become. This is just as true of the way they discuss in small groups as it is of the class discussion. Every time a group of children take part in a discussion they will either be involved in making knowledge negotiable, or in creating it assertable. Obviously the way in which the discussion originates will be important but, even within the wholly unhelpful constraints of a non-negotiable curriculum content, it may still be possible to facilitate task-focused peer-group discussions in which the children are able to make the point their own. This is most likely to happen when they are invited to consider values and other issues for which there is no absolute answer, and to aim to identify their differences rather than points of agreement. After all, the purpose of education is not to list what is already known, but to identify what is still to be learned, and to devise strategies for becoming a knower. When children are 'doing discussion' they are learning ways of knowing: each discussion that enables them to consider related matters puts them nearer to a belief in knowledge as negotiable, ownable and exciting.

Note

1. An interchange from a later moment in the same discussion demonstrates this even better:

   1. *A:* I wouldn't mind . doin' macramé
   2. *D:* macramé
   3. *B:* macramé [yeah
   4. *E:*   [I wouldn't mind doin' some of that

References

Barnes, D. (1976). *From Communication to Curriculum*, Harmondsworth, Penguin.
Berry, M. (1981). 'Polarity, Ellipticity, Elicitation, and Propositional Development: Their Relevance to the Well-Formedness of an Exchange', *Nottingham Linguistic Circular*, no. 10, pp. 36–63.
Boomer, G. (1985). *Fair Dinkum Teaching and Learning: Reflections on Literacy and Power*, Upper Montclair, NJ, Boynton Cook.
DES (1984). *English from 5 to 16: Curriculum Matters 1 (An HMI Series)*, London, HMSO.
DES (1986). *English from 5 to 16: Responses to Curriculum Matters 1*, London, HMSO.
Edwards, A. D. and Westgate, D. P. (1986). *Investigating Classroom Talk*, Lewes, Falmer.
Foucault, M. (1972). *The Archaeology of Knowledge*, London, Tavistock.
Halliday, M. A. K. (1985). *An Introduction to Functional Grammar*, London, Edward Arnold.
McLaughlin, M. L. (1984). *Conversation: How Talk is Organised*, London, Sage.
Phillips, T. (1983). 'Now You See It, Now You Don't. Some Participant and Observer Perceptions of Language for Learning', *English in Education*, vol. 17, no. 1, pp. 32–41.
Phillips, T. (1985). 'Beyond Lip-Service: Discourse Development After the Age of Nine' in G. Wells and J. Nicholls (eds), *Language and Learning: An Interactional Perspective*, Lewes, Falmer.
Phillips, T. (in preparation). *Talk amongst Yourselves, That's Not My Style: Reflections on the Relationship between Interactive Mode and Active Learning*.
Schourup, L. C. (1985). *Common Discourse Particles in English*, London, Garland.
Sinclair, J. McH. and Coulthard, R. M. (1975). *Towards an Analysis of Discourse: The English Used by Teachers and Pupils*, London, Oxford University Press.
Willes, M. (1983). *Children into Pupils*, London, Routledge and Kegan Paul.

7 Is there a task in this class?[1]

DAVID HALLIGAN*

Understanding classroom texts

There is a sense in which the study of text is a 'frontier science' not only because it has been the most recent aspect of the language system to be subjected to analysis, but also because it stands mid-way between that which may be revealed by a study of the language system itself and that which has to do with the uses to which men and women put that system. It is the audible point at which the disciplines of linguistics, psychology and sociology meet. It is the point of messy questioning. It seems to me to be a point of some regret that there has been a deal of academic coyness about this meeting, a certain standoffishness which makes text linguistics shy of human intentions and psychologists and sociologists shy of one another as well as of the structure of the language data which is their daily nourishment. It is, in fact, to a notable exception that I have found it most useful to turn in seeking a way through the maze in which we find ourselves when we begin systematic exploration of classroom conversations.

The collaboration between sociolinguist and psychotherapist that produced the approach to the study of spoken interaction described in *Therapeutic Discourse* (Labov and Fanshel 1977) has provided a way of examining conversations of central interest to teachers and other educationalists. The authors of that study foreground their concern to examine not simply matters of diagnosis or the evaluation of outcome, but 'what is actually done in the therapeutic interview' (1977: 3). Central to the problem which they – and we – seek to address is how speakers come to hear particular forms of words as expressing particular meanings, and the central feature of their solution to the problem is the formulation of what they call discourse rules.

From the point of view of the issues to be discussed in this chapter a particularly important discourse rule is that which Labov and Fanshel call the 'Request for Information'. They write it as follows:

* The author is now a member of HM Inspectorate but the substance of this paper is derived from work for a doctoral thesis carried out before he joined the Inspectorate.

If A addresses to B an imperative requesting information I, or an interrogative focusing on I, and B does *not* believe that A believes that

(a) A has I
(b) B does not have I

then A is heard as making a valid request for information.

The rule enables the clarification of a familiar issue in classroom discourse study; that is, the interpretation of questions. The most familiar form of classroom question, 'guess what's in my mind', fails to fulfil the conditions set out by Labov and Fanshel for requests for information. It fails because A, who is in this case the teacher, is clearly known to all the participants to have I. The teacher does not ask the class the date of the Battle of Hastings because he or she wonders when the event occurred, but because the child is required to show that, in response to that question, it can produce the magic formula '1066'. Labov and Fanshel remark on this sort of questioning, 'common in school situations', and call it a request for display. They do not go on to formulate the rule, but by adding a modification to the request for information it is possible to see what it would look like. The modification would go like this: 'If a request for information is invalid because A has I, but B believes that A has the right to make a request for I, then A is heard as making a valid request for display.'

Even at this early point it is worth pausing to consider some of the characteristics of these two 'rules', for they, as much as the 'rules' themselves, are of some importance in the context of the study of classroom discourse. The first is that they rest on the subjectivity of the participants in the events to which they relate. For instance, the meaning of the utterance, 'What was the date of the Battle of Hastings?' resides not only in its structure as a bit of language but also in the knowledge and beliefs of the participants in the exchange. The meaning of the words is context-dependent, and an important part of that context is how the participants see the situation in which they find themselves. The second is that they view the subjectivity of each participant in relation to the subjectivity of other participants. The meanings that participants in a conversation can develop depend on the relationships between them. It seems clear, therefore, that to understand classroom conversations it is necessary to adopt an approach which enables discussion of how the classroom text is made up with reference both to the intentions of individuals and to the relationships between them.

Who controls the meaning?

It now becomes possible to say something about the pattern of the conversation which is facilitated by different sorts of request. In the case of the request for display the participants – pupils and teacher – share a belief that A has I. There is thus nothing problematic about the nature of I. It is what A decides it will be. So, in relation to that wretched battle, 'the second half of the eleventh century', 'the third quarter of the eleventh century', '1066' or '14 October 1066' are all possible answers but exactly which one constitutes I rests with the teacher to define. Consequently the familiar pattern of teacher–pupil–teacher–pupil–teacher exchange as the teacher questions his or her way to the pre-ordained goal, follows on the request for display. I would wish to call this patterning a 'style of discourse' and to call this particular style the style of display since it depends for its initiation on that particular request.[2]

In the same way a request for information gives rise to a style of information. No longer does one participant have a special right to define I, except of course in a conversation between only two participants, where only one of the participants will have I. In a multi-person conversation, however, more than one person can legitimately chip in as the participants seek to establish an adequate formulation of the I in question. Few human beings in Anglo-Saxon culture can be fortunate enough not to know the date of the Battle of Hastings but, if I can be allowed to postulate one who might ask a group of more erudite friends when the event took place, the conversation might then proceed with each participant adding a little more precision until all were agreed that 'I' had been reached along the lines of the sequence I have just presented. Since the questioner does not have the right to define the answer that is required, control of the discourse passes out of the questioner's hands. The classroom, of course, remains a special case. If the teacher continues to retain control of the turn-taking aspect of the conversation the pattern of teacher–pupil–teacher may persist even though the conversation is being conducted in the style of information. None the less, if this really is the style of information, the teacher will have surrendered, or will not be laying claim to a very important aspect of the control of the discourse, namely, when this particular speech act has been completed. Should the teacher retain that control, then, in claiming a special right to define I, the teacher is still operating the style of display.

Along with the perceptions of individual participants in a conversation, and the relationships between them, this approach takes into account the meanings being exchanged. The essential difference between the styles of information and display is *who is in control of the meanings* which may be generated. In both cases the possibilities of meaning have a finite quality. In the case of display, that finite quality derives simply from the right of one participant to be arbitrator. In the case of information it derives rather from the participants reaching a mutual agreement that, together, they have I. There is, however, another case in which the meanings generated do not have this finite quality, and that is a case in which the participants are able to generate disputable meanings. This is the case of the style of proposition. The essence of this style is that I is not specially held to be the possession of any participants: its nature is not definite but disputable. The rule for the speech act to initiate this style of discourse can be formulated as follows:

If A addresses to B an imperative requesting information I, or an interrogative focusing on I, and B does not believe that:

(a) I is not disputable

(b) any other member has a special right to define I

then A is heard as making a valid request for a proposition.

This is a speech act of great importance for the organisation of discourse in learning situations. As with requests for display, I have stated it in terms close to those used for requests for information because again the surface structure of an utterance which enacts it may be very close to the surface structure which enacts either of the other two acts. It is the fulfilment of the contextual conditions that defines the act in any particular instance. The importance of this speech act in the discourse of learning lies in the possibilities offered by the contextual conditions, and centres on the concept of disputability, because it is that quality of a proposition that enables other members of a group to take up the proposition, agreeing with it, adding to it, modifying it or denying it in their subsequent discussion. Like requests for display and information this request has an effect on the sequences which follow it. But this can only happen if not only do the members believe that the proposition is disputable, but also if they believe that no one member has a final right to act as arbitor of truth or falsity. That is the importance of condition (b), which I shall call the 'reciprocity condition' because of its demand that no one member of the group dominates the others. It is failure to fulfil this condition that in part accounts for the sort of discourse observed in formal classrooms.

Labov and Fanshel set out to find a way of describing what the participants in a therapeutic conversation *do*. I have been seeking to argue that it is possible to use the essence of their approach to describe at least an aspect of what people involved in an educational conversation *do*. A way of summarising my hypothesis would be to say that what speakers do is establish a way of interacting with one another which enables meanings to be generated between them, rather than being imposed by one of the participants as in the stereotypical classroom dialogue between teacher and pupil.

Participant relationships, and discourse styles

I now want to present an example to show the interaction process at work in practice. The following conversation was recorded in the course of a longitudinal study of a class of eleven- and twelve-year-olds in the English lessons which took place during the first year of their secondary schooling. (A fuller description of this work and presentation of the documentation appears in Halligan 1984). The school in which these recordings were made was an inner-city, multi-ethnic one, and the pupils, in terms of conventional measurements and standardised tests, were not able ones. The transcription which follows is of the first recording which I made of one particular group of boys. In the lesson which preceded the recording I had read the class a short story (Callender 1968). The story is about Mr Spencer, who has a magnificent banana tree on which grows superb fruit. He will neither pick the fruit for himself nor share it with his neighbour, Bulldog.

The latter becomes incensed at his selfishness and declares that, before a specific time, he will steal the fruit. Mr Spencer keeps an armed vigil before the tree but, momentarily turning away from the tree just before the deadline expires, he looks back to see the bananas gone and becomes the victim of 'An Honest Thief'. The group of boys were sent off to a small room with a tape-recorder which they had to operate themselves and a card on which some questions were written. The pupils were told they could alter or ignore the questions if they wished. The object was to produce, through discussion, a reading of the story. Here are the questions:

1 What sort of man was Mr Spencer? Do you know anyone like him?
2 Bulldog and Mr Spencer were 'bad men'. What do you think this means? Do you know anyone who has a reputation like that?
3 How on earth do you think Bulldog managed to steal the bananas?
4 What do you think the title means?
5 Can stealing ever be right?

And here, in full, is the text of the boys' discussion:

1 *Mark:* Here are some ideas for talking about 'An Honest Thief'. Can, you choose which ones you want? What sort of a man was Mr Spencer? John?
2 *John:* He was you know, you know, a mad man.
3 *Mark:* Thank you. Do you know anyone like him? Leroy?
4 *Leroy:* No.
5 *Mark:* That all?
6 *Leroy:* Yes.
7 *Mark:* Bulldog and Mr Spencer were bad men. Was Bulldog and Mr Spencer bad men?
8 *Sam:* Yes, they were bad men, of course they was, don't you know that?
9 *Mark:* What do you think this means? Er, Paul?
10 *Paul:* Well, it means they were always hitting people 'n' that.
11 *Mark:* Do you know anyone who has a reputation like that?
12 *John:* No.
13 *Mark:* Sam
14 *Sam:* Mark . . . (*followed by something inaudible*)
15 *Mark:* Thank you.
16 *John:* Shut up.
17 *Mark:* How on earth do you think Bulldog managed to steal his bananas?
18 *John:* Cos he was, when he was/
19 *Sam:* /He was.
20 *Mark:* One at a time please.
21 *John:* Cos he looked at his watch right, he shouldn't have looked at his watch.
22 *Sam:* No.
23 *Mark:* Leroy, what do you think?
24 *Leroy:* Because Bulldog was up in the tree and when Spencer looked at his watch he nicked the bananas.
25 *Mark:* What do you think Paul?
26 *Paul:* I think the same as Leroy.
27 *Mark:* What do you think?
28 *John:* So do I.
29 *Sam:* Same as me of course, you stupid idiot.

30 *John:*   I think as Leroy as well.
31 *Mark:*   What do you think the title means? The Sun Eyes.
32 *John:*   The Sun Eye, The Sun's Eyes.
33 *Sam:*   No that ain't the title, that's the title of the book/The title of the story.
34 *Paul:*   /The title of the story.
35 *John:*   Whoops.
36 *Mark:*   What do you think 'An Honest Thief' means?
37 *John:*   Here it is.
38 *Sam:*   I think 'An Honest Thief' means that he gives you a fifty-fifty chance.
39 *Mark:*   Correct. Can you ever steal, can stealing ever be right?
40 *Chorus:* /No.
41 *Sam:*   /No it cannot, its against the law.
42 *Mark:*   Why?
43 *John:*   Cos if you steal you get put in jail.
44 *Mark:*   Thank you that's all for now. Just a minute . . . (*They stop the tape*)

45 *Mark:*   Do you think Bulldog was a thief?
46 *John:*   Yes, I do, I do.
47 *Paul:*   He stole the bananas so he's got to be a thief, an'e.
48 *Sam:*   Yea.
49 *Mark:*   Do you think Mr Spencer was a bully?
50 *Chorus:* Yea.
51 *Sam:*   Sure he was a bully definitely.
52 *Paul:*   Cos he was a really bad man.
             (*Inaudible*)
53 *Mark:*   How do you know he was a bully?
54 *Paul:*   /Because.
55 *Sam:*   /Because he said he could beat Spencer when he came to meet him.
56 *Paul:*   Yea, and he, they also, cos they said in the story/about
57 *Mark:*   Do you think Mr Spencer was a show off?
58 *Chorus:* Yea.
             (*Inaudible*)
59 *Mark:*   They was getting all juicy but in the end he loses them all.
60 *Chorus:* Yea.
61 *Sam:*   That's it.
             (*They stop the tape*)

62 *Leroy:*   I think Mr Spencer was very selfish because he don't want nobody else in the town to have things.
63 *John:*   And if say somebody else had a banana tree, right, and he, and it was bad. Bulldog and he asked if he could have some what would Bulldog say?
64 *Mark:*   I reckon that Bulldog he would probably have given some because he's kind.
65 *Sam:*   Mr Spencer had to lose the bananas because he kept praising them and
66 *Mark:*   Yea.
67 *Sam:*   kept looking at them every day/and watering them.
68 *Paul:*   /He should have
69 *Mark:*   And they're all juicy.
70 *Leroy:*   If he'd have picked it on about Monday or Tuesday he wouldn't have lost them.
71 *Paul:*   Yea.
72 *John:*   He should have picked it when he said.
73 *Leroy:*   Yea.

74 *John:*   He should have picked them when his wife
75 *Sam:*   But he was too big-headed.
76 *Paul:*   In the end they would have all gone bad.
77 *John:*   He should have picked it.
78 *Sam:*   Yea but . . . he was too big-headed.
79 *Leroy:*   He kept on saying couple of days.
80 *Mark:*   That's all for now folks.

A curious feature of this recording is that the boys chose to switch off the tape-recorder in such a way as to divide the recordings into three sections. The three sections illustrate the three styles of discourse I have been discussing. There is a classic moment in the first section, for example, where Sam responds to Mark's reading of the question about the meaning of the title of the story (turns 36–9). I once showed a transcription of these four turns to a group of teachers without playing the tape. They immediately assumed that Mark was a teacher, so recognisable was his behaviour as that of a teacher. It is what I have described as the style of display, with Mark assuming not only the right to pose the questions but the right to arbitrate when the requested display has been given and so to move on to the next question. The meanings which can be generated in the conversation are determined by one participant alone. Things change after the break in the recording. For one thing Mark, although still 'in charge', in the sense that it is he who asks the questions, now asks questions of his own making. More important though, from the point of view of this discussion, is the way in which the others make their contributions. Thus turns 23–30 contrast sharply with 49–52. In the first sequence each makes his contribution as called upon by Mark; in the second Paul can come in with an extra contribution to add to the first offering from Sam. The definition of what constitutes the requested information no longer rests absolutely with one participant as the style of the discourse shifts from display to information. A sharper contrast still is presented by the third section of the conversation. Here Mark has surrendered his right as the poser of questions and meaning seems to grow from one turn to another. If this section of the conversation is presented in summary form, it might read as follows:

> Mr Spencer lost the bananas because of the delay in picking them (Sam, 65, 67) even though they were ripe (Mark, 69). He would not have lost them if he had picked them earlier (Leroy, 70) when he said he would pick them (John, 72), and when his wife advised him to pick them (John, 74), but he would not follow her advice because he was too vain (Sam, 75, 78) and would have left them on the tree until they rotted (Paul, 76).

The style of discourse enables the pupils to produce a 'reading' of the story as they establish a proposition by means of successive modification and additions. No one of them is in control but rather a reciprocity exists in their relationships which enables them to generate meaning together. The essence of the contrast between the three sections of the recording and the three styles of discourse that they represent is that the third allows meaning to grow and flourish between the participants while the second allows only its exchange, and the first only the exchange of the meanings selected by one of the participants. To create the conditions which will enable pupils to generate propositions should be a major aim of the educational project.

Those conditions as specified by discourse rules of the type I have been using have much to do with the relationships between the participants in the conversation. It is Mark's dominance of the group in the first section of the recording which is an essential condition of the style of display: he must have the *right* to make the request. It is his surrender of that right which makes possible the subsequent changes. To begin to ask questions about the creation of the necessary conditions for the style of proposition is to have to address the relationships between the participants. This is a central part of the context with which these speakers have to deal.

To enrich my understanding of what the boys were doing in their conversation I have to turn to the contextual knowledge which I had of them at the time of making the recording. As a group within the class they were known by the other pupils and even by some of the teachers as 'The Gang' or as 'Mark's Gang'. They would sit together in lessons. They would be always together in the playground. They were not everybody's favourite pupils because always doing what the teachers wanted and being well behaved were not part of the expected pattern of behaviour for them. Indeed, although only eleven or twelve years old at the time, they were beginning to show some features of the counter-school peer group to which sociologists of education have drawn attention ever since becoming concerned with the internal sociology of the school. It is part of the process of socialisation described in Willis's classic study of 1977 and encapsulated in its title *Learning to Labour*. In his study, the counter-school group refer to themselves as 'the lads', distinguishing themselves sharply from their more conformist peers whom they dub 'ear'oles'. Willis emphasises the crucial importance of the friendship group.

Willis suggests that the 'lads' make their decision to split definitively from the 'ear'oles' somewhere in the second or third year of their secondary schooling. Although our group offers some evidence of the earlier existence of the sub-culture, it is by no means decisively split off and, for all of its members, there are crucial decisions yet to be made. The relationships at the point of the recording, with the boys only at the beginning of their time at the school, were far from stable and over the year of the study there were to be several changes in its membership. Paul and Sam were both to leave the group and something of the tension that led to that is present here. Turns 7 and 8, for example, show Sam resisting the request for display by reminding Mark that the latter already knew the answer to the question he had posed.

In a recorded interview I later asked Paul why he had left the group and his reasons were quite clear. The others were stopping him getting on with his work because they spent too much time in lessons 'just chatting an' that and mucking around and putting me off my work'. Sam was never to be as forthcoming as Paul in talking about relations in the group, but he did assign the problems within it to the role of Mark, pointing out that the others always 'behaved' better if Mark was not present. Now, if all this is put together a picture begins to emerge. To produce their most productive talk the group have to deal with internal problems. Some degree of reciprocity must be produced so that Mark, acknowledged leader of the group, does not dominate it in such a way that the only meanings to be exchanged are those which he allows. These problems reside in the relationships between the boys, but they reflect much wider issues in the choices that the boys must make about their attitudes towards school and towards the role of school as a socialising agency.

Somewhere in the midst of all this lies the forgotten task: to discuss the questions about the story, and hopefully to come to some reading of it. In the third section of the recording, that wider interpretation of the task seems to have been fulfilled. Certainly the task was to answer some questions, but, as the Rules of requests for display, information and proposition make clear, what a question actually is is no simple matter. It will be read differently according to the context of interaction within which the participating members of the group find themselves. That reading of the task gives rise, of course, to very different outcomes in terms both of the way the conversation is structured, i.e. the style of the discourse, and in terms of the sorts of meanings which can be generated.

Discourse style – the language produced – is at the centre of a network. On the one hand, it arises out of the interaction of the participants in the conversation. That interaction itself is made up of a combination of factors. There are the histories of the individuals themselves, together with the history of them as a group; there is the task as presented to them; and the immediate social setting of the classroom and the school. Behind this lies that wider context of the society in which the school and its community are located. On the other hand is that which different discourse styles make possible in terms of the power they give to speakers to generate meanings and so to learn. The contexts in which the children operate do not, in any simple or necessary sense, determine what they will do, but they do represent, in the way they are responded to, the problems and possibilities of the world in which the children must function. Because the pupils can negotiate in the small group much of what happens between them, they are enabled to generate meanings which will change the ways they interact and thus the way they come to read the task. To relate to one another with a degree of reciprocity is to make possible the generation of propositions rather than the giving of displays. Human agency, the intention of the participating children, acts, therefore, on the task and gives it that quality of instability which I have been seeking to explore.

If Mark is prepared to surrender his dominance of the group he makes possible collaboration within it and he makes it possible not only for Paul and Sam to remain in the group but allows the group access to what they have to say. *Doing* the task, which can only be accomplished by the collaborative formulation of propositions, demands the resolution, at least for the time being, of the inter-actional problems in the group. I have said that both Paul and Sam were later to leave the group. That did not happen straight away and the group was able to hold together through the first two terms of the year. During that time it was forever unstable but it did not break up, and that, on the evidence of what Paul and Sam told me, all hung on the role of Mark. The styles of discourse that they used varied, but they were often able to use the style of proposition. Finally, however, the group did break up or, more accurately, contract down to its core members, those who were the nucleus of 'The Gang'. When this happened, towards the end of the year, the style of discourse changed: once again it retreated to that of display: the challenge to Mark's authority, represented by those members of the group whose membership was always problematic, was removed. Long after the study was finished I found out that Paul went on from strength to strength in the community of the school and, through truancy, Mark effectively opted out without, except in name, completing his secondary education. The crucial choices, 'lads' or 'ear'oles', for or against school, were made once and for all.

There was certainly work to be done when those boys went off to tape-record a discussion of the questions I had given them, but the task, narrowly conceived as those questions, is only a small element of it. It is the visible portion, the official agenda and, if we are really interested in it, we can attend to only a small part of what it actually is by concentrating solely upon it. Attention to conversational text forces us to look behind the surfaces of task and of utterance and into the intentions of speakers as they confront the immediate and wider social contexts with which they must deal.

So is there a task in the class?

Each group of pupils has to interpret a task for itself. If the task I have used by way of illustration was 'to make a reading of the story', it can also be said that there is always the prior task of making a reading of the task itself. Meanings are social products and so are constrained by the social circumstances in which readers find themselves. So it is for pupils making sense of tasks. If pupils need help in coming to formulate their readings of tasks, they also need help in coming to an understanding of the social situations which condition those formulations. This is to argue that the social relationships of the classroom, between teachers and pupils and between pupils and pupils are not simply an enabling condition of learning, something which may go wrong and so prevent learning, or something which must be made to go right so that learning may take place. It is also to argue that those social relationships are themselves an important area for the content of learning. Moreover, that is not a statement of what ought to be the case but of what is anyway going to be the case. One way or another all pupils have to make some sort of sense of the social world in which they find themselves and the nature of the conversational text is such that, if we are to work with it and to seek its development, we must live with that.

So there isn't simply *a* task in this class, there are a large number of them and they are continually being negotiated, reviewed and revised as the pupils, in coming to terms with one another, come to terms with those few written words which are the official task. I have argued that an approach to classroom discourse suggested by the work of Labov and Fanshel can provide a way of describing some of these processes at work, but that is an argument for *observers* of classrooms. There is also a need for a pedagogy which makes those processes visible for pupils. That is because the task in the class is first and foremost the class itself.

Notes

1. The title of this paper is borrowed and misquoted from Fish (1980). He is concerned with the instability of literary texts; I am concerned with the instability of the task.
2. At this point I have departed substantially from Labov and Fanshel (1977).

References

Callender, T. (1968). 'An Honest Thief' in A. Walmsley (ed.), *The Sun's Eye*, London, Longman.

Fish, S. (1980). *Is There a Text in This Class: The Authority of Interpretive Communities*, Cambridge, Mass., Harvard University Press.

Halligan, D. J. (1984). 'Social Context, Discourse and Learning', PhD thesis, London University Institute of Education.

Labov, W. and Fanshel, D. (1977). *Therapeutic Discourse*, New York, Academic Press.

Willis, P. (1977). *Learning to Labour*, Farnborough, Saxon House.

PART THREE

The dynamics of classroom communication

8 The literate potential of collaborative talk

GEN LING CHANG AND
GORDON WELLS

It is just after recess on Thursday, 19 February 1987. The place a combined third- and fourth-grade classroom in an inner-city school in Toronto. Outside, although the sun is shining in a cloudless sky, the temperature is −15°C. Inside, too, it is the arctic climate that is the focus of attention as the children engage in the exploration of self-chosen topics arising from the school-wide theme of 'The Enchantment of Winter'.

The project had started for these children with a reading of Robert Service's poem 'The Cremation of Sam McGee'. Now, three days later, almost all of them have chosen their projects, most of them arising from the brainstorming session which followed the reading of the poem. After the initial macabre fascination with Sam's mode of cremation, it is the Yukon itself – its vast size and harsh climate – which has captured the children's imagination and most of the projects have a natural history flavour.

Two of the children, Joao and Eric, started by deciding to study the terrain and after reading in a book about three-dimensional mapping techniques, they have decided to make a model of Dawson City and its surroundings using a photograph as a starting point. In the following extract, they are sitting on the floor with some of the necessary materials around them, preparing to begin the construction.

1 *Joao:* Eric, look! See, here is going to be the small mountain.
2   We're going to build it up how it is in the book.
3   Where's the book? (*He picks it up to show it to Eric*)
4   You know, building it up and everything.
5 *Eric:* Yes.
6 *Joao:* Here it is, see. It says 'Building it up'.
7 *Eric:* No, it doesn't mean –
8 *Joao:* So the small one then the big one (*referring to the already*
9   *cut pieces of cardboard*).
10   We can make a little river and the town on the edge too.
11 *Eric:* Yes, that's what I mean.
12 *Joao:* Yeh, OK.

13 *Eric:* That's what we were talking about.
14 *Joao:* Yes, we're starting.
15 *Eric:* And we can do little boats because of the little trees.
16 *Joao:* Yes, OK. So we have to glue this (*the cardboard*).
17 *Eric:* And these are the ⟨*****⟩
18 *Joao:* Yes. No, we're not going to put a church.
19 *Eric:* I know I know.
20 *Joao:* No, we're not going to do any of that, OK?
21   We are going to plan it how we planned it in the paper.
22 *Eric:* Yes.
23 *Joao:* OK, let's go.

Joao and Eric have already decided on their goal: to build a model of a particular location in the Yukon. What they still have to determine is the specific form their model is going to take and the means for achieving it. This extract forms part of the process of reaching shared understanding, which is essential if they are to engage in joint action. So, despite its limitations, it is an example of the sort of talk that we wish to concentrate on in this paper: what we shall call 'collaborative talk'.

Enabling and empowering learning

So what is collaborative talk? Conceived quite generally, collaborative talk is talk that *enables* one or more of the participants to achieve a goal as effectively as possible. This may, as in the opening example, be a goal involving action, such as making a model or buying the right number of rolls of wallpaper to paper a room. On the other hand, the goal may be much more abstract, such as understanding a scientific principle or planning a piece of research. Or it may involve the interplay between thought and language that occurs in writing, as, for example, in the composition of a paper to be delivered at a conference. The occasions for collaborative talk may thus be very diverse. But what they all have in common is that, at some level of specificity, one of the participants has a goal that he or she wishes to achieve and the other participant engages in talk that helps the first to achieve that goal.

In most cases, the participants in collaborative talk are of approximately equal status, each able to take either of the roles of principal actor or facilitator and to benefit accordingly. Typically, too, the purposes of the collaboration are achieved when the task is completed or, at least, when the principal actor is able to continue with the next step. The talk has then served its instrumental purpose and, in the light of the effectiveness of this outcome, can be judged to have been more or less successful. This was the case in the extract from the two boys' discussion quoted above, just as it was in the collaborative talk that preceded and accompanied the preparation of this chapter. And the potential value of such enabling peer collaboration should not be underestimated.

However, the benefits of collaborative talk need not be limited to the function of facilitating achievement of the task. Where one of the participants has greater expertise than the other, he or she can engage in interaction with the learner with the deliberate intention of enabling the learner to acquire some procedure, knowledge or skill that will be useful in other situations beyond that in which he or she is currently engaged. In these cases, collaborative talk not only facilitates the task, it also empowers the learner. Indeed, we do not think it would be too strong a claim to say that, under ideal conditions, it has the potential for promoting learning that exceeds that of almost any other type of talk. It is the ideal mode for the transaction of the learning–teaching relationship.

For collaborative talk to have this empowering effect, however, it must meet two essential conditions. The first of these has already been addressed: it must be based on the assumption that the learner has ownership of the task and the teacher must strive to ensure that this ownership is respected. In practice, of course, ownership is a matter of degree, for the learner may not yet have sufficient confidence to take full responsibility for every aspect of the task or the necessary executive procedures for planning and carrying it out. A major objective of such talk, therefore, will be to help the learner develop conscious and deliberate control over his or her mental processes, not only in order to complete the task in hand, but also so that he or she becomes progressively more able to take responsibility for his or her own learning more generally (Bereiter and Scarda-malia, in press).

The second essential condition arises from the first: the expert's contributions to the dialogue should be contingently responsive to the needs of the learner, as these needs are understood in the light of the immediate situation as well as of the longer-term goals of education. To date, there has been little mention of this important characteristic of interaction in discussions of teacher–student talk, although its importance is clearly recognised in studies of much younger children. Schaffer (1977), for example, considers the contingent responsiveness of the caretaker's interactive behaviour to be essential for the infant's earliest social and intellectual development. In studies of language acquisition, too, the same quality has been found to characterise the conversational style of parents whose children are accelerated language learners (Cross 1978; Wells 1985). The content of adult–child conversation changes, of course, as the child increases in competence and experience, but the learning process is continuous, as are the conditions that facilitate it. At every stage, the same conversations which provide the basis for the child's acquisition of the language system also simultaneously provide evidence about the way in which the community makes sense of experience and about how the resources of language can be used for thinking and communicating. Therefore, since there is no reason to believe that there is any radical change at the age of school entry in the basic strategies that the child uses to learn from the evidence provided in such conversations, there is equally no reason to believe that contingent responsiveness ceases to be important as a feature of adult contributions that facilitate the learning process.

Whether in incidental learning situations in the home or in the more deliberate situations that teachers arrange in the classroom, the principles that should guide the adult's participation in collaborative talk are essentially the same. Adapted from Wells (1986), they can be stated as follows:

1 Take the child's attempt seriously and treat it as evidence of his or her best effort to solve the problem unaided.
2 Listen carefully to the child's account and request amplification and clarification as necessary to ensure that you have correctly understood.
3 In making your response, take the child's account as a starting point and extend or develop it or encourage the child to do so him or herself.
4 Select and formulate your contribution in the light of the child's current manifested ability as well as of your pedagogical intentions, and modify it, as necessary, in the light of feedback provided by the child.

Put much more succinctly, these principles can be summed up in the injunction to 'lead from behind'. What is important is that it is an understanding of the learner's conception of his or her task and of the way to set about it that provides the basis for the teacher's decision as to how best to help the child to progress from where he or she is now towards the more mature understanding that the adult already possesses.

When the requirement for contingent responsiveness is met, therefore, collaborative talk can fulfil its empowering function. Not only the learner is empowered, however; so also is the teacher. For it is precisely through frequently engaging in collaborative talk that the teacher is able to increase his or her understanding of children's thinking in general, and it is *only* by engaging in such talk with a particular learner while he or she is engaged on a specific task that the teacher can become knowledgeable about that learner's purposes and current state of understanding, and thus able to make his or her contributions contingently responsive to the learner's needs.

The characteristics of collaborative talk

In order to achieve the benefits of having two minds focusing collaboratively on a problem, the participants must achieve intersubjectivity in their representation of the task in hand and of their proposals for dealing with it. Each needs to know the other's understanding and intentions, and both must take the appropriate steps to ensure that mutual understanding is maintained. There is a need, therefore, to be explicit. In order to explain the matter in hand sufficiently clearly for the other participant to make an informed response, each is forced to construct a more coherent and detailed verbal formulation than would be necessary if he or she were working on the problem alone. In the process, gaps and inconsistencies become apparent and can be repaired, with the result that the problem is seen with greater clarity.

However, it is not only the adequacy or inadequacy of the offered information that is revealed in these circumstances, but also the connections that are made between the parts. In developing the account, the role of cause and effect relationships, of inferences, generalisations, extrapolations, and so on, is also made apparent, as are also failures to make such connections. In sum, the need for mutual understanding in collaborative talk requires each participant to make his or her meaning clear to the other, and hence also to him or herself, with the result that thinking is made explicit and, thus, available for inspection and, if necessary, for extension, modification or correction.

Then, having achieved a shared understanding of the task, participants can now, from their different perspectives, offer opinions and alternative suggestions. Once again, there is a need for explicitness. But more importantly, opinions and suggestions need to be justified and supported by relevant arguments and reasons need to be given why one alternative is more appropriate than another, if decisions are to have a principled basis. As a result, participants in collaborative talk can not only learn from each other's differing knowledge bases, they can also learn the need for disciplined thinking and develop some of the strategies for achieving it.

Depending on the stage reached by the principal actor in the execution of his or her task, the collaborative talk may focus on one or more of the following components: specifying the goal more precisely; planning the means for achieving it; generating and choosing between alternatives; reviewing achievement to date; and modifying what has been done.

Choices and connections: collaborative talk in one classroom

In the first part of this chapter we have been concerned to give an idealised account of collaborative talk and to justify our claim for its pre-eminence as a mode of teacher–learner interaction. However, we want to acknowledge immediately that the ideal conditions that we have assumed in the theoretical discussion are rarely encountered in reality. There are three reasons why the ideal can rarely, if ever, be achieved. First, the sheer number of children who need to be supported and the constraints imposed by the organisation of the school day mean that many interactions are cut short or interrupted. Second, since most of the children work in small groups rather than individually, there are issues of group collaboration to be addressed as well as the substantive issues raised by the tasks themselves. Third, there are limits to the resources of personal knowledge as well as of books, materials and equipment that the teacher can draw on immediately in meeting the needs of particular children as they arise spontaneously in the course of the day. For all these reasons, the ideal can rarely, if ever, be achieved.

In turning to an examination of examples taken from one particular classroom, therefore, we wish to make it clear that our purpose is not to evaluate, but rather to explore the potential of collaborative talk as it is conducted in practice. To do this we shall focus our discussion of the extracts on the following four questions:

- In what ways is the talk collaborative?
- What aspects of the task are addressed in the participants' talk?

- What aspects of learning are being enabled in the talk?
- How are the participants contingently responsive to each other?

'So you've changed your topic'

Let us return to Joao and Eric, who were introduced at the beginning of this chapter. In the extract below they have not yet begun to construct their model. As the teacher joins them, the two boys in their enthusiasm both start speaking at once:[2]

```
 1 Joao:  (We're) doing a model
 2 T:     Wow
 3 Eric:  I know what the model's going to be
         (Joao and Eric both talk at once for 8 seconds as they describe their intentions so
         neither can be heard)
 4 T:     Hold it! I hear that you're making a model. I hear something
 5        about houses. What's this going to be about? What's your topic?
 6 Joao:  Yukon
 7 Eric:  Yukon
 8 T:     You're making –
         (Joao and Eric again speak together making the next few lines difficult to
         understand)
 9 Joao:  In the Yukon they have shops. I saw it in the ⟨*⟩
10 Eric:  You can make – you can make igloos
11 Joao:  They say they have shops ⟨**⟩ and it has a big mountain beside it
12 Eric:  (to Richard, who has come to look) and we can do the other side ⟨**⟩
13 T:     So you're going to do a little town?
14 Joao:  (nods)
15 T:     Wow!
16 Joao:  And we could make a big mountain and ⟨put those things⟩ on top
17 T:     Uh-huh uh-huh
18 Joao:  And then it would be covered with snow
19 T:     Uh-huh
20 Joao:  And then um – we could make a little shop here and park
21 T:     What questions are you answering particularly?
22 Joao:  Um – . . . Like 'Where did they get the name from?'
         So we wanted – we wanted to do the model
23 T:     So you – you've changed your topic a little bit
24        So you're making a model of the Yukon . showing a town?
25 Joao:  Yeh
26 T:     And some of the things you've learned about what it's like
27        to live in the Yukon, is that it?
         (During the next few turns Eric is trying to secure the teacher's attention by
         calling her name. He has been left out of the preceding discussion.)
28 Joao:  But the mountain is small for the size of the town .
29        like the mountain ⟨≛ –⟩
30 T:     Which town is this? Is it a particular town? D'you know
31        the name of it?
32 Joao:  It's the Yukon.
33 T:     That's the name – that's the name of the big territory
34        Can you find the name of a town?
```

35 *Eric:* We don't know.
         (*T hands book to Joao and talks to Sandra briefly while Joao and Eric consult the book*)
36 *T:*   (*turning back to boys*) OK . This is a map that shows
37   very few towns
38   There's one
39 *Joao:* I know . Whitehorse
40 *Eric:* Whitehorse
41 *T:*   Whitehorse . That's a famous . town in the Yukon
42   Uh-huh . Whitehorse
43 *Joao:* Is Alaska there too?
44 *T:*   Pardon?
45 *Joao:* Alaska Alaska (*pointing to two occurrences of the name on map*)
46 *T:*   This is the Alaska Highway – the Alaskan Highway
47 *Joao:* It's very complicated becuse it says United States and
48   then the United – it's over there see
49 *T:*   Yeh
50 *Joao:* The United States and then United States
51 *Eric:* ⟨**⟩
52 *T:*   OK Why might it be like that? Do you understand why?
53 *Joao:* Maybe . it's the ⟨shore's down that *⟩ too?
54 *T:*   Yeh Alaska belongs to the United States
55 *Seth:* (*who is on the edge of the group also looking at a map*)
         I found it I found it
56 *T:*   You did?
57 *Eric:* (*looking at book*) It says Yukon – Yukon's three things and
58   ⟨**⟩ you can find – you can look through every page . that
59   has the Yukon in it
60   One of them might be a photograph of a town.
61 *T:*   That's true that's true.

The first point to note is the teacher's 'active listening', indicated in the opening lines by her 'Wow' and 'I hear that you're making a model', etc. By echoing what the boys have said, she is assuring them that she has heard and is interested. She is also letting them know what she takes to be the salient points in what she has heard and indirectly inviting them to consider whether these are the points that they too judge to be the most important. At the same time, the particular phrasing of lines 4–5, 'I hear something about houses', suggests that there is some problem about comprehensibility – a problem to which the solution might range from being more informative or explicit to speaking one at a time.

The teacher's first turn ends with a question about the issue that underlies their decision to make a model: 'What's this going to be about? What's your topic?' (5). However, although their first replies seem to provide some sort of answer, it is clear from what follows (9–20) that they have not really understood the purpose of her question. For the two boys continue to elaborate on the details of the model they want to make rather than considering the question to which their model is addressed. In spite of this the teacher continues to listen and echo back to them (e.g. 'So you're going to do a little town' (13)).

But, interspersed with her expressions of support, she continues to address the problem of articulating a statement of enquiry by posing questions that might elicit the issue the boys are investigating: 'What questions are you answering particularly?' (21) and 'So you're making a model of the Yukon . showing a town? . . . And some of the things you've learned about what it's like to live in the Yukon, is that it?' (24, 26–7). This last question, it will be noted, also acts as a model of the sort of question which the boys' intention to construct a model could appropriately address.

By juxtaposing these two kinds of response, the teacher is making a critical distinction for the children between the action goal of making a model and the topic goal, that is to say the question that is directing their enquiry. This is clearly an important distinction for them to understand, for it is only when the two goals are brought into interaction with each other that an enquiry can be productive. Moreover, it is a distinction that is too often overlooked in discussions of goal-setting with students, although it has begun to figure in recent research on writing (Freedman 1985).

That it is the need for an articulation of a statement of enquiry rather than a concern that they should stick to a previously agreed topic is corroborated by the teacher's ready acceptance of the change that has taken place: 'So you – you've changed your topic a little' (23). At the same time, this observation also emphasises the teacher's recognition of the boys' ownership of the task and her willingness to accept their decision to change their topic. In so doing, she also demonstrates another important feature of planning: that the setting and revising of goals and sub-goals is an ongoing and recursive process as the various components interact with each other.

In fact, the following talk (24–61) exemplifies the revision of planning in operation, as the agreement that the model will be of a single town rather than of the whole of the Yukon Territory leads to a scaling down of the original intention and to the search for a specific town to be the subject of the model. With the help of the book provided by the teacher, Eric comes up with a strategy for solving the problem (58–60), and it is by using a photograph of Dawson City that they are able to form the specific plan that is being discussed in the extract with which this chapter opened.

'I think he got a point'

During the next week, the model progressed apace and, by the time we meet Joao and Eric again, they are reaching the final stages.

1 *Joao:* We're going to – we're going to cover it with white tissue paper, Eric
2 *Eric:* ⟨That's what we've got to do⟩
3   That's for when they have snow . and after . by mistake it
4   could avalanche on here (*pointing to the base of the mountain*
5   *on the model*) and some houses will be crushed
6 *T:*   I wonder if that's a danger here (*pointing to the equivalent place on the*
        photograph)
7   I think you're quite right about some <u>mountains</u>

8 *Joao:*   I thought it was summer (*meaning in the photograph*)
9 *Eric:*   Yeh but in winter – but if it's in winter . .
10 *Joao:*   Yeh . yeh the seasons could change
11 *T:*   That's true
12   And they don't move their houses here . . do they?
13 *Eric:*   <**> Yeh they can't like lift it and go 'ow ow' (*miming*
14   *lifting a very heavy weight*) unless they just go 'da da da
15   da' (*said in a sing-song voice, which seems to represent the use of magic*)
             (*all laugh*)
16 *T:*   I don't think they're going to do that . .
17   Well if you have a look here (*pointing to photo in book*) . .
18   See where the houses are . along the river . and then .
19   What does this look like?
20 *Joao:*   That's a mountain
21 *T:*   Part of the mountain
22 *Eric:*   (*pointing to model*) These are one of these mountains
23 *T:*   Uh-huh uh-huh
24   You know you don't have to have the same number of houses
25   in here as in the photograph (*pointing to book*)
26 *Eric:*   I know
27 *Joao:*   Yeh but some of – like one or two over here would be OK
             (*pointing to base of mountain on model*)
28 *Eric:*   Yeh but if we put one or two over next to the houses . we
29   won't have room for the tissue paper
30   Here almost squashed even
31 *T:*   Right . sounds like this is something you boys have to talk
32   about a little more
33   You both have good points
34 *Joao:*   Yeh I think he – he got a point because . if we put tissue
35   paper over it . that –
36 *T:*   Is that what you plan to do with these houses?
37 *Eric:*   Yeh
38 *Joao:*   And then we could put like . little – put it like little
39   streets coming through here
40 *T:*   Uh-huh . Interesting
41 *Eric:*   Yeh we could like er . if you still want to make the thing,
42   right? we could make – you could put pine trees all around there
43 *Joao:*   Around the mountains
44 *T:*   Very good
45 *Joao:*   OK Let's go

As is evident in this and the earlier extract, collaborative talk emphasises both the personal and the social aspects of learning. The social is made important because successful completion of the task depends on the combined efforts and expertise of both participants; the personal because each collaborator has his own resources, ideas and approaches to the task. But most importantly, the commitment to collaborate obliges the participants to recognise the relevance of each other's expertise and, where necessary, to realign their own knowledge systems. It is this balancing of the social and the personal that enables learning to occur.

From a superficial reading of these transcripts, it might appear that, of the pair, it is Joao who plays the dominant role of 'knower/doer' and that Eric is the 'helper'. However, a closer examination of their talk, particularly the extract currently under consideration, makes it evident that each has his ideas about the task of making a model of Dawson City. It is not surprising, therefore, that their differing perspectives should come into conflict when, as in this extract, they have to reach a practical decision on how to proceed. However, it is not their differences that are noteworthy. Rather, it is the way in which collaboration on the task to which they have committed themselves both brings out each child's differing abilities and makes it possible for each to enable the other's learning in the joint thinking and doing that the task demands. As the teacher commented on reading the above extract: 'These two boys have a fascinating style of working through their (mis)conceptions with a lot of talk that appears confusing on the surface but on reflection their logic is evident.'

The nub of the problem is that Joao wants their model to be an accurate representation of the scene in the photograph, while Eric is more concerned with achieving internal consistency within the model itself. The problem is brought into focus by the question as to whether they should add more houses to the model. Joao wishes to site some more at the foot of the mountain. But, following through the implications of Joao's plan to use tissue paper to represent snow on top of the mountains, Eric argues that, if an avalanche were to occur, houses placed at the foot of the mountain would be crushed (3–5). Although Joao accepts this objection, he does not abandon his plan for, a moment later, he again suggests adding more houses at the foot of the mountain (27). This time Eric counters with the objection that if the houses were too tightly packed together, there would not be room for the tissue paper that they intended to put on the roof of each house (28–30) and to this practical (i.e. constructional) objection Joao agrees and concedes that Eric has 'got a point' (34). They could, however, represent streets going between the houses (38–9) and, in place of the houses at the foot of the mountain, Eric suggests, they could put pine trees (42). With this agreed, the practical Joao calls for a resumption of activities: 'OK Let's go'.

To this interaction, it is interesting to note, the teacher contributes very little by way of suggestion or new information. It is as if, as she herself put it in a subsequent discussion, her presence is sufficient to enable the two boys to listen to each other's perspectives and take account of the arguments behind them. And this is the impression one gains from examining her role in the discussion. She listens to what each of the boys has to say and, in her responses, implicitly accepts the validity of both points of view. 'I wonder if that [an avalanche] is a danger here', she says to Eric (6), pointing to the foot of the mountain in the photograph – the spot that is in dispute as the site for additional houses on the model. But Joao's wish to achieve an accurate representation of the photograph is also recognised when she tells them that they do not have to have the same number of houses in the model as in the photograph (24–5); and 'You both have good points' (33).

In this respect, her most interesting contribution to the discussion is line 12. Perhaps sensing that Joao has not fully appreciated the implications of Eric's argument, the teacher jokingly points out that people in the Dawson City shown in the photograph do not move their houses with the changing seasons and, therefore, by implication, that even if their model depicts a summer scene, they should take account of such a hypothetical winter catastrophe by not siting houses in a position from which they would have to be removed if they were to change their model to represent the same scene in winter. It is not possible to tell from the ensuing remarks whether the two boys took in the full significance of this one utterance, the force of which depends on the initial 'and' which makes connection with Joao's preceding concession that the seasons could change, and the 'here' which contrasts the city in the photograph with the boys' representation of it in the model. The point we are making, however, is not that this utterance succeeded in convincing Joao, but rather that it illustrates very clearly the teacher's concern both to make her contributions contingently responsive to each of their perspectives and, at the same time, to encourage them to follow through to a logical conclusion the incompatibility of their implications. As she says a moment later, 'sounds like this is something you boys have to talk about a little more' (31–2).

Attaining literate thinking through talk

The preceding analysis of the collaboration between Joao, Eric and their teacher has illustrated the potentially empowering nature of collaborative talk and highlighted the centrality of concerns such as problem-solving, ownership, challenge and intersubjectivity of understanding. If we now look at the attributes of language use which are intinsic to the enactment of these concerns – such attributes as explicitness, connectivity, justification, relevance – it will be seen that they are precisely those that are held to be particularly characteristic of written discourse (Chafe 1985). They are also attributes of thinking processes that are considered to develop as a consequence of becoming literate (Cole and Bruner 1971; Goody 1977). Since, however, we are dealing here with spoken language, it seems that we should reconsider the traditional definition of literacy and, in the present context, ask what literate thinking is and how it develops.

Until quite recently, answers to these questions would almost certainly have taken for granted that the linguistic-cognitive processes of reading and writing must be centrally involved (e.g., Olson 1977). However, as a result of further comparisons of spoken and written language, including cross-cultural studies (Scribner and Cole 1981; Heath 1983; Tannen 1985), a more complex picture has begun to emerge. While it would probably still be agreed that literate thinking is most likely to occur in connection with reading and writing, it is now recognised that thinking which displays many of the same characteristics can occur in relation to oral interaction between those who are literate when the purposes of the interaction demand it (Olson and Astington 1986). Langer (in press) cites the following example:

> When a group of people read one of the classics and then discuss the theme, motives, action and characters at a Great Books meeting, I would say they were

using literate thinking skills . . . Further, when those people see a movie and then discuss the motives and alternative actions and resolutions, I would again say they were using literate thinking skills even though they had neither read nor written. And if the people engaged in that very same conversation about a movie but did not know how to read or write, I would still say they had engaged in literate thinking.

If we accept this argument, then we must also accept that the process of becoming literate can potentially take place through speech as well as through engagement with written language. For it is not the mode of language use that defines literate thinking but rather the manner in which language is employed. Thinking is literate when it exploits the symbolic potential of language to enable the thought processes themselves to become the object of thought. Under appropriate conditions this can occur in either writing or speech.

Throughout this chapter, it has been assumed that the prime function of schooling is to develop effective thinking. We can now make this assumption more explicit by stating that what schools should be attempting to promote is the development of *literate* thinking. On a previous occasion, we argued for the pre-eminent role of writing in performing this function (Wells and Chang 1986), though we would have to add that not all writing has that effect (Wells 1987). On that occasion, we also made a plea for the recognition of a similar role for talk, whilst recognising that it is only certain types of talk that have these literate consequences. In this chapter, our aim has been to show that one type of talk that has this potential is what we have called 'collaborative talk'. It now remains to show just how this can occur.

As an example, let us consider the discussion between Joao and Eric of their reasons for and against locating more houses in their model of Dawson City. Both boys have to make their arguments explicit; they also have to make them relevant to their own position as well as to that adopted by the other. Although these requirements are reduced somewhat by the physical presence of the objects referred to, there is no doubt that they are felt and, within the children's capabilities, responded to as well. Decisions concerning relevance and presentation thus come into play, and these are certainly instances of literate behaviour.

Another important aspect of literate thinking is the recognition of the need to consider alternatives and to justify them by appeal to systematic knowledge. This, too, is illustrated in the collaborative talk between Joao, Eric and their teacher, when each has to extrapolate from his or her knowledge about seasonal variation in climate, topography, land relief, and so on, in order to decide whether to site more houses at the foot of the mountain. Although the discussion is brief, it illustrates how the collaboration that is necessarily involved in a task such as making a model can lead children purposefully to access their mental dictionaries of knowing and understanding and, in the process, to become more aware of them.

Reflecting on what one has done – questioning the outcome of one's efforts – is another important feature of literate thinking. For the testing of one's assumptions of knowing and not knowing may lead to or at least call for a realigning of or adding to one's existing knowledge systems. Although this kind of literate thinking is a common epistemic characteristic of expert performance, it is one which has to be deliberately acquired (Scardamalia and Bereiter 1985). Encouraging children to question their own efforts is one way to help them to adopt this practice.

So far we have drawn attention to the literate consequences of addressing the content of the task: the need to make one's intentions and one's understanding of the topic intelligible to another and at the same time to oneself. But we should also recognise the potential benefits that derive from the goal-orientated nature of collaborative talk. The tasks in relation to which the talk occurs make demands for planning and execution, which themselves may become the subject matter of talk. It is important to emphasise, however, that it is not the talking through of plans that is claimed to be advantageous in itself; rather it is when planning and similar processes are raised to the level of conscious attention so that they may be brought under intentional control that such talk warrants being described as literate.

A good example of this conscious attention to goal-setting occurs when Joao and Eric are asked to formulate the question they are addressing in the making of their model. This episode qualifies as literate, we would argue, because in responding to the request to identify their question, Joao and Eric are developing self-regulatory procedures. They are learning to adopt a 'what is my question?' and 'where am I going?' stance to the task they undertake.

Thinking of the kind that we have characterised as literate does not only occur, of course, when activities are carried out collaboratively. It might also have occurred if the children in this classroom had been working on their own, although it would probably have been in an attenuated form. However, because they needed to achieve intersubjectivity of understanding about their intentions, which was essential if their joint efforts were to be productive, the children were encouraged to turn their thinking back upon itself – reflectively selecting and evaluating in order to construct an intelligible, coherent and convincing verbal formulation. It is above all because it can foster the growth of this critical reflectiveness that collaborative talk has such important potential for the development of literate thinking.

In this chapter, we have only had space to consider two examples of collaborative talk, taken from recordings made in the course of one class project. As a result, there is a danger that we have read more into what was said than the participants themselves were aware of. We must also admit that our claims about the potential benefits for the development of literate thinking that derive from engaging in collaborative talk may not have been realised in the learning that actually took place as a result of these particular interactions. On the other hand, although of limited significance when considered in isolation, the extracts which we have analysed take on a different significance when they are treated as a small but representative sample of the learning opportunities that each child enjoyed during the course of those two weeks.

However, it is with the teacher's comments that we should like to end. They are taken from a discussion that followed a viewing of that part of the recording that included the first discussion with Joao and Eric.

> That part with Joao and Eric – it's just like that business that kids need time to talk about what they're going to write about to work out their ideas, and then to do rough copies to find out what they really think, and then revise . . . That really interested me. I kept seeing little parts where it's like Joao and Eric – that nudging them to make the connection between two ideas, asking them what their topic is. I mean it's the same as the writing process – having them tell you what they're doing, where they're going, what their questions are . . . and having them review the process and what they're doing.

Attending to the extracts that we had analysed, the teacher has clearly made a very similar interpretation, understanding and knowing for herself the significance of the talk in which she had been involved. Although she does not use the term herself, there is little doubt that what has excited her is the potential for the development of literate thinking that is to be found in collaborative talk.

Notes

1. We are grateful to the Toronto Board of Education, the Ontario Ministry of Education and the Ontario Institute for Studies in Education for their support of the Language and Learning Research Project, on which this chapter is based. We would also like to express our gratitude to Ann Maher for her willingness to allow us to observe her class at work and for her helpful comments on the video and audio recordings we made.
2. In this and the later extracts, the significance of the conventions of transcription is as follows: < > = transcription uncertain; * = unintelligible word; portions of utterances spoken simultaneously are underlined.

References

Bereiter, C. and Scardamalia, M. (in press). 'Intentional Learning as a Goal of Instruction' in L. B. Resnick (ed.), *Cognition and Instruction: Issues and Agendas*, Hillsdale, NJ, Lawrence Erlbaum.

Chafe, W. L. (1985). 'Linguistic Differences Produced by Differences between Speaking and Writing' in D. R. Olson, N. Torrance and A. Hildyard (eds), *Literacy, Language and Learning*, Cambridge, Cambridge University Press.

Cole, M. and Bruner, J. S. (1971). 'Cultural Differences and Inferences about Psychological Processes', *American Psychologist*, vol. 2, pp. 867–76.

Cross, T. G. (1978). 'Mothers' Speech and its Association with Rate of Linguistic Development in Young Children' in N. Waterson and C. Snow (eds), *The Development of Communication*, Chichester, Wiley.

Freedman, S. Warshauer (ed.) (1985). *The Acquisition of Written Language: Response and Revision*, Norwood, NJ, Ablex.

Goody, J. (1977). *The Domestication of the Savage Mind*, Cambridge, Cambridge University Press.

Heath, S. B. (1983). 'Protean Shapes in Literacy Events: Ever-Shifting Oral and Literate Traditions' in D. Tannen (ed.), *Spoken and Written Language*, Norwood, NJ, Ablex.

Langer, J. A. (in press). 'A Sociocognitive Perspective on Literacy' in J. A. Langer (ed.), *Language, Literacy and Culture: Issues of Society and Schooling*, Norwood, NJ, Ablex.

Olson, D. R. (1977). 'From Utterance to Text: The Bias of Language in Speech and Writing', *Harvard Educational Review*, vol. 47, pp. 257–81.

Olson, D. R. and Astington, J. W. (1986). *Talking about Text: How Literacy Contributes to Thought*. Paper presented at the Boston University Conference on Language Development, 19–21 October.

Scardamalia, M. and Bereiter, C. (1985). 'Fostering the Development of Self-Regulation in Children's Knowledge Processing' in S. S. Chipman, J. W. Segal and R. Glaser (eds), *Thinking and Learning Skills: Research and Open Questions, Vol. 2*, Hillsdale, NJ, Lawrence Erlbaum.

Schaffer, H. R. (1977). 'Early Interactive Development' in H. R. Schaffer (ed.), *Studies in Mother–Infant Interaction*, London, Academic Press.

Scribner, S. and Cole, M. (1981). *The Psychology of Literacy*, Cambridge, Mass., Harvard University Press.

Tannen, D. (1985). 'Relative Focus on Involvement in Oral and Written Discourse' in D. R. Olson, N. Torrance and A. Hildyard (eds), *Literacy, Language and Learning*, Cambridge, Cambridge University Press.

Wells, G. (1985). *Language Development in the Pre-School Years*, Cambridge, Cambridge University Press.

Wells, G. (1986). *The Meaning Makers: Children Learning Language and Using Language to Learn*. Portsmouth, NH, Heinemann Educational.

Wells, G. (1987). 'Apprenticeship in Literacy'. *Interchange*, vol. 18, nos 1–2, pp. 109–23.

Wells, G. and Chang, G. L. (1986). 'From Speech to Writing: Some Evidence on the Relationship between Oracy and Literacy' in A. Wilkinson (ed.), *The Writing of Writing*, Milton Keynes, Open University Press.

9 The roots of oracy: early language at home and at school

MARTIN HUGHES AND
JACQUI COUSINS

In this paper we want to present some preliminary material from a project currently under way in Plymouth – the Early Years Language Project – which is concerned with the spoken language of young children before and after they start school. The material has direct relevance for a number of issues central to any discussion of oracy, including the major influence of *social context* on spoken language, the way language is used to *make sense* of situations (particularly those which are novel or threatening in some way) and the importance of *story-telling*. Much of the material is in the form of conversations involving a five-year-old traveller's child called Sonnyboy. In addition, interview material will be presented which bears on an issue of crucial educational importance, that of *teachers' theories of spoken language*.

Previous research on early language at home and at school

The first author's (MH) interest in this area comes from a study he carried out with Barbara Tizard, which described and compared the conversations that a group of four-year-old girls had with their mothers at home and with their nursery teachers at school. When its findings were published (Tizard and Hughes 1984), they created a certain degree of controversy, because they were interpreted in various quarters as claiming that parents were better teachers than teachers, a claim to which many teachers, not surprisingly, took exception. The message of the book was in fact slightly different, namely, that, so far as conversations with adults were concerned, young children of all social backgrounds seemed to be learning more through talking to their mothers than they did through talking to their nursery teachers. The book certainly did not intend to suggest that children did not gain other benefits from attending nursery school, or that young children should spend their first five years at home with their mothers, although that was how it was sometimes interpreted.

The study did not set out to demonstrate the educational superiority of either teachers or mothers. It took its starting point from a series of claims which were being made in the 1970s about early language and social class. These claims were typically of the following form:

1 Working-class children do badly in school because they lack certain language abilities when they start school.
2 The reason for this deficit lies in the severely limited linguistic environment of the home: in particular, the conversations between working-class children and their parents are often barely adequate.
3 This deficit can to some extent be compensated for by the early introduction of working-class children to the formal education system, particularly to the 'linguistically enriching environment' of the nursery school.
4 The task of the education system in compensating for this deficit can be further helped if working-class parents are encouraged to model their conversational techniques on those of trained nursery teachers.

This position – which is sometimes referred to as the 'verbal deprivation theory' or the 'language-deficit model' – was particularly widespread during the 1970s. At a theoretical level, versions of the theory can be found in the work of Bernstein (1971) and Tough (1976), and in the Bullock Report (DES 1975), although these authors would not necessarily subscribe to all or any of the claims exactly as listed above. More pertinent, perhaps, is that the language-deficit model was pervasive in the informal theories of language to which *teachers* of young children subscribed at the time. When, in the course of the study, schools and classes in working-class areas were visited, comments such as 'no one talks to these children' or 'all they hear at home are grunts and swear words' were frequently encountered. Such claims, incidentally, were not restricted to the urban working classes, but were also made about other children who appeared to be failing in school, such as children from ethnic minorities, children in isolated rural communities, and the children of travellers.

At the time the study started (the late 1970s) there was little hard evidence either for or against these claims. It was clear that the only way they could be tested was by directly recording the natural conversations between adults and children at home, and comparing these conversations with those taking place in nursery school. The only major research which had attempted anything similar was the Bristol Language Study carried out by Gordon Wells and his colleagues, who had concentrated on recording and analysing conversations at home, and whose publications were then starting to appear (e.g., Wells 1978).

The methods evolved to record and transcribe children's conversations, and the efforts made to ensure that they were as natural as possible, are described in full in Tizard and Hughes (1984). Basically, the study involved thirty girls aged between 3¾ and 4¼ years, fifteen of them from middle-class and fifteen from working-class backgrounds. They were recorded in the mornings talking to the staff at their nursery schools and in the afternoons talking to their mothers at home, an observer being present throughout to ensure that full details of the context were available.

The study revealed a picture that was profoundly different from that put forward by the language-deficit theorists. The conversations in the working-class homes were just as prolific as those in the middle-class homes: there was no question of these children 'not being talked to' at home, or suffering from any other major form of verbal deprivation. Indeed, study and analysis of the transcripts of these conversations revealed how rich the home learning environment was for all the children. A large number of varied topics was discussed – such as work, the family, birth, growing up and death, as well as more unusual matters such as whether the Queen wears curlers in bed – with many of the richest conversations taking place while the children and their mothers got on with the everyday business of life such as having lunch, planning a shopping trip, or feeding the baby. Furthermore, it became increasingly clear that young children were impressive learners – particularly through their determined, logical questioning as they struggled to overcome their lack of knowledge or to make sense of a complex and confusing world.

In contrast, the analysis of the conversations between these same children and their nursery teachers was disappointing. The richness, depth and variety which characterised the home conversations were sadly lacking, as was the sense of intellectual struggle and of a real attempt to communicate being made on both sides. Instead, the children at school were often on the receiving end of a sequence of bland questions about their play activities, to which they frequently gave minimal replies. This contrast between home and school was especially pronounced for the working-class children, who were particularly likely to be quiet and subdued in their conversations at school. The working-class children often took part in long and sustained discussions at home, but showed little evidence of this with their teacher. It was easy to see how theories of verbal deprivation might arise: faced with an inarticulate child in the classroom, teachers might easily conclude that the child was just the same at home.

Many of these points can be illustrated by two conversations involving the same working-class child, Joyce. In the first conversation Joyce was rolling out clay at school when her teacher sat down next to her:

1 *Teacher:* What's that going to be, Joyce? (*No reply*) How are you making it?
2 *Joyce:* Rolling it.
3 *Teacher:* You're rolling it, are you? Isn't that lovely? Oh, what's happening to it when you roll it?
4 *Joyce:* Getting bigger.
5 *Teacher:* Getting bigger. Is it getting fatter?
6 *Joyce:* Yeah.
7 *Teacher:* Is it, or is it getting longer?
8 *Joyce:* Longer.
9 *Teacher:* Longer. Are my hands bigger than your hands?
10 *Joyce:* My hands are little.
11 *Teacher:* Your hands are little, yes.

12 *Joyce:*   It's getting bigger. Getting long. And long. Look.
13 *Teacher:* Mmm. What's happened to it, Joyce?
14 *Joyce:*   Got bigger.
15 *Teacher:* It has. My word.

This conversation is by no means untypical and contains several features which crop up repeatedly in the school conversations. For example, the conversation is almost entirely dominated by the teacher's educational motives (concerning the topics of shape and size) which she puts into effect using a series of questions to which she already knows the answers. Joyce's replies are minimal and do not convey any degree of interest in the topic. Not surprisingly, Joyce's teachers told us before the recordings were made that she was a girl whose language was 'poor'.

A very different picture of Joyce emerges in the following conversation at home. She is sitting in the kitchen eating a sandwich lunch while her mother prepares the evening meal:

1 *Joyce:*   Mum, it was good to have something to eat while you was at the seaside, wasn't it? (*Mother cuts sandwich*)
2 *Mother:*   Was good, I agree.
3 *Joyce:*   Well some people don't have something to eat at the seaside.
4 *Mother:*   What do they do then? Go without?
5 *Joyce:*   Mm.
6 *Mother:*   I think you'd have to have something to eat. (*Kettle boils and mother makes tea.*)
7 *Joyce:*   Yeah, otherwise you'd be (*unclear*) won't you?
8 *Mother:*   Mmmm. When we go with David's school we'll have to take something to eat. We go on the coach that time. (*They are going on an outing with the older child's school.*)
9 *Joyce:*   Mmm. To the seaside?
10 *Mother:* Mmm. Probably go for a little stroll to the seaside.
11 *Joyce:*   Mmm? Yes, I still hungry.
12 *Mother:* When?
13 *Joyce:*   When we was at the seaside wasn't I?
14 *Mother:* We weren't. We had sandwiches, we had apples.
15 *Joyce:*   But we . . . but when we was there we were still hungry wasn't we?
16 *Mother:* No, you had breakfast didn't you?
17 *Joyce:*   But, we were thirsty when we got there.
18 *Mother:* Yes, suppose so, yeah we were.
19 *Joyce:*   What happened? We wasn't thirsty or hungry.
20 *Mother:* Why weren't we? What happened?
21 *Joyce:*   Well, all that thirsty went away.
22 *Mother:* Did it?
23 *Joyce:*   Mmmm.

Here Joyce emerges as a child who, while undoubtedly limited in her ability to express herself, nevertheless struggles to overcome these limitations. At turn 1 she has already produced a more complex utterance than anything she came up with in the school conversation, as she tries to make sense of a past event in her family's life. The ensuing conversation is much more balanced than the one-sided school conversation, as both Joyce and her mother grapple to recall what had happened on that day, and to work out what Joyce found puzzling about the memory. The conversation might not have been totally successful, but it nevertheless contains the essence of a real-life conversation, in which both sides are taking part because they want to communicate with each other. Note also the way the conversation takes place against a backcloth of shared experience, to which Joyce's mother adds by her reference to a future school trip (8–10). Shared experience is an important feature of the home conversations, and its absence at school presents a considerable barrier to communication.

By the time of Tizard and Hughes (1984), similar findings from the Bristol Language Project had already appeared (e.g., Wells 1981), and it seemed that the language-deficit position would soon crumble under the weight of research evidence. However, as we shall see, that was a somewhat optimistic belief.

Teachers' theories of language

The Plymouth Early Years Language Project arose directly from concerns expressed by a group of Plymouth headteachers about the language abilities of children starting infant school. These headteachers appeared to be putting forward a version of the language-deficit model, in that they were of the opinion that large numbers of children were starting school in Plymouth with little or no spoken language, and that this was directly attributable to the linguistic environment of their homes.

One of the first steps taken by the Plymouth Early Years Language Project was to visit all the schools in Plymouth which admitted children at five years, and interview the headteacher and the teacher in charge of the new entrants. The interviews focused on the problems faced by teachers of reception classes, on the nature and extent of language problems amongst their new entrants, and on their views concerning the possible causes of these language problems. These interviews are still being analysed, but it is clear that some version of the language-deficit model is held by the great majority of interviewees. The following are some verbatim quotes from our pilot interviews in Plymouth and elsewhere in Devon:

> At a conservative estimate I would say that at least 70 per cent [of children starting school] have very little experience of having adults to talk with.

> Parents don't talk to them . . . it's all home really, isn't it? . . . sounds awful . . . we get them straight from home so that's all you can blame it on.

> Adults don't talk to their children, or are monosyllabic, or use only foul language . . . There are no books in some homes. It all comes down to parental neglect, inadequacy.

> The parents simply don't talk . . . They eat, sit and oggle the box until bedtime and they don't have a story-time.

> Language is the major problem. Children are unable to express themselves – they haven't done much talking at home. Conversation is not valued – nods and grunts are adequate for communication.

These interviews were carried out in 1986, two years after Tizard and Hughes (1984), and at least eight years after Gordon Wells started to publish the findings of the Bristol Language Project. Clearly, the publication of research findings does not by itself bring about transformation in teachers' theories, and perhaps, given the extent to which research findings often conflict with each other, this is just as well. But there has been no conflicting evidence here, and it does raise the question of what *would* change teachers' theories of language, given that the situation confronting them daily – of children who are inarticulate at school – presents them with prima facie evidence for a language-deficit model.

The child's point of view: a case study from a traveller's child

So far we have been considering the problem of school entry from the teachers' point of view. But it is important if not essential to consider the *children's* point of view as well. What sense do they make of school? What assumptions and expectations about school do they bring with them from their home culture? How does school measure up to these expectations? How does language fit into this? How do children respond to the unfamiliar words – or to the new meanings attached to already familiar words – which they encounter from their first day at school? And finally, how can we help children bridge the two worlds of home and school?

In the course of the Plymouth Language Project, recordings have been made of children's language at home (prior to school entry) and in the first few weeks of school. These recordings are still being analysed, and hopefully will provide answers to some of the questions raised above. In the remainder of this chapter, however, we want to present some material from a child who started out as incidental to the study, but whose recorded conversations bear in a fascinating way directly on the main concerns of the project.

The child in question, Sonnyboy, is a five-year-old member of a travellers' community which is in semi-permanent residence on a site in Plymouth. Travellers are generally despised and not wanted, and their treatment by the authorities can be seen as a severe form of discrimination. The Plowden Report (DES 1967) referred to their children as 'probably the most severely deprived in the country', while the recent Swann Report on Multicultural Education (DES 1985), which devoted a chapter specifically to the educational needs of travelling children, claimed (1985: 740) that 'In many respects the situation in which travellers' children find themselves also illustrates to an extreme degree the experience of prejudice and alienation which faces many other ethnic minority children.' Sonnyboy's life certainly bears little resemblance to any romantic image of a gypsy family wandering along country roads in a painted horse-drawn caravan. Like most modern travellers, his family lives in a modern caravan (or 'trailer') pulled by a powerful truck. Their main income comes from dealing in scrap metal, and they move from one inadequate site to another – their current site is next to the corporation rubbish tip. According to his mother, Sonnyboy was a very active, boisterous baby who was never able to 'look before he leapt any-where', and while chemicals, rusty iron, and glass on the tip were seen as natural enough hazards and within his ability to cope – in the same way that he was expected to be careful with knives or sharp scissors – she was more worried about him going under a trailer or running out in front of a truck.

The extent to which the modern travellers' culture, with its TV and trailers, can still be regarded as an 'oral' culture, is no doubt open to debate. Nevertheless, there appear to be two important elements in Sonnyboy's immediate background which are often associated with an oral tradition.

The first element is that of *story-telling*. Despite the arrival of TV, many travellers still spend time in the evenings talking in their trailers, and the children are often expected to sit and listen quietly to the conversations, negotiations and discussions of the adults within their trailers – indeed to join in would be considered 'brazen and bold'. However, story-telling is considered differently, and it is during these often spontaneous sessions that the child is encouraged to join in, take turns and to challenge (often noisily) others' efforts. As we shall see later, Sonnyboy's ability to tell stories was quite considerable, and there can be little doubt as to how this ability was acquired.

The second element is harder to define, but it has much to do with the use of spoken language in order to *make sense* of situations. All human beings, of course, use language in this way, but it seems to be particularly pronounced amongst the travellers. It is characterised by a constant challenging of what others say, usually by questioning it from many different angles, by a lengthy process of turning over a topic in conversation, trying to fit what is new into an existing framework and, above all, by an insistence that things make sense. As we shall see, the comment 'That don't make no sense' occurred frequently in Sonnyboy's conversations at school.

Sonnyboy came to our notice when the second author (JC) was trying to get a radio-microphone to work in Sonnyboy's school. Sonnyboy was attracted by the recording equipment which was clearly familiar from his own background, indeed his opening remark was: 'Did you know me *Da's* got one a those? Me Da's got a *lot* a things like that – CBs, truck radios . . .'. Sonnyboy soon discovered how to get the equipment working and became research assistant and technician. In return, many of his own conversations in school could thus be recorded.

As mentioned earlier, Sonnyboy was very insistent that the rituals and routines of school should make sense, and thus he was able to articulate differences between his home culture and that of school which other children may have felt but kept quiet about. For example, he was used to being involved in the financial wheeling and dealing of the travellers' life, and was particularly scathing about the absence of real money in the classroom 'shop' and 'café': 'That don't make no sense . . . You can't have a café without money' and 'How can you go buying things without money?' He also found the notions of 'playtime' and 'snacktime' rather puzzling, coming as he did from a culture where the duration of an activity tends to be 'as long as it takes' rather than determined in advance. About playtime: 'Don't you know that we plays *all* the time in our class . . . It don't make sense . . . Is it a sort of teatime, only we don't get the tea like in me trailer?'; and about snack-time: 'I eat my packet when I get hungry . . . stupid to have a time in't it, for eatin' and that?'

Another difference between the cultural norms of his own background and that of school concerned the extent to which children are allowed access to sharp and possibly dangerous tools. This difference emerged when Sonnyboy wanted to know why the school scissors were blunt and wouldn't cut thick material:

Teacher: Well, sharp scissors might be a bit dangerous.
Sonnyboy: Dangerous? An' what about the knives?
Teacher: What knives?
Sonnyboy: The knives what I can cut with.
Teacher: At home?
Sonnyboy: Yeah.
Teacher: Well, that's different at home because there's only you to watch.
Sonnyboy: Nobody watches me – an' it's a real knife, an' it's me business to be careful.
Teacher: But what if you get cut?
Sonnyboy: Then I wash it under the tap an' then I'm careful next time.

The following conversation illustrates not only the challenging nature of the travellers' questions, but also their no doubt painfully acquired experience that nothing in this world comes free. The conversation involves both Sonnyboy and his cousin Emily, another member of the travelling community. The two children were packing away a collection of small dolls.

Emily: I loves them little things.
Sonnyboy: Yeah . . . I loves the little sand things – that tiny wee spade . . . and this little bucket . . .
Teacher: Do you think it would be a good idea to ask Cathy to get some? (*Cathy runs a playgroup for the travellers' children on their site.*)
Emily: What for?
Teacher: So that you'd have some at home.
Sonnyboy: And who'd pay for them? Would Cathy pay?
Teacher: No, it would be part of the kit.
Emily: I don't know what you mean. Kit – who's Kit? Me da's called Kit – would me da have to pay?
Sonnyboy: Not your da – it's not that sort of kit, Emily. It's the sort a box with things in that you play with . . . like toys and things for all the little ones.

Sonnyboy's final comment illustrates another important feature of the conversations he was involved with, namely his ability to make sense of school *for other children*. In doing this he revealed a remarkable ability to see possible misunderstandings, and to communicate the nature of these misunderstandings to all concerned. In the next conversation, for example, he notices that David, on his second day at school, is confused by the ambiguity of the word 'letter'. The teacher had gathered the children and had asked David to give her the letter (which he was holding in his hand) more by gesture than by words. David had been neither looking nor listening and as a result had missed the context clues.

Teacher: Go and get your letter David.
David: (*looks round vaguely . . . goes to story corner*)
Teacher: Go on lovie, go and get your letter.
Sonnyboy: He don't know what you mean, Mrs S——. He don't know what sort of
    letter. He thinks it's in the book.

Sonnyboy's contribution demonstrates his capacity to be 'inside' another child
and instantly to interpret the misunderstanding.

A few days later another occasion arose when Sonnyboy was able to act as
interpreter between David and his teacher. This time David was trying to do a
jigsaw puzzle and what the teacher said, just before she was interrupted and went
away, was again ambiguous:

Teacher: Why don't you try turning it round.
    (*David turns piece over*)
Sonnyboy: She never meant that way, she never meant turn it over like that. You've
    got to look at the picture.
David: What picture?
Sonnyboy: The picture what it makes with all them bits in.
David: Have . . . what picture?
Sonnyboy: Did you not do puzzles before? I done a million . . . This don't make no
    sense 'cos you haven't seen no picture. You got to make a picture with all
    that.
David: I got a puzzle at home . . . I got a box for it.
Sonnyboy: You got a picture on top o' the box?
David: Yeah.
Sonnyboy   Makes sense with pictures.

Sonnyboy's concern for David was not restricted to explaining ambiguous
remarks from the teacher: he also went out of his way to defend David against
other children who were less sympathetic. The next conversation, for example,
took place while a small group of children were looking at some photographs
which the second author (JC) had taken on her first day at the school. In one
photograph David is looking nervously over a piece of scaffolding:

Sonnyboy: Look at this, David – that's you near the scaffolding.
David: Mmmm. Yeah.
Sonnyboy: That's the scaffolthingy round the school – was that the day when you
    first came?
David: Yeah.
Other child: (*laughing*) And he was eating the scaffolding in his mouth!
Sonnyboy: Don't be stupid and taunt him like that! You know very well it was his
    first day and he was awful shy.

The final aspect of Sonnyboy's oracy which we want to consider was his ability
to tell stories. It is impossible to convey on a written page the quite remarkable
capacity that Sonnyboy has, especially for a five-year-old, to capture and hold an
audience of other children through his use of voice, gestures, pauses and
intonation, presumably all learnt while sitting listening to the stories of adult
travellers back home in the trailer. What can be conveyed, however, is the way
that Sonnyboy was able to take the familiar stories of the classroom and

personalise them by adding to them from his own experience. In the following story, for example, Sonnyboy creates his own version of the Enormous Pumpkin story by incorporating references to dogs (which fight and bite each other) and particularly to the 'fine horses' which have such a central place in the travellers' traditional stories:

> Will you come and listen to me story?
> A long long time ago there was this old man and he grew a pumpkin. And it was a very magic sort o' pumpkin – cos when he went to get it up it was very, very big and enormous lookin'. He called for his mam to give him a hand at pullin' it – but that was no use. So – so then he called for his boy and the biggest one o' his girls – and he said to them PULL, PULL – it was no use again. So after a bit he thought and he thought – and he thought about what he can do. Then he thought about his dogs and they had sharp teeth and they could hold on tight and PULL, PULL, dogs – but the dogs started fightin' and they all let go their tails and was bitin'. The man went mad at them then and got his fine horses and they was stronger 'an anyone in the world – they can pull a big waggon – PULL, PULL – horses can pull, and they did – and the old man had his pumpkin for supper and so did his mam and all the children.

In the next example Sonnyboy is telling his cousin Emily his version of the story of 'The Avocado Baby', while he turns the pages of the book to show her the pictures. His audience grows as other children gather round to listen:

> *Sonnyboy:* You know this 'un – it's about that strong kid – the one that ate that pear thingy . . .
> *Emily:* What kid?
> *Sonnyboy:* You remember the one – that poor babby boy as weak as a floppy dolly – that poor little boy, a poor weak little babby. His mam and his da fretted an' fretted about him bein' that weak. Then they buyed him this pear thingy – not a pear like on an ordinary tree – a great big magic pear that hung in a magic place. An' his mam cut it and mashed it an' he ate it all up an' from that minute he got stronger an' stronger, an' – till he could break his bed to bits.
> *Emily:* He never done that – you jus' made that bit up.
> *Sonnyboy:* An' that's just what you do with stories. You can make 'em up all you like, all you wants to.
> *Emily:* You cannot, Sonnyboy. You got a read them words.
> *Sonnyboy:* Nah – I knows that story. I know about him gettin' strong wid pear – and his mam buyed a lot o' them so's he'd get the strongest in the whole world, stronger than the thief what came in the night and all the wild devils who creep round the house and bit his dog to death . . .
> *Emily:* That's a real creepy story. It never says it like that.
> *Sonnyboy:* *My* story does – how 'ould you know?

These exchanges between Sonnyboy and Emily illustrate two fundamentally different notions of the idea of a 'story'. For Emily, the story is quite clearly contained in a written text: that is the story and Sonnyboy has to 'read them words'. For Sonnyboy, however, a story is something which is essentially spoken, which can be altered to suit the occasion, and which is as much the property of the current story-teller as it is of the original story-writer.

Conclusions

Quite clearly, Sonnyboy has exceptional talents, both in understanding the difficulties his classmates have in making sense of school and in entertaining them with his stories. In addition, he is characterised by an unusual determination to make sense of school, and by an equally unusual confidence to voice his doubts and confusions where other children would remain silent.

But while Sonnyboy may be an exception, he also illustrates a number of important generalities. He shows the difficulties all children face in moving from the culture of home to the very different culture of school. He shows the importance of creating conditions where children can voice their confusions and misunderstandings concerning school, which may often be ones we have totally overlooked. His concern for David and Emily shows the value of a *human bridge* between the two cultures of home and school – that is, someone who can interpret school to puzzled children and ease their confusions, not a role which we would naturally expect a five-year-old to play, but which we might entrust to an older sibling or parent. And finally, he illustrates the importance of *story-telling* – not just as a means of entertaining others in the trailer or the classroom, but as a way in which children can themselves bring together different aspects of their experience into a more coherent and unified whole.

The last word must belong to Sonnyboy. We mentioned earlier that he had come to act as an unpaid research assistant, setting up the equipment for the second author (JC) and helping to obtain the tape-recordings of other children. Like the best research assistants, however, he was also developing his own theories about the matter being investigated, in this case the language of children in school. He was particularly concerned about one boy, Peter, who was very quiet, and Sonnyboy was constantly trying to think of ways of eliciting talk from him. When JC returned to the school after an absence of about a month, Sonnyboy bounded along the corridor and greeted her with news of their 'subject':

> *Sonnyboy:* You'll be delighted wid Peter.
> *JC:* Will I? Why's that?
> *Sonnyboy:* Well, you'll be delighted wid his talkin'.
> *JC:* Really, Sonnyboy?
> *Sonnyboy:* Yes, you will – he just talks and talks . . .
> *JC:* That's very interesting, Sonnyboy – why do you think that is?
> *Sonnyboy:* (*instantly, giving JC one of his broadest beams*)
> It's because you left!

Acknowledgements

We are very grateful to other members of the Early Years Language Project team – Mary Chessum, John Gulliver, Graham Hammond, Lorraine Hubbard and Marilyn Goldsborough – for allowing us to use material from the project in this paper. We should make clear, however, that the views expressed here are our own and are not necessarily shared by other members of the Project team. We are also very grateful to Ann Brackenridge for her help in preparing the manuscript.

References

Bernstein, B. (1971). *Class, Codes and Control*, London, Routledge and Kegan Paul.
DES (1967). *Children and their Primary Schools*, London, HMSO (the Plowden Report).
DES (1975). *A Language for Life*, Report of the Committee of Enquiry chaired by Sir Alan Bullock, London, HMSO.
DES (1985). *Education for All*, London, HMSO (the Swann Report).
Tizard, B. and Hughes, M. (1984). *Young Children Learning*, London, Fontana.
Tough, J. (1976). *Listening to Children Talking*, London, Ward Lock.
Wells, G. (1978). 'Talking with Children: The Complementary Roles of Parents and Teachers', *English in Education*, vol. 12, pp. 15–38.
Wells, G. (1981). *Learning through Interaction: the Study of Language Development*, Cambridge, Cambridge University Press.

10 Putting context into oracy: the construction of shared knowledge through classroom discourse

NEIL MERCER, DEREK EDWARDS
AND JANET MAYBIN

This chapter is based on an approach to the study of classroom language which we have developed in recent years, an approach which is concerned with the function of classroom talk as a medium for the development of a common (i.e. shared) knowledge. We are not concerned with patterns of communication, or discourse structures, for their own sake. Our interests are psychological rather than linguistic. The central issue for us is how teachers and children establish shared understandings of curriculum content, so our examination of various sorts of classroom communication is made in order to see how information, arguments, ideas and analyses are expressed.

We have very recently completed the second phase of a research project which allowed us to pursue our interest in such things as how teachers introduce new topics to children, how they check children's understanding, the kinds of question that are asked by both teachers and children, the assumptions that are made about what is already known, and the kinds of misunderstanding which arise (and how, if at all, they are resolved). To do this, we observed primary schoolchildren and their teachers engaged in the process of learning and teaching. During the most recent phase of the research, upon which we will draw most in this chapter, we went to three schools in Buckinghamshire and video-recorded teachers and small groups of children working together through three consecutive sessions on specific curriculum topics (that is, one topic carried through by a teacher with the same group of children over three sessions, making *nine* recorded sessions in all). As well as analysing these video-recordings, we interviewed the teachers and children about what was said and done.

We have tried, through this research, to develop a theoretical account of the process of sharing knowledge; an account which draws heavily on the work of Vygotsky (e.g. 1978) and Bruner (e.g. 1986). We see knowledge as something which is social and communicated, and not just the product of the thought and actions of individuals. This research is fully described in Edwards and Mercer (1987), and in that and other publications we provide details of theory and analysis in ways that would not be appropriate here (see Mercer and Edwards 1981; Edwards and Mercer 1986a; 1986b; Edwards and Maybin, 1987).

We will concentrate here on the particular, and problematic, notion of *context*, and argue for the importance of this concept for understanding the nature and function of talk in education. We have chosen this topic in the hope that we will be dealing with matters of interest to all who are studying oracy.

It is important to begin by identifying the precise nature of our interest in educational talk. It has become apparent that, as a developing field, the study of oracy includes a wide range of different interests. Many of these interests are essentially 'applied', arising in some way out of educational concerns. But there appears to be some disagreement amongst researchers and teachers about which of these interests should be the prime objects of attention.

For example, it is clear from the output of current curriculum development projects on oracy (of which the Wiltshire Project is probably the best known British example) that the oracy theme encompasses all of the following: encouraging children to make more use of talk for learning (e.g., encouraging children to talk more to each other and to the teacher about what they are studying); helping children gain a more effective command of oral communication (i.e. developing 'communication skills'); and encouraging teachers to make more use of children's talk as data in assessing their knowledge and understanding (instead of relying almost entirely on children's written output). These are all worthwhile interests, so long as they are recognised as distinct. Usually, however, they are not. This is particularly apparent in the development of procedures and checklists for 'oral assessment' in schools. It is often unclear whether 'oral assessment' means that children's oral performance is being assessed in order to judge their competence as effective communicators, or that their talk is being used to judge the extent of their understanding of curriculum content.

To take just one school-based example, in an interesting article on Investigational Science, one of the teachers involved in the Wiltshire Project (Acres 1987) describes how pupils were asked to talk together about how they would design an experiment to investigate extra-sensory perception. Their talk was then assessed by the teacher, using a checklist by which each pupil was given a score for such performance characteristics as 'accuracy and precision', 'stamina', 'enthusiasm', 'ability to respond to a prompt', 'ability to counter argument', with just one reference to 'content and understanding'. It would seem, therefore, that the teacher/assessor's main interest was in evaluating *communication skills*, as demonstrated through the presentation of scientific knowledge. However, Acres's (1987: 22) main conclusion is that 'the discussions and assessment gave me a much clearer insight into the way pupils thought about their investigations'. So it seems that the teacher was in fact using the talk to make an assessment of the children's *understanding of the principles of scientific method*. But this would seem to require quite a different form of assessment from that described. Acres then took the step of asking the pupils for their views of the oral work, and from this we can learn something of what they were doing that was being assessed. Although all were favourably inclined to the activity, the individual pupils offered very different justifications for what went on: 'Assessment of talk is a good idea because it means you're not copying everyone else'. 'I think it was good discussing the experiments because it helps you understand more'. 'I thought it was very good 'cos some people can't do writing' (Acres 1987: 22).

An interesting question is this: could these different conceptions of the purpose of talk in class influence the children's views of what constituted 'good' talk in that particular setting? If so, individuals might, in good faith, offer up quite different kinds of 'performance' for assessment. We provide the question, but not the answer. And we do not offer here an improved methodology for oral assessment. We chose the above example simply to illustrate the 'state of the art', to demonstrate problems within a broad field of activity in which we, too, are involved, and to offer a perspective on these problems which we hope will assist their solution. But from this, and other, observed instances, it is clear that we cannot assume that participants always share a basic understanding of what they are trying to achieve through classroom talk or even by participating in specific language activities. That is, the *educational ground rules* (Mercer and Edwards 1981) upon which the oral work is based, do not generally seem to be well established in the shared understanding of the pupils and their teachers and assessors. Educational ground rules have both social and cognitive functions. They represent both a set of social conventions for presenting knowledge in school, and also a set (or sets) of cognitive procedures for defining and solving problems. These rules are problematical for both teachers and pupils, for reasons which stem from the fact that they normally remain implicit, they are hardly ever discussed and negotiated. We may describe these ground rules as a *regulatory aspect of the context* of classroom discourse (Edwards and Mercer 1987), and so we will now turn to a consideration of the broader issue of 'context' in the analysis of classroom talk.

Context

By 'context' we do not mean, in any simple sense, the physical features of the environment which co-exist with the discourse, or the non-verbal context which accompanies it. Those things may provide raw material for the construction of contexts. We mean everything that the participants in a conversation know and understand, over and above that which is explicit in what they say that contributes to how they make sense of what is said and done. This may include personal and culturally derived information which has its origins in talk, events and experiences distant in time and place from the current conversation. Physical correlates of the talk – for example, the room in which we sit, the equipment in it – only become contextual if and when they are *invoked* by the discourse explicitly or implicitly (we have, in fact, just explicitly invoked them now!). Let us now look at a fragment of classroom discourse which illustrates very well how physical context is invoked. In the transcript which follows, the speech of the participants is shown in the left hand column. The right hand column consists of our 'context notes', made when viewing and reviewing the video-recording, which serve to remind us of relevant non-verbal information. (Other information on transcription conventions is given in the Appendix to this chapter.)

Discourse sequence 1: physical and mental context

Teacher:	Right. So Sharon how are you then going to decide on your angle? 'cause I mean you've got to have certain measurements./ Turn it around and let's see if we can give her any ideas. How is she going to decide on her angle?	Teacher writes 'ANGLE' under 'TIME' in matrix.
		Sharon turns pendulum to face teacher.
Anthony:	on that/ draw angles on there.	Anthony points to top plate of upright.
Jonathan:	Or hold/ [set a protractor on the top.	
David:	[she could put angles at the top.	All gesturing to top of pendulum.
Teacher:	She could/ could/[at the top (. . .)	
Jonathan:	[place a protractor up there with sellotape.	
Sharon:	(. . .) or just draw it.	
Teacher:	Or just draw it. What else could she do? If she didn't do that what else could she do? To make sure she always had it/ you know at the level she wanted? It doesn't really[mat(ter . . .)	
David:	[put the ruler down here and make/ the height from the ground/ from the table.	David holds bob out and points to distance between bob and table.
Teacher:	So where would/ what would she mark then/ to measure the height from the ground?// What could she mark// on the pendulum?	Teacher pauses, pupils don't respond.
Jonathan	Oh on on here.	Jonathan points to two places, different heights on the upright on his pendulum.
Teacher:	Right. She could put marks across couldn't she? And it doesn't matter if there's/ er/ it matters if they're even. Right/ so you could start? How's she going to make sure that the bob* of the pendulum is next to that mark**/ 'cause that's going to be a bit of a problem.	Teacher indicates upright on pendulum with pencil at 3 different heights. *Grasping bob **Indicates mark on upright, made earlier with felt tip pen.

| *Jonathan:* | Get a right angle thing and a big ruler. | Jonathan gestures a right angle out from upright. |

In this sequence we have a piece of discourse which is clearly context-dependent. We need to know about the equipment, gestures, and so on, to make proper sense of what is happening. How hard, if not impossible, it would be to make sense of the talk without the 'context notes' in the right-hand column of the transcript. But there are two rather less obvious features of this context-dependence which are equally important. These are: the fact that *all* of the dialogue can be said to be dependent on context for its meaning; and the fact that context is not physical, but mental. We shall consider each of these in turn.

The dependence of all the dialogue on a current, or previously established, or implicit context, is clear from examining particular words. 'Pendulum', for example, has a general, abstracted meaning, but here 'the pendulum' refers to the wooden structure on the desk. The words 'ground', 'mark', and so on, also have specific situational referents. David uses 'ground' first, to refer to the table top. The teacher then continues this usage. These particular meanings are ones that participants in the dialogue all understand; they are part of their common knowledge. In order for the teacher and pupils to develop a shared understanding of the work they are doing on pendulums, it is crucially important that they are able to relate discourse to context, and build, through time, a joint frame of reference.

The notion that context is *mental*, not physical, is an essential part of the link between discourse and knowledge. The physical circumstances of any talk could support an infinity of detailed descriptions. The physical circumstances of talk, the situational context and the record of previous speech, are available to linguists and psychologists for scrutiny. But this observable context is both more and less than the mental context carried forward by the talkers. It is too much, because it contains more than they remember, more than they have perceived or defined as relevant. It is too little, because it omits all of the general knowledge structures and history of experiences which are used in our rememberings to transform and rework what we see and hear (Bartlett 1932; Bransford 1979). The transform-ations from physical to mental contexts of conversation are qualitative as well as quantitative, but we shall not explore those issues here (see, for example, Edwards and Middleton 1986a).

This is one of the reasons why the contextualisation of discourse may be highly problematic, not only in education but in the rest of social life. Here is a brief anecdotal example. A friend had arranged to let his house during a period abroad. All this had been done at very short notice, so that on the day of his departure he still had to hand over the key and some practical information to a representative of the estate agents involved. The representative was late, so much so that the friend thought he might miss his train. The doorbell rang; the friend invited the caller in, and showed him around his home with special attention to switches, taps and locks. The caller diligently accompanied the owner round the house, but on finally being offered the key he seemed quite bewildered. 'Why should I want that?' he said, 'I'm the taxi come to take you to the station'. For the owner, the whole conversation had, tacitly, invoked the contextual framework of a handover of property from one person to another and to his mind followed the appropriate ground rules for such a transaction. The taxi driver presumably also 'made sense' of the early part of encounter, but must have done so by contextualising the discourse in quite a different way, satisfying the maxim of relevance (Grice 1975) by recourse to a different referential framework.

Displaced contexts

It has often been claimed that the language of formal schooling differs from less elevated forms of discourse by being relatively 'displaced', 'disembedded', or 'context independent' (Bruner 1971; Donaldson 1978; Bernstein 1971). It supposedly transcends the here and now, invoking abstract generalisations rather than simple descriptions of what is physically real and present to the senses. There are a number of problems with this notion, of which we will focus here on just two.

One of these is that evidence from our own researches supports that of others (e.g., Cooper 1976; Driver 1983) who found that most classroom talk is overwhelmingly tied to the concrete activities and situations that occur in classrooms. Moreover, in the primary school lessons we have observed, when teachers invoked 'displaced' contextual information, this was very largely a matter of drawing on shared experiences and discourses which *were generated by the pupils and the teachers themselves* in previous lessons. This makes good educational sense, as it ensures that nearly all of the talk, instruction and exploration, questions and answers, is founded on a self-contained body of common knowledge. Only very rarely did teachers invoke wider, out-of-school experience to contextualise activities or talk.

The notion that the proper business of the lesson centres on what is 'done' in class, rather than by reference to the wider world, apears to be understood by pupils themselves. They appear to operate within a ground rule to the effect that, if the teacher asks a question related to work done in class, then the answer is to be found in what the lesson has actually covered. This is well illustrated by the next sequence of discourse, which is taken from a lesson on clay pottery in a primary school. In it, the teacher is trying to get the children to think out, and express, a procedure for ensuring that *solid* clay pottery figures (as opposed to hollow pots) will not explode, through the expansion of trapped air, when baked in the kiln.

Discourse sequence 2: making the pot hollow

| Teacher: | Let the air out/ now that's because it's hollow/ but the same thing happens with a great lump of clay/ you/ you've pushed it | Teacher to John |

around so much that you've probably got air trapped inside/ also when it's a thick lump/mm it/ it's to do with the way it's heated up in the kiln/ it may burst open/ hey/ steady on girl/ steady on girl/ steady on/ now/ mm/ can you think what you might do to make it like Katie's/ you've not made it in two pieces so what do you think you might have to do to make it like Katie's? (Teacher is here elaborating a point about air in clay introduced in an earlier session.)

Teacher to John, pointing at Katie.
John looks blank.

Katie: Put a hole straight through

Teacher: Not a hole straight through/ exactly. Put a hole come on keep going dear don't stop*   *To John

Peter: Is that spare clay?

Teacher: Any idea Peter?

Peter: No

Teacher: No   Teacher sounds incredulous.

Peter: No. Can I have the knife please John?

Teacher: What/ listen/ what sort of a shape is Sarah's/ is it solid/ what is it?

Peter: Hollow

Teacher: Hollow/ hollow/ now think of that word hollow/ and what are you going to do to yours/ hey/ come on think   Peter and John both look blank.

John: (. . .)

Teacher: Pardon/ what do you think you're going to do to yours then/ make it/ make it what?   John looks blank, and looks down at the table.

Katie: Hollow

Teacher: Why is Katie having to tell you/ you've got a brain/ you know really don't you?

John: Yes

Teacher: Well shout up then

Peter: How do you make it hollow?

Teacher: How do you think you make it hollow?   Teacher sounds exasperated.

Patricia: You done it/ mm/ on Monday/ when you ⎡made the pig and the hedgehog

John: ⎣Made two thumb pots

Teacher: Well/ you've not made two thumb pots love/ you've done it without making two thumb pots/ so how can you hollow something out. Think about a man that made the first boats and they chopped down trees/ they've got a lump of tree

	piece of a tree trunk/ now/ what did they do/ they?	Rising intonation on final 'they' and pause.
John:	They got something and hollowed it out	
Teacher:	So what does it mean/ hollowing it out. What does that mean?	
Peter:	Hollow out	
Teacher:	Yes/ so what do you have to do?	
Peter:	Dig it out	
Teacher:	Pardon	
Peter:	Dig it out*	*Peter gestures a digging action.
Teacher:	Dig it out/ yes/ so you're going to have to dig some out from/ from underneath where nobody can see/ alright	
John:	Yes	John nods, looking abashed.

The first child (Katie) tried to answer by referring to the procedure used for *hollow* pots – piercing them. This of course will not do. The teacher eventually evokes the response 'hollow' from Katie. David tries a direct question, which fails, and the other children refer back to the quite different procedure they used in earlier lessons. The teacher is clearly exasperated, apparently convinced that she is asking for no more than common knowledge – 'common sense', in fact. The pupils respond on the basis that what they are required to do is remember what they have been taught. Only when the teacher herself provides a new context of shared knowledge (the idea of 'dug out' canoes) do the pupils grasp what she is after. The teacher was apparently exasperated by the pupils' refusal to look to wider contextual horizons. Yet it was precisely within narrower 'lesson-bound' contexts that she generally strove to maintain the content of classroom talk.

The above examination of classroom talk has emphasised its context-embeddedness. It might be inferred that the fragments of discourse we have examined were particularly 'context-tied' because they dealt with practical matters, with manipulating clay and wooden pendulums. But we would argue strongly that *all* educational discourse relies for its intelligibility on speakers' access to particular, implicit contextual frameworks. The wooden pendulums of the past, the patterns of question-and-answer engaged in yesterday, all contextualise the talk of today and tomorrow. Educated people are those who have gained access to a particular, implicit contextual framework. Their talk is not 'explicit' in the sense of requiring no prior knowledge of a listener. The discourse of educated people talking about their specialism – mathematics, philosophy, literary criticism, music – is explicit only to the initiated.

We believe it is important for the study of oracy that more attention is given, by researchers and teachers, to how classroom talk is regulated by context. Contextualisation is the development of intersubjectivity (the shared understanding, by teachers and children, of what they are doing), and so a central issue in the educational process. Responsibilities for 'failure to learn' need not be attributed to particular teachers or children, but to inadequacies of the educational framework within which education takes place. In other words, they may be failures of context. They may be locatable in particular events within the dynamics of discourse in a particular classroom over a given period of time, or attributable to inherent features of the process of teaching and learning, as tacitly defined by participants who must invoke their own conceptions of education and its ground rules to make sense of what they do.

To emphasise this point, let us return to educational ground rules, the regulatory aspects of context. This regulation becomes particularly important and contentious when the educational issue is that of *assessment*. All those examples in previous research which encouraged our own thinking on these matters were, in some way, to do with this – Bernstein (1971) and Labov (1970) on evaluations of ways of talking, Donaldson's (1978) critique of Piagetian assessments of cognitive development. To take a more recent example, we turn to the assessment of oracy in primary schools reported by the Assessment of Performance Unit (1984) of the Department of Education and Science.

The APU's national testing of pupils' oracy is aimed at broadening the scope of traditional assessment, beyond more formal speech-giving and interview activities, to include 'a more varied range of communicative tasks which approximate more closely to the range of purposes for which pupils need and use talk in their real life situations' (APU 1984: 14). They acknowledge, however, that the classroom is a highly restrictive communicative context, and that the simulation of a range of 'real life' communication tasks within this setting might be seen as unavoidably artificial. However, their responsibility is to make the best possible assessments under such difficult circumstances. And they have gone to some pains to encourage pupils to perform the tasks in an atmosphere as relaxed and natural as possible, for example by using friendship pairs. But the criteria used by assessors, particularly for the more detailed analytical marking, implicitly evoke educational ground rules which import an arbitrary prescriptive element into what purports to be a value-free or objective analysis.

For instance, in the primary survey, pupils were asked to tell a story about a series of four pictures featuring snails, hedgehogs and a dog, to an audience of two children who could also see the pictures. According to the analytic marking schemes, good marks should be awarded to a description which includes the following – an opening statement which set the scene followed by an account of the main event, and then an elaboration which gave more detailed information. Pupils who mixed, for example, details of the landscape and of the main event, were penalised. 'Particularly striking lexical usage' (examples given are 'rather fuzzy hedgehogs' and 'an unfortunate snail') gained pupils higher marks, as did descriptions which ascribed 'purposes, thoughts and feelings' to the animals (for example, 'all the hedgehogs and snails are deciding how to get him out'). Pupils who linked events only through time, without suggesting causes and motivations, were penalised, and skeletal accounts were also awarded low marks. The successful stories were, therefore, those which showed pupils' readiness to use an essentially *literate* model with a clear beginning, middle and end, and the anthropomorphic metaphor of a certain genre of children's literature. Pupils were also expected to give an elaborated description of details in the pictures, in spite of the fact that the listeners could see these details perfectly clearly for themselves. The expectation that language work should conform with essay-type conventions, and that pupils should be prepared to present detailed redundant information to adults, are familiar ground rules to successful consumers of British education. It is questionable, however, whether literary criteria such as these should so strongly influence the nature of what is meant to be an *oracy* test. Moreover, there is no good reason to believe that these essentially arbitrary ground rules were ever made explicit, in advance, to the children being tested.

We are not being cynical by criticising these and other aspects of current practice. Rather, we are suggesting that, to progress further, the study of oracy must take more seriously the notion of context. Through talk itself, teachers and assessors can create suitable contexts for pursuing their educational goals. They can carefully create contexts, frameworks for shared understanding based on joint knowledge and action, which will provide children with both a rationale for understanding and evaluating present activity and a strong foundation for future development.

Conclusion

To sum up, therefore, we are arguing that contextualisation is a vitally important, and highly problematic, aspect of oral communication. We have highlighted two important aspects of this contextualisation: the intersubjective nature of context, as shared knowledge constructed (and continually reconstructed) by people talking together; and the operation of implicit ground rules, according to which the participants interpret and act upon each others' communications. As we have shown, these are especially problematical in situations where the issue is one of assessment, evaluation or prescription of what is taken to be good oral performance.

References

Acres, J. (1987). 'Investigational Science', *Oracy Matters* (publication of the Wiltshire Oracy Project), no. 9, pp. 18–23.

Assessment of Performance Unit (APU) (1984) *Language Performance in Schools: Primary Survey Report 1982*, London, Department of Education and Science.

Bartlett, F. C. (1932). *Remembering*, Cambridge, Cambridge University Press.

Bernstein, B. (1971). *Class, Codes and Control, Vol. 1*, London, Routledge and Kegan Paul.

Bransford, J. D. (1979). *Human Cognition*, Belmont, Calif., Wadsworth.

Bruner, J. (1971). *The Relevance of Education*, Harmondsworth, Penguin.

Bruner, J. (1986). *Actual Minds, Possible Worlds*. Cambridge, Mass., Harvard University Press.

Cooper, B. (1976). 'Bernstein's Codes: A Classroom Study', University of Sussex Educational Area Occasional Paper no. 6, mimeo.

Donaldson, M. (1978). *Children's Minds*, London, Fontana.

Driver, R. (1983). *The Pupil as Scientist?*, Milton Keynes, Open University Press.

Edwards, D. and Maybin, J. (1987). 'The Development of Understanding in the Classroom', *EH207 Communication and Education*, Unit 16, Milton Keynes, Open University Press.

Edwards, D. and Mercer, N. (1986a). 'Context and Continuity: Classroom Discourse and the Development of Shared Knowledge' in K. Durkin (ed.), *Language Development in the School Years*, Beckenham, Croom Helm.

Edwards, D. and Mercer, N. (1986b). 'Discourse, Power and the Creation of Shared Knowledge: How Do Pupils Discover What They Are Meant To?', paper presented to the First Annual Congress on Activity Theory, Berlin, 3–5 October.

Edwards, D. and Mercer, N. (1987). *Common Knowledge: The Development of Understanding in the Classroom*, London, Methuen.

Edwards, D. and Middleton, D. J. (1986). 'Joint Remembering: Constructing an Account of Shared Experience through Conversational Discourse', *Discourse Processes*, vol. 9, pp. 423–59.

Grice, H. P. (1975). 'Logic and Conversation', in P. Cole and J. Morgan (eds), *Syntax and Semantics, Vol. 3: Speech Acts*, New York, Academic Press.

Labov, W. (1970). 'The Logic of Non-Standard English', in F. Williams (ed.), *Language and Poverty*, Chicago, Markham.

Mercer, N. and Edwards, D. (1981). 'Ground Rules for Mutual Understanding: Towards a Social Psychological Approach to Classroom Knowledge', in N. Mercer (ed.), *Language in School and Community*, London, Edward Arnold.

Vygotsky, L. S. (1978). *Mind in Society*, Cambridge, Mass., Harvard University Press.

Appendix: Transcription conventions

The names of the children have been altered to protect their identity, and the teachers are all identified as *Teacher*. Our aim has been to present these sequences of talk as accurately as possible, using some conventions for the transcription of discourse, but at the same time ensuring that they remain easily readable and comprehensible. Our purpose has not been to produce an analysis of linguistic structure, but to provide the sort of information that is useful in analysing how people reach common understandings with each other of what they are talking about. So, while commas are avoided, and certain conventions are used to indicate such things as pauses and simultaneous speech, we have retained the normal written uses of capital letters and full stops to mark the start and end of sentences. The conventions used are as follows:

(. . .)	Words undeciphered.
/	Pause of less than 2 seconds.
/ /	Pause of more than 2 seconds.
[	Simultaneous or interrupted speech.

PART FOUR
Spoken language and the media

11 Oral models in the Press

ROGER FOWLER

In this chapter I will first of all reflect on a general theoretical problem in linguistics – the boundary between speech and writing, and the relationships between the two modes. I will then look at a genre of discourse in which the boundary is not clear-cut: English newspapers, which are printed publications but with a noticeable predilection for oral styles of writing. I will focus on some of the linguistic constructions which are used to make print evoke speech. Next, I ask some questions about the functions of oral models in the Press, specifically about the kinds of text–reader relationship that are implied. Finally, I suggest that this topic has educational implications, though since I am a linguist rather than an educationist I shall not dare to say very much about that side of things.

Traditional structural linguistics, and contemporary mainstream linguistics of the generative kind, have little to say about written language. The textbooks tell us that, historically, writing is derived from speech, and that today many communities do not possess a written form of their language: therefore speech is the basic form and writing merely a derived version. Structuralist grammars are supposed to represent speech, the assumption being that writing can be accounted for by simply adding a few orthographic rules. The descriptively adequate grammars of which Chomskyans dream, and of which they sometimes write little fragments, are presumably in principle neutral as between speech and writing, the rules representing the linguistic competence which underlies constructions in either medium. I would guess that for the Chomskyan – based firmly in the structuralist heritage, despite Chomsky's denial of this (see, for example, Chomsky 1964: ch. 1) – speech is instinctively a kind of norm, the written medium a deviation to be accounted for (by someone else) in the messy world of 'linguistic performance'. Interestingly, many of the example sentences discussed by transformationalists are obviously made up and often exceedingly bookish – 'Jill and Mary perform on the accordion and the harmonium respectively', 'Not all of the soldiers were hit by many arrows', and the like – sentences which would sound odd, or be difficult to process, in real speech. Perhaps this bookishness is of no theoretical significance, possibly merely indicating that linguists tend to be middle-class, and therefore a trivial fact of linguistic performance.

The serious point is that, intuitively, one can tell the difference between speech and writing. One can tell when someone is reading from a typed script, and one can tell when they depart from it. And we can agree also that there is a limit to what can be read out: certain kinds of language, e.g. laws, charters, insurance policies, are virtually *unspeakable*, so remote are they from the lexical and syntactic patterns of speech. Conversely, speech is very hard to transcribe; on top of lexical and syntactic patterns which make transcribed speech look unnatural, there is all the essential apparatus of intonation and paralanguage for which writing makes no provision. The two modes seem to be decisively different in many respects and at all levels: semantics, syntax and phonology.

How does one theorise this difference? One thing that is clear to me is that the competence–performance distinction of Chomsky makes the job of theorisation more, not less, difficult, because it requires us to take decisions of an absolute kind. On the one hand, we might be tempted to say that the substantive differences between the modes indicate the existence of different linguistic codes, that is that different 'competences' are available to the speaker and the writer. This would clearly be a gross misuse of the Chomskyan notion of competence which, if it means anything, surely means 'competence in one language', and spoken and written English are obviously one language, not two. On the other hand, locating the distinction between speech and writing at the level of linguistic performance, that is essentially a stylistic difference dependent on context, tells us nothing if it is left at that, and minimises the major structural differences to which I have alluded.

The way forward, it seems to me, is to abandon binary distinctions and to relativise the situation. (The move to 'variable rules' made by Labov in the 1960s to cope with regular sociolinguistic variation which could not be accommodated in a generative grammar is instructive, though my solution does not follow Labov exactly; see Labov 1972.) The fact that communicatively competent speakers of English can recognise some discourse as speech and some as writing does not mean that there exist just two modes. We are certainly justified in adding others, such as *script*, which would be a prepared written text designed to be performed orally as if it was speech, for example the text of a radio or television news bulletin or a commentary on a documentary programme; *writing in speech style*, print designed to be read but to evoke in the reader the image of a speaking voice, for example a newspaper editorial in the tones of Peregrine Worsthorne. We lack technical terms for the various distinctions that need to be made at this point, but a longish list including some rather complicated categories could be produced.

Such a list might then be assimilated to a pluralistic model of sociolinguistic varieties; perhaps these variants of speech and writing (let's call them 'modes') are complementary to what Halliday calls 'registers'. So instead of two modes, speech and writing, we would have as many modal varieties as could be differentiated: script, conversation, writing in speech style, formal print, and so on. The speaker or writer would on this theory have internalised a set of modal varieties from which he or she would select one which was appropriate within a given context.

This pluralistic model would seem to offer more discrimination in description than the binary one does; but that is not to say that it is a correct model of discourse processes, or indeed that description along these lines is even feasible. As a matter of fact, the low yield from the register project over the last twenty years suggests that the idea of a language as a set of discrete varieties is simplistically formulated or, more likely, incorrect. No one has formally described any single register such as 'scientific English' in such a way as to identify it and to distinguish it utterly from something else, say 'advertising English'; and I do not believe that we would have any more luck in describing autonomous modes such as 'script' or 'speech style'. But it is possible to improve the theory by amending the status of 'variety'.

Just as I find it misleading to think of a language as consisting of a set of registers and a set of modes (and other categorisations, such as a set of dialects), so I find it a distortion, and inhibiting, to think of a text as 'being in such-and-such a register' or mode or dialect. This misconception would imply that a text is marked exclusively by a single consistent set of linguistic features all signifying register X or mode Y. This conception ignores the manifest stylistic and modal heterogeneity of most texts, and the neutrality or ambiguity of most segments of most texts. It seems to me to put the cart before the horse: I would prefer to say not that a text is in a mode (or register or dialect) but that modes and registers and dialects are 'in' texts. I have put 'in' in quotation marks because modes are not actually present in the linguistic structure, but rather, they are perceived in texts by hearers or readers.

To make sense of this notion of potential rather than actual structure in texts, we need an idea of the text which is less formalistic and literal than that usually employed by linguists; and the post-structuralist theory of the text, well articulated, for example, by Roland Barthes (1979), fits the bill. I do not have the space to explain this in detail, but the essence is that the text is co-produced by writer and reader (or speaker and hearer) negotiating the significance of a piece of language on the basis of their more or less shared knowledge of the world, society and language itself. So a mode is not an objective linguistic structure, but an idea in the minds of language users: this is what I refer to as a 'model' in my title. A model is an intersubjective category, that is, an idea which is shared in the relevant community, which is projected onto the text in the process of making sense of it. Models have the status of what are called 'schemata' in cognitive psychology, categories or structures which readers' shared experiences allow them to detect in the objects of perception. In Western art, for example, perspective is a schema: a conventional expectation that paintings are to be viewed as having depth, three-dimensionality. Now three-dimensionality is, obviously, not an objective property of a representation on canvas; the relevant objective properties are technical devices such as convergent lines and variable shading which act as *cues* to the viewer to experience the painting as a representation with depth.

The idea of cueing implies that a particular mode or a particular register or a particular dialect can be assigned to a text even on the basis of some very small segment within its total language: it does not have to be saturated with markers of the variety, or structured with tyrannical consistency. The effectiveness of fragments has occasionally been acknowledged in sociolinguistics and dialectology: Halliday (*et al.* 1964: 87) in his earliest treatment of 'register' maintains that just one sentence from a sports commentary, a church service or a school lesson 'would enable us to identify [the situation type] correctly'. Hudson (1980), who gives priority to the concept of 'linguistic item' and is sceptical about 'varieties', provides a sympathetic theoretical framework which would accommodate such observations. Labov (1972) and Trudgill (1974) are also suggestive from this point of view. Their research does not attempt to give a complete profile of any dialect, but focuses on small phonetic details which are characteristic of an accent. Some of these, called by Labov 'stereotypes', have, as he puts it 'rise[n] to overt social consciousness' (1972: 248) and can be used to symbolise an accent and the social values associated with it. So for example, the pronunciation /toyd/ for 'third' in New York metonymically symbolises Brooklynese by virtue of the concentration of three highly significant features: /t/ for 'th', the highly recognisable diphthong /oy/, and the lack of the prestigious post-vocalic /r/. Readers will be able to think of many other examples from their own sociolinguistic experience where some small detail is taken as representative of a whole variety of language and can economically call up the social values associated with that form of language.

The principle that a variety can be cued by a stereotypical detail explains how modally complex texts like newspapers can exist: a lengthy piece of text like a newspaper can contain within it diverse signals so that at different points within the paper the reader is encouraged to realise the text as different kinds of language. Large distinctions such as, for example, those between sports reporting, reviews of the arts and reports of proceedings in Parliament are signalled in this way, as are more subtle differences – for example, the *Guardian* always carries a report on some humorous, curious or personal story in a particular place at the foot of the front page, and this is somewhat different in tone from anything else on the page. Newspapers are full of differences of this kind. But I am going to concentrate on just one – signals of the (fictional) presence of a speaking voice or a speech situation.

It will be useful at this stage to list some of the features of language which may be used to make a printed medium suggest the presence of speech.

1 Typography and orthography
  (a) phonemes
  (b) contrastive stress
  (c) intonation and paralanguage
  (d) information structure
2 Register
  (a) lexis: words, idioms, clichés, proverbs

(b) informality

(c) naming: first names, diminutives, nicknames

3 Syntax and morphology

(a) contractions of auxiliaries and negatives

(b) elisions, incomplete sentences

4 Deixis

(a) pronouns

(b) time and place

5 Modality

(a) subjectivity: judgement, qualification, hedging

(b) status: permission, obligation

6 Illocutionary

(a) speech acts, questions, exclamations, imperatives, etc.

(b) reported verbal processes

The *typographic* devices include anything that can be done to break up the monologic uniformity, the greyness, of conventional print. The tabloids employ many different typefaces on the same page to suggest variations of stress, tone and pace; the so-called 'quality' papers in a lower key use dots and dashes to break up their sentences and to trail off reflectively at pregnant points. Short or incomplete sentences implying many short intonation contours model the 'information units' into which, according to Halliday (Kress 1976: ch. 12) speech is segmented. Misspellings and simplifications of spellings draw attention to phonemes; there is a literary model here in the techniques of representation of dialect speech by novelists such as Dickens and Lawrence. Moving to *register*, we will see in a moment that even one single slang word slipped into a printed text crystallises the text as something that is not quite proper printed; and in general an impression of a colloquial style can be built up by an accumulation of informalities. *Morphological* and *syntactic* contractions such as 'don't', 'not likely', need no comment. *Deixis* is crucial for the experience of print as if spoken. The deictic situations of speech and writing are by definition quite different: there is no 'here and now' in printed communication, no direct contact of participants either in relation to one another or to the communicated content. In the modes of print which mimic speech, deictic forms such as personal pronouns and the various indicators of time and place are deployed to build a fictional speech situation with its own implied participants, drawing in the reader as a party to the speech event. *Modality* – expressions of judgement, qualification, permission, obligation, etc. – can be exploited to give the impression that behind the printed page there exists a real individual giving voice to his or her subjective opinions, making recommendations and concessions which signify a certain status, a certain authoritative role. Editorials in the 'quality' papers are prone to a high level of activity in the area of modality. Finally, let us consider the area of speech acts or *illocutionary* acts. The philosophers Austin and Searle have developed the theory of speech as action, the notion that in speaking one is not only saying something but at the same time performing actions such as claiming, promising, warning, and so on. Like modality, speech acts are vital to the presentation of writing as speech, because they evoke a speaker who does the deed and a hearer who is the object of a speech action. The more 'popular' the newspaper, the more requests, commands, promises and claims fill its pages. My last sub-category, reported verbal processes, recognises that in addition to pretend direct acts, much newspaper reporting consists of the recording of speech acts by politicians and other people.

I want now briefly to illustrate some of these speech-evoking features from two editorials: an extract from a *Guardian* leader and a complete leader from the *Sun*. First, the extract from the *Guardian* of 16 April 1986, which is speaking of the bombing of Libya on the previous day by American planes which took off from British air bases:

> Mad dogs (to use the easy rhetoric) cannot be cowed or trained by example. If
> they are murdering now, they will go on murdering. And what, pray, does the
> great avenger of Lakenheath do then? He presents himself at the bar of world
> opinion as the man who sent his bombers to pound civilians (and the French
> 5 embassy in Tripoli). He didn't mean it, but it happened; inevitably so. The last
> high level intelligence from the White House was of Nicaragua's invasion of
> Honduras. Rubbish: even the Hondurans said so. The world – not just
> Europe, the Third World – has grown sceptical of Mr Reagan's narrow vision,
> and leery of the way he compensates for foreign policy revolts on Capitol Hill
> 10 with risk free adventures against states which can only soak up his firepower.
> Ramboism without risk.
>   But we are only at an interim stage as tit follows tat. Mr Reagan's judgment
> is that, along this road, a cowed Gadafy will sink into impotence. He will
> ultimately be judged – by his own electorate – on the wisdom or frailty of that
> 15 judgment. Mrs Thatcher, however, is sadly exposed: girding her electorate for
> reprisals, defending to her people the blank cheque she gave America's
> bombers. And all the while there is a fatal hole in her arguments.
>   Remember the copious evidence of Libyan terrorism she threatened to
> expose to the House yesterday? Did it not exist a few months ago when Britain
> 20 declined to join economic sanctions against Libya? Did it not exist even on
> Monday when Sir Geoffrey left such sanctions out of his European package?
> Why on earth – if the evidence of evil is so strong – balk at peaceful reprisals by
> Britain? Why not even mention them today?
>   . . . Mrs Thatcher is adrift. Even she wouldn't try sanctions: but she
> 25 condones the bombings and the loss of civilian life. It is a bleak bind, and one
> that may come to haunt her. But did her closest ally think of that, any more than
> he thought through the stages beyond the rubble of Tripoli?

If we compare the text with the categories listed in the table, it quickly becomes clear that many of the more mechanical markers of oral mode are present. The sentence beginning 'He didn't mean it' in line 5 has no less than three of these features: a morphological and a syntactic contraction, and the terse clauses which imply the intonation units of speech. There are plenty of colloquial expressions, for example 'rubbish' (7), 'leery' (9), 'why on earth' (22), 'bind' (25). Such expressions would seem odd in a printed discourse on such an intensely serious subject if it were not for the fact that we as readers have conventionally been led to expect newspaper editorials to read as if they were delivered by an individual speaker: they would be indecorous in print, but are not out of place in a text tinged with an oral mode. The same goes for the numerous mundane, uncreative metaphors such as 'at the bar of world opinion', 'soak up', 'girding her electorate', 'adrift', etc. Moving to categories 4–6, i.e. deixis, modality and illocution: this leader makes linguistic selections which add up to an illusion of a speaker engaged in debate with a hearer within a real communicative context. Among printed genres, newspapers happen to be deictically rather distinctive compared with, say, novels or textbooks: they are literally dated, and they are generally read on the date which is printed at the top of every page. So 'today' literally means today, at least for the reader. What actually happens is that the leader writer, composing his piece during the previous night, adopts the temporal perspective of the imminent 'today', i.e. the intended reader's perspective. Thus a point of orientation is created for the reader, the foundation of a speech situation which he or she can literally occupy and which he or she can imagine the writer sharing as co-locutor. There is a lot of literal temporal reference in this text, as befits an editorial intervention in a political and military narrative which unfolded hour by hour over several days with uncomfortable speed and unpredictability: see, for example, the third paragraph.

Within the deictic context that the text conjures up, modal and illocutionary devices reinforce the impression of a speaker confronting a hearer. Although modal auxiliaries indicating necessity and obligation, common in middlebrow editorials, happen to be rare here, there are plenty of expressions of judgement referable to a speaker with strong opinions: 'inevitably' (5), 'rubbish' (7), 'sadly exposed' (15), and so on. Finally, the reader is drawn into the debate by a series of rhetorical questions, particularly in the third paragraph, which demand that he or she should do two things: access and reflect upon presumed shared knowledge – in the area of 'the copious evidence'; and imagine, and strike an attitude toward, the motives and considerations of the other participants referred to, Thatcher and Reagan.

I will comment on these patterns shortly. Let us first look briefly at how the *Sun* manages an oral mode of writing (see overleaf). The editorial, which starts off as a response to the 1986 New Year's Honours List, differs from the *Guardian*'s most obviously in the use of a variety of typographical devices. Each sentence is set out as a separate paragraph. The half-a-dozen different typefaces used – apparently randomly distributed since they do not appear to correlate with any regular features of content or structure – emphasise still further the discontinuities between sentences. Everything is done to fragment the text into a sequence of separate assertions, like speech in the brevity and disjunction of the units, unlike printed prose which strives to maximise cohesion (in the sense of Halliday and Hasan 1976) and to subdue vocal interruptions. The heading, a patriotic allusion to the wartime Mr Chad, is striking in its insistence on the sound of the word which prose normally spells *what*. The social significance of

Wot, no Bob on the list?

WHO, of all possible contenders, most deserved an award for his achievements in 1985?

Just about every person in the land would put forward one name.

Pop star Bob Geldof aroused the conscience of the world over the heartbreaking plight of the starving peoples of Ethiopia and the Sudan.

Floodgates

He was responsible for releasing the floodgates of charity that meant the difference between life and death for millions of men, women and children.

Yet there is no mention of Bob Geldof in the dreary New Year Honours List.

No mention, either, of any of the helpers who made Band Aid the most uplifting story of the year.

Instead, we have the usual plague of ever so worthy politicians and ageing members of the showbusiness fraternity.

Bob has this consolation.

The whole honours system has become so discredited that men and women who really matter ought not to give a damn whether they are on the list or not.

Fairy tale

JUST look whom radio listeners have chosen in a landslide vote as their Woman of the Year.

Princess Anne.

Only a short time ago that would have seemed as unlikely as Australia winning a Test.

The Princess was best known for her temper and for slagging off her husband in public.

Dedicated

She has earned the award by her marvellous, dedicated work for hungry children all over the world.

Maybe there is a lesson here for another royal ugly duckling.

Instead of constantly complaining that she is misunderstood, why does not Princess Michael find herself a good cause?

Join the club

SINCE days before Christmas, paralysis seems to have swept over Britain.

If you were at work yesterday you qualified for the most exclusive club in the land.

We were working, too.

Wasn't it fun?

Editorial from the *Sun* (Tuesday 31 December 1985).

this device, which has to do, I think, with an appeal for working-class solidarity, is too complex to analyse here and this spelling is best just taken as a cue to a model of oral performance. Note that the whole editorial is printed in a larger typeface than that used for running text elsewhere in the paper, perhaps asking us to imagine a loud declamation of something very important.

If typography is patchy and un-prose-like, so also is register. There is a general colloquialism in vocabulary: 'pop star', 'dreary', 'ever so worthy', 'not give a damn', 'ugly duckling'. One expression stands out against the background of this routinely casual language like a sore thumb: 'The Princess was best known for her temper and for *slagging off* her husband in public'. Spoken of in the language of vulgar gossip appropriate to 'Coronation Street', the Princess is domesticated, assimilated to the petty world of family and community passions and strife which this newspaper regularly cultivates. 'Slagging off' is a shock; and a lot of work can be done by one foregrounded expression like this. There is also another area of vocabulary worth noting, in tone somewhere between the pompous and the pathetic: 'heartbreaking plight of the starving peoples', 'floodgates of charity'. Clichés like these might be embarrassing in print, but here they are a feature of the language of an imagined *vox populi*, impatient, forthright, brushing aside the decorum of literary details.

Finally, notice that modality and speech acts are, as might be expected, prominently involved in the process of building an image of a badgering, populist speaker. The editorial starts with two rhetorical questions posed on behalf of the readership, who, as the second sentence indicates, are assumed to agree totally with the suggested answer. It concludes with a direct address to the reader, deictically located within an interpersonal context sketched by the pronouns 'we' and 'you'. The reader is, as the *Sun* might put it, directly 'fingered' here. If he was working during the Christmas holiday, he, like the reformed miners celebrated in the other article on the page, can be congratulated, and, like the *Sun* journalists, feel self-righteous; if he wasn't working, the *Sun* will cast him in among the rabble of printers, striking miners, teachers, and other militants, subversives and time-wasters that this newspaper constantly condemns. The last paragraph of this editorial amounts to a threat.

My last comment amounts to an interpretation, a statement about one of the functions of oral mode, and it is now time to turn directly to the general question of function.

In different ways, newspapers model an oral mode of language. The differences are internal and external: there is a major external difference between the *Sun* and the *Guardian*, and there are large internal differences within one paper, between, for example, pages devoted to entertainment and to foreign news. All these internal and external differences deserve to be studied in careful descriptive projects, but setting aside the differences for the moment, there remains the general question: why should a publication which is necessarily printed, and which is necessarily impersonal – we do not know or meet the writers, they do not know us as individuals – affect a personal, speech-like, form of rhetoric? Part of the reason could be a lack felt in the essential impersonality of mass communication, a need to imagine and situate the individual subject whom by definition one does not know. This explanation, it seems to me, has some plausibility but does not go anything like far enough.

What is the *product* of the newspaper industry? Not, it seems, newspapers themselves, because the sale of newspapers is not profitable. Advertising revenue may yield a profit, or at least offset the losses involved in producing and distributing the papers. Nowadays, most national and local newspapers are owned by multinational companies with highly diversified interests, and the profits come from the other branches: the entertainment industry, property speculation, and so on. Newspapers are bought and run to be used as instruments in the reproduction of the social, political, and economic conditions which favour capitalism, and within that economic framework, the proprietors' business enterprises in general. The product of the newspaper industry is *readers*. Not just the *quantities* of readers boasted in the sales figures – that is just to impress the advertisers. What are produced are readers with attitudes favourable to the success of the businesses which own the papers: that is to say, ideologically appropriate readers. Newspaper language, like all language, continuously articulates ideology. But printed communication is not very good at implanting beliefs in readers, because readers can remain anonymous, sit back without response, and never read the publication again. Conversation and dialogue are much more effective because they target or situate the addressee, they make assumptions about what the addressee is thinking, and force the addressee to take a line in relation to those assumptions. It is the ideological power of conversation which causes the newspapers to cue oral modes.

Stuart Hall (1978: 61) suggests that the language of a newspaper is 'the newspaper's own version of the language of the public to whom it is principally addressed'. What has to be emphasised here is that arriving at that version of the reader's speech is a *constructive*, not a *reflective* process. I am sure that the editor of the *Sun* would like us to believe that there is in nature such a person as a '*Sun* reader' (a category referred to frequently in the paper, by the way, as if such persons do exist) whose ideas about work, fun, money and sex are exactly reflected in the paper, hence the paper's mass popularity. As an extension of this account, it might be claimed that the language of the paper reflects that of its readers. But this claim would be empirically fatuous: no one actually speaks like the *Sun*, it is in no sense a transcription! Newspaper language is a pretend oral mode which does two things for the reader. First, by appearing to be conversation, it offers the reader a dialogic position to occupy: situates the reader, offers him or her a role, forces him or her to take up a position on the ideas expressed. Second, the oral model, containing cues like 'slagging off', encourages the reader to imagine that he or she *might* speak like that, or at least take part in a conversation expressed like that.

The crucial point is that if we can imagine taking part in a certain mode of discourse, we can entertain the ideas, the ideology, that are encoded in that mode of discourse. I cannot explain and justify this claim in detail here, but the arguments have been worked through in several familiar sources elsewhere: in Berger and Luckman (1967), in Halliday (1978), in Fowler *et al.* (1979), and associated work in 'critical linguistics' (e.g., Chilton 1985). There is a good account of the processes involved as they figure in the media in Hartley (1982), though he has little to say on how linguistic details carry ideological significance. In summary, what happens is that newspaper writers imagine a category of reader to be addressed who holds views favourable to the interests of the paper: in the case of the *Sun*, for example, the beliefs that trade union activity subverts economic success and that trade unions are ruled by 'militants' (i.e. communists). Any specific reader may not, of course, believe such things, and the job of the language is to make the ideas seem so natural and commonsensical that he accepts them. The newspaper offers the reader the opportunity to participate in a discourse in which such beliefs are comfortably encoded. The fact that the discourse is orally modelled leads to the reader's being semiotically, and therefore ideologically, situated more precisely than an impersonal prose model could manage. The values of the discourse appear to be unproblematic, 'common sense' – what everyone believes. One of the tasks of critical linguistics is to show how common sense is artificially constructed, and the role of language in effecting this construction.

Looking at newspapers in this way seems to me to have a number of implications or prospects for education. First, newspapers and magazines make up the major amount of print consumed by young people (or indeed, all people) and we ought to be clearly aware of their status as ideological practice. Second, critical linguistics provides simple methods for reading the ideology and could be the basis of a classroom practice of analysis, however informal. Third, the case of newspapers reminds us that the world of discourse is not neatly divided simply into two modes, written and spoken. Among the most interesting – and common – classes of discourse are those which exhibit multi-modality, or modal structures which are at the interface of writing and speech. This fact should get full recognition in programmes designed to help young people towards achievement in communicative competence.

References

Barthes, R. (1979). 'From Work to Text' in J. V. Harari (ed.), *Textual Strategies: Perspectives in Post-Structuralist Criticism*. Ithaca, NY, Cornell University Press.
Berger, P. L. and Luckmann, T. (1967). *The Social Construction of Reality*. Harmondsworth, Penguin.
Chilton, P. (ed.) (1985). *Language and the Nuclear Arms Debate: Nukespeak Today*, London, Frances Pinter.
Chomsky, N. (1964). *Current Issues in Linguistic Theory*, The Hague, Mouton.
Fowler, R., Hodge, R., Kress, G. and Trew, T. (1979). *Language and Control*, London, Routledge and Kegan Paul.
Hall, S. (1978). 'The Social Production of News' in S. Hall, C. Critcher, T. Jefferson,

J. Clarke and B. Roberts, *Policing the Crisis: Mugging, the State, and Law and Order*, London, Macmillan.

Halliday, M. A. K. (1978). *Language as Social Semiotic*, London, Edward Arnold.

Halliday, M. A. K. and Hasan, R. (1976). *Cohesion in English*, London, Edward Arnold.

Halliday, M. A. K., McIntosh, A. and Strevens, P. (1964). *The Linguistic Sciences and Language Teaching*, London, Longman.

Hartley, J. (1982). *Understanding News*, London, Methuen.

Hudson, R. A. (1980). *Sociolinguistics*, Cambridge, Cambridge University Press.

Kress, G. (ed.) (1976). *Halliday: System and Function in Language*, London, Oxford University Press.

Labov, W. (1972). *Sociolinguistic Patterns*, Philadelphia, University of Pennsylvania Press.

Trudgill, P. (1974). *The Social Differentiation of English in Norwich*, Cambridge, Cambridge University Press.

12 Scripting for creative video: from talk to writing and back again

STEPHEN PARKER

Background

Although television is considered to be a visual medium, television programmes in every genre – news, situation comedy, documentary – communicate through the spoken word in large measure. Within that dimension television would seem essentially to stress the oral skills of those appearing in the programme. What is far less obvious to the viewer of the broadcast programme is that the spoken word has wherever possible been written down first. It is the relationship between the spoken and the written text when video programmes are produced in the classroom, in imitation of broadcast television, which I wish to explore, concentrating on the notion of 'scripting' and making reference to issues which have emerged in working with classes of children, aged eight, ten and fourteen.

Anyone who has experienced a whole-language classroom context will know that language is seldom tidily divided between the four modes of reading, writing, speaking, listening. It is now an orthodoxy of classroom procedure that a written end-product will involve exploratory talk at one or many of the stages of production. Project work as a curriculum focus in the English primary school has traditionally blurred watertight demarcations between subjects in the curriculum, times in the timetable and the language modes. Although in theory we can explore the language modes in project work as separate strands, in practice they are interwoven, one supporting and interpreting another. Creating a video programme with a class of children requires many of the attributes of the project approach; group or syndicate class organisation, negotiative teaching style, integration of subjects, flexible use of time, and a complex interrelationship of reading, writing, speaking and listening.

Current thinking on language in the curriculum emphasises the use of language for 'real or realistic purposes', to quote from DES (1984). This in turn underlines the importance of language models; that children should be exposed to realistic models of language and should replicate them in order better to understand and later better participate in the communication systems of the adult world. Television clearly plays a significant part, at least quantitatively, in the lives of children and adults alike. Since it is a medium, it offers not just one single language model. As there are many broadcast programmes, so there are many structures, conventions and styles of presentation. The medium offers a wealth of material across a wide range of spoken language models for curriculum developers.

What is a script?

We usually expect adult speakers in a real-life context to use some kind of a script where *written* text is used to prompt and guide *spoken* text. For example, politicians, union delegates, teachers or speakers at a conference, almost all will have paper before them in formal situations. According to the style and skill of the speaker, the nature and extent of the script will vary; from single key words at one end of the scale to every word that is spoken at the other. In all kinds of formal situation the speaker is highly likely to have at least worked out ideas beforehand on paper, even if not referring directly to some kind of written prompt whilst speaking. In many contexts, little attempt is made to disguise this use of writing, although we expect the speaker's intonation patterns to be those of natural speech, and the delivery to be fluent, without any stumbles in the reading.

Scripting is a constructed, or perhaps reconstructed, version of natural speech. A script, whilst imitating the patterns of spoken language, uses writing to develop what is possible in speech in three significant ways: to extend it in length; to shape its direction; and to increase the density of its meaning. To expand briefly on these three qualities, very few speakers under pressure can *reliably* sustain spontaneous dialogue for an extensive but precise length of time, without 'hesitation, deviation or repetition' (to quote the rules of a well-known radio panel game) whilst still making good sense to the perceived audience. What Carl Bereiter (1980) called the 'epistemic' in relation to writing has significance here. A script is an epistemic use of writing in that it is intended to contain a higher density of meaning than a speaker could generate by more informal, more spontaneous means.

Although it might seem that the principles of scripting have more to do with the written word than with the spoken, it is a very important principle to all who create television that what is spoken sounds as if it were natural speech, and not writing. It is a first principle that scripting should conceal itself. In the media of radio and television, very little of what is broadcast is unscripted, and this is true of all their genres – drama, documentary, news, features, and so on. For those studying the media, it is safest to assume that the fullest written script has been used wherever possible in any programme.

Within that guideline, though, there is a continuum from completely un-scripted to fully scripted material. Completely unscripted material is rare. Although a commentary on a football match has a high degree of unpredictability about it, it is clearly possible for the commentator to prepare information about each team and each player beforehand, and, importantly, the genre has a well-known repertoire of stock phrases about passes, tackles and goal-scoring which will come quickly to the tongue of the practised commentator. Such phrases will be described pejoratively by the critic as 'clichés' but in reality it would be impossible for anyone reliably and fluently to invent a flowing commentary match after match under considerable pressure and perhaps when tired from long travel. Stock phrases and linguistic conventions are themselves a kind of script, or at least a set of alternatives available to a speaker which facilitate choice of expression under pressure.

Similarly the chat-show host will have prepared questions for the guests. Sometimes the interview will have been rehearsed or at least the questions to be asked will have been discussed beforehand with the interviewee. The opening and closing remarks by the host can be constructed word for word beforehand. Such unscripted parts of the programme as there are will only be slots within a scripted framework.

This tight control and lack of spontaneity is not part of the way children normally conceive of television. Partly because of the skill of the broadcasters, and partly because children are so familiar with relaxing in front of the set, television is to them completely natural, spontaneous and hence unscripted. This is easy to understand. How often on the screen do you see an actor or presenter actually reading something? Because of the ubiquitous autocue, even the news 'readers' appear to consult the written word only fleetingly. Television has evolved the ability to create an illusion of natural speech, spontaneously generated.

Children's reactions

How do children react, then, to producing their own versions of television? To characterise children's first experience of a video camera in stages, first they treat it as if it were a mirror, pulling zany faces or doing funny walks, or (as if it were a porthole with people on the other side) they come right up to it and peer in. In the second stage they become highly enthusiastic about co-operating with partners to produce instant video. 'Let's do Starsky and Hutch, Tom and Jerry.'

Eight-year-olds have no idea at all that scripting is involved in creating a programme. Because they are so familiar with the medium in many of its conventions and genres, they will spring forward in front of the camera with no preparation or forethought at all but full of energy and enthusiasm to create programme material – only to stutter to an embarrassed halt within just a few words. The young child who can from the outset perform even the most familiar material or simplest story to a camera for more than a minute is rare. The large majority, after a very few words, simply dry up. It is the speed with which it happens and the contrast with their previous enthusiasm which is most amazing. Only the most vocal are able to continue, but still looking embarrassed in a variety of ways, voices getting fainter and thinner. Since their original conception of a programme is of a co-operative effort, they have no one left to work with and the thing squeaks to a halt by default.

It is interesting also that the groups who have not yet performed do not realise what has happened. They seem to think that their classmates are being inexplicably inept, and tend to jeer – until it comes to their turn, and their David is slain by Goliath. The reaction of all age groups is similar, though the fourteen-year-olds seem to have a much greater awareness of the constructed nature of the medium and hence more caution at the outset.

I think that what they realise in front of the camera is that television material is fabricated and not natural; that the camera as audience is remote, silent and gives no feedback, yet is intrusively apparent; that presentation before a video camera removes the speaker from the normal data and context of talk; older children are aware that it captures what they do and say – their performance can be repeated over and over, to an unknown audience which is likely to be critical. These realisations combine to create one major reason for their drying up – pressure. The effect of pressure on oral performance seems to be a subject largely unexplored by educational research, but as all teachers know from personal experience, nervous tension affects the nature of performance. The scale of formality described by Joos (1962) recognises that as an audience changes in number or relationship to the speaker, so the level of formality in the linguistic structures increases, along a scale from 'casual' to 'frozen'. We might add as a hypothesis that there is a corresponding increase of pressure on the nerves of the speaker.

The scripting process

Once children have realised how vulnerable their fluency is under the pressure of a camera, they are easily persuaded that a script would be a good idea. They are also incidentally later more tolerant of performances by individuals who are dependent on reading the script word for word. The stages in the production of a script seem to me to be: exploration; drafting; rehearsal; performance; and evaluation.

Exploration

This is a three-pronged stage, involving exploration of the medium; a genre within it; and the subject matter of the programme.

Medium

The exploration phase needs to take account of television 'grammar' – the technical process of making video, including terms for camera operation. Younger children understand this most directly if it is handled as a practical hands-on session. This is probably true of all ages but the older children seem to enjoy learning in a more abstract way the terms television uses – pan, zoom-in, close-up, and so on – which put a concept label on their extensive intuitive knowledge of the medium.

Genre
Next comes the selection of an appropriate television genre to replicate, and consideration of its techniques. As a medium, television contains models of speech across the whole available range. Guided discussion allows children to analyse indirectly the structural features of the chosen programme type, as they describe from recollection the features of particular examples. The next stage is to advise them on how to simplify the model into a replicable form for a simple one-camera set-up. A first line of simplification is in terms of length. Most broadcast programmes are too long at 30 minutes since the scripting task would be considerable and the production task enormous. For this reason advertisements are a highly successful model with all age groups. Scripting a twenty-second advert is not, by definition, an epic task. The format is brief but it has strong impact, offering a range of structural patterns which are well known to all including the youngest children. Many have a narrative structure and language patterns – rhymes, jingles, mnemonics – which are easily memorised for performance. The genre often uses the voice-over technique, which allows that part of the script to be read unobtrusively, greatly reducing the pressure on the performer.

Drama is also a genre with which all ages are very familiar, though it presents some difficulties, including turning a script into natural-seeming dialogue without a great deal of rehearsal. Young children enjoy several aspects of drama – the imaginative play, creating a narrative, dressing up, having the camera as an audience which is more easily ignored than a large group of people. Enjoyment seems to reduce the pressure on them, and so drama is a genre I have used with ten-year-olds, who are capable of handling a larger structure than the eight-year-olds. Historical drama with advertisement inserts allows them to enjoy the 'in' joke of anachronism too.

On the other hand, fourteen-year-olds enjoy the notion of 'studio' and the simulation of real-life pressures of recording, where the camera is an obvious part of the genre. Studio documentary is a format which is easy to analyse and replicate, so the fourteen-year-olds can produce programmes on such themes as 'Education Now'. By using their classroom as a reference point, they have before them concrete substance to talk about in describing the effects of education budget cuts or curriculum change. Interviewing their classmates reduces the pressure which might be created if they interviewed outsiders. On the other hand, with a more experienced group, interviewing outsiders is just the kind of increase in pressure which would stimulate their further development in oral skill.

In between the longer structure of drama and the simulated seriousness of documentary, the magazine programme is very useful for eight-year-olds because of its variety, which both holds their interest and allows for a range of genres to be held together as a single entity. It can be produced by different groups in the class working as a syndicate on such items as drama, interviews, competitions, jokes, and so on. Songs can be a useful ingredient, too, because of their powerful mnemonic quality. The model is well known from such shows as the BBC's 'Blue Peter' and Saturday morning miscellanies.

Content

Last of the three phases is the more familiar classroom process of compiling, within a small group, the content of the proposed programme, through discussion, research, negotiation, argument. Because of children's familiarity with project work, this is a stage which seems most straightforward, though it does mean that the younger children concentrate less on the context of the new medium because of their traditional concerns.

Drafting

Use of a proforma for the script layout saves a great deal of explanation and reminders of what is necessary to construct a programme. The proforma used by Weiss and Lorac (1980) contains the three essential features as columns down the page: vision; camera directions; and sound. In this layout, the camera directions need only be abbreviations (e.g., ZI for 'zoom in'); the sound is the spoken script plus shorthand notes on music background or sound effects. Vision is expressed through sketches of the major events on screen at any one time, like a cartoon strip set out down the page. Planning the visual element has a strong effect on the sequence and detail of the written script. The process does require the scriptwriters to 'see' the finished product and hence plan in depth – not the natural inclination of young children. Adults can be very self-conscious about their drawings, and generally prefer written descriptions to sketches. Some fourteen-year-olds have reached that stage of abstraction (or insecurity) but can be encouraged to use pin-men drawings as a working compromise.

For the eight-year-olds I have found that a simpler format is necessary, the complexity of three distinct but interrelated columns being too much for them to handle. So the camera directions are omitted and the other two columns amended to 'What we say' and 'What you hear' to personalise them. Young children do not readily make compromise drawings. They spend a long time on the simplest-seeming drawings, and get bogged down with detail, hence cannot produce the number of drawings needed for a longer programme sequence. They may consequently produce very little written script. Some of the more articulate will orally expand on the written text, but many will depart from it altogether, as if the writing and the speaking were completely unrelated activities. Here the rehearsal stage is a help if children practise the effect of their script and revise it as a result. The early stages then involve teaching them how to spend less time on the individual drawings so as to produce a complete overview; write a fuller script or a script which can be expanded spontaneously in performance; and revise the script in the light of what is discovered in rehearsal.

Rehearsal

The concept of rehearsal implies repetition to produce a spiral of increasing mastery of the scripted material, hence increased fluency. For younger children a first rehearsal tends to show up so many omissions and misunderstandings in their script that they need to revert quickly to the drafting stage, and time constraints begin to force severe compromises. But eight-year-olds have great difficulty in achieving a true spiral of increasing mastery. Those who are fluent tend to improvise unpredictably on each occasion. Those who are not fluent may be completely thrown by these unpredictable improvisations or make different mistakes every time. It is a particularly convoluted spiral, and time restrictions usually curtail the pursuit of perfection.

Ten-year-olds show more patience with the process of repetition, but again their ability to repeat exactly as a form of learning is limited. As a group they too tend to forget on each run through a different sequence of words or actions, making the spiral progression slow and unpredictable.

Fourteen-year-olds, though, are capable of a rehearsal stage which is, first, a test of the feasibility of their script, with minor modifications, and second, a partial learning of the sequence of its speech events. Cumulative rehearsals greatly improve their fluency in the final recorded performance.

Another possible extension of script use at this stage is to brief a 'technical crew'. It is more involving as a class project if each group acts as the camera and recording crew for one other group. This means that a copy of the performing group's script has to be available to the technical crew and be understood by them so that they can make the recording with its camera moves and cuts. This a very demanding (and potentially frustrating) use of the script, with a further range of spoken language applications, outside the scope of this chapter.

Performance

There are perhaps four ways in which a written script can be translated into a spoken performance: memorisation; reading aloud; signposting; and free range.

With eight-year-olds there are considerable limitations in their ability to handle any of these alternatives. Most are unable to remember much more than a line or two of a written script, although one solution is to make the programme piecemeal like a film, with the participants memorising short snatches of text which are recorded in sequence – the Hollywood technique for dealing with dumb blondes: 'Walk to that chalkmark over there, honey, and then say "How could you leave me, George?"' The technique fits the conventions of drama, where the script is written in short scenes which call for a change of camera position. At the other end of the scale, reading the whole script aloud to the camera is of limited use, since many have difficulty in reading with any fluency, particularly when decoding their own writing. It is possible to hold flash-cards of a sign-posting kind or even full text alongside the camera as a kind of primitive autocue. The wild-eyed gaze askance of a performer still looks very odd to the viewer, and intonation patterns can sound very unnatural, but it is perhaps the best training for future, more advanced use of written script as prompt for oral performance.

For many fourteen-year-olds the various alternatives are genuine options. Many are capable of memorising lengthy passages of script, either word for word or for their general sense. The ability to scan a text at speed for information may be well developed, allowing the use of the fully written-up text. After rehearsal, many are able to use a script for its signposts, selecting these out rather than reading the text wholesale. Some prefer to work with flash-card prompts held alongside the camera, and are able to sound and look unprompted at the same time.

Across all age groups, those who can 'free range' are an interesting phenomenon. By this term is meant those who, knowing the rough outline of the script, can improvise within it. This innate ability can be a mixed blessing, particularly among the younger groups, because a programme is usually a team effort and others in the team can be completely thrown by the wrong cue or unexpected comment, no matter how appropriate. Their talent is well placed in the link position – as presenter, host, announcer – because of their ability to improvise and keep going when all around them fails.

Evaluation

It is important to allow the class to watch the programme immediately after the recording. The recording process is always very tense, often frustrating, but the degree of concentration is usually very high in all age groups. No matter how strong the teacher's affiliation to the priority of process over product, for those involved in programme-making there is no doubt that product is the ultimate concern. The process is past; the product is here to stay. For all ages the first stage in viewing any recording is to find oneself and laugh with embarrassment, then to find one's friends and laugh even harder at their mistakes. There is no way of avoiding that reaction. With the eight-year-olds I have gone only a little further, asking them what they felt went best, and what they would like to do again leaving it as a free discussion.

The ten-year olds, more aware of broadcast standards, are rather more concerned for perfection, and so can make some discriminating judgements, often of a self-deprecating kind. The fourteen-year-olds are interested enough in the mechanical processes of making video to want to see the programme more than once, to compare it with the script and to suggest detailed changes which would have improved its quality. If they are referred back to the written record of what they intended to say and do, they can be guided towards high-level and committed critical commentary. The script is the evidence of their intent, and the recording is the measure of their success in achieving that intent.

Conclusions

The processes involved in producing a script are complex. They require considerable teacher mediation along three dimensions; the analysis of broadcast models, the direction of the writing task, and the organisation of group practical activity in the recording. In helping children develop facility in scripting, the process is one of assimilation, simplification and approximation: the assimilation of broadcast models, simplification of those models to allow for replication, and an increasingly close approximation of the models as facility increases over the years of schooling.

Scripting gives children an applied demonstration of the practical usefulness of writing in its relationship with speech, both at the macro level of organisation and at the micro level of linguistic choice. There is the opportunity to analyse success from the recording later, and hence for further guided development.

The process puts great pressure on oral ability; probably more so than any other classroom activity, excluding performance before larger audiences such as the whole school. In that respect it offers an important extension to the range of classroom audiences.

Although emphasis here has been on performance talk through scripting, the complex interactions necessary to produce the material and then record it require a great deal of task-orientated problem-solving talk, off camera – information exchange, explanation, negotiation, and so on. Participants have a great deal of shared responsibility for the success of the venture. Scripting is just a part of more extensive oral interaction involved when video is used creatively.

'Seeing ourselves as others see us' is undeniably fascinating and a universal motivator. One of the fourteen-year-olds leaving the classroom after the final lesson in a production series said to me: 'I knew what they all looked like (pointing at his friends) – but I never knew I looked like that'. Not a great philosophical statement perhaps, but if we are truly training children for life, their language performance and how others perceive it is of critical significance. A video camera offers a mirror for self-analysis and thereby a potential starting point for the self-motivated development of oral skills.

References

Bereiter, C. (1980). 'Development of Writing' in L. W. Gregg and E. R. Steinberg (eds), *Cognitive Processes in Writing*, Hillside, NJ, Lawrence Erlbaum.
DES (1984). *English from 5 to 16*, London, HMSO.
Joos, M. (1962). *The Five Clocks*, The Hague, Mouton.
Weiss, M. and Lorac, C. (1980). *Communication and Social Skills*, London, Wheaton.

PART FIVE

Language at play: children's rhymes and games

13 Children's oral culture: a transitional experience

ELIZABETH GRUGEON

> Entry into school in our society provides . . . a ritual entry into a formal apprenticeship towards adult communicative skills. But since we do not look upon the early years of language use as different but merely as a lesser form of what is to come, this ritual entry does not have the nature of its transitional experience truly evaluated. The *oral* language experience of children is looked upon as a preparation rather than a separate stage of experience, and we do not always give sufficient thought, nor recognition, to the social as well as the cognitive reorganization of experience and its processing that is necessary for the child to enter into literacy.
>
> Cook-Gumperz and Cook-Gumperz (1981)

Cross-cultural apprenticeship

Terndeep and Bukshow are bilingual eight-year-old Punjabi Hindus who go to school in Bedford. In 1987 I recorded them playing 'A sailor went to sea, sea, sea'. They played with deep concentration; the combination of word and action was particularly elaborate and required split-second timing. As the game progressed they used clapping movements which became ever more complex, but by maintaining eye-contact their timing never faltered. They were singing a version I had not heard before; their sailor also goes to India and China. As they sing 'A sailor went to India' they introduce wide encircling arm movements; as they change to 'A sailor went to China' they bow with hands clasped together. What is fascinating is that Terndeep and Bukshow are playing a game which originated from a 1930s song by Fred Astaire and Ginger Rogers, but which successive generations of children have made their own, turning it over the years into a demanding, highly-structured game which requires a constant concentration on co-ordination between the players. The climax of *their* song/rhyme is a memory-testing round-up of all the parts of the body and other items referred to.

Shabana, Gazala, Kushna, and Afsana are also members of families from the Punjab. Their version of the same song involved even more complex patterns and movement, as different parts of the body were mentioned. As the transcript of their rhyme demonstrates (see below) they develop the original song to an astonishing extent.

A sailor went to sea, sea, sea,
To see what he could see, see, see,
But all that he could see, see, see,
Was the bottom of the deep blue sea, sea, sea.
A sailor went to chop, chop, chop,
To see what he could chop, chop, chop,
But all that he could chop, chop, chop,
Was the bottom of the deep blue chop, chop, chop.
A sailor went to knee, knee, knee,
To see what he could knee, knee, knee,
But all that he could knee, knee, knee,
Was the bottom of the deep blue knee, knee, knee.
A sailor went to toe, toe, toe,
To see what he could toe, toe, toe,
But all that he could toe, toe, toe,
Was the bottom of the deep blue toe, toe, toe.
A sailor went to China
To see what he could China
But all that he could China
Was the bottom of the deep blue China.
A sailor went to India
To see what he could India
But all that he could India
Was the bottom of the deep blue India.
A sailor went to head, chop, knee, toe, China, India
To see what he could head, chop, knee, toe, China, India
And all that he could head, chop, knee, toe, China, India
Was the bottom of the deep blue head, chop, knee, toe, China, India

If I try to remember all the parts of the body mentioned, and the accompanying actions, I am severely tested. The girls, however, finish this first rhyme, stop briefly to draw breath, pick up a skipping rope, and begin a new chant, the familiar 'Roses are red, violets are blue, sugar is sweet and so are you . . . A . . . B . . . C . . . D . . . E . . . F . . . G . . .'. Shabana and Afsana turn the rope whilst Kushna jumps. They turn faster and faster until she misses a letter and Gazala jumps in. Younger children gather round the big girls, waiting for a turn. And in this way, the songs and games are passed on, always from older to younger children. The songs, chants, and skipping rhymes that these children are singing *belong* to them, they are part of their playground and street life. They cross cultures and class, both constituting and becoming the property of a particular culture which belongs exclusively to young girls.

Not all the songs that children own are intended to accompany clapping and skipping: some simply celebrate being. The children's comments about the celebratory rhymes that I recorded reveal that these also are learned through a form of apprenticeship. In July 1987, for instance, three five-year-olds who had been at school for eight weeks, sang and danced the kind of celebratory song which Stewart (1978) calls 'playing with infinity'.

Do your dances, do your dances, do your dances
Ping, pang, pong
Look at that bird right in the sky
Oh my god, it's shot my eye
With a wiggle and a woggle
And a wiggle and a wee,
Do your dances, do your dances, do your dances,
Ping, pang, pong
Look at that bird right in the sky
Oh my god it's shot my eye
(*continues for as long as it can be kept up*)

When I asked how the girls come to know this rhyme, Susan said, 'A girl came along and she taught it to us'; much as my own daughter Jessica had replied, 'Janine told me, of course', when I had asked her a similar question some years earlier. Five-year-old girls arriving on the playground, it seems, enjoy a period of apprenticeship to older girls (cf. Brice-Heath 1983)

Continuity and adaptability

I first became aware of the power of the singing game when I observed my daughter Jessica becoming involved during her very first weeks at school in the same initiation process that Shabana and her friends, and Susan and *her* friends were experiencing nearly ten years later. After less than half a term Jessica had a repertoire of ten different songs, varying in length, and with accompanying patterns of dancing or clapping. The transcriptions of her songs are set out below.

1. My friend Billy had a ten foot willy
    Showed it to the girl next door
    thought it was a snake
    and hit it with a rake
    and now it's only four foot four.

2. Batman and Robin in the batmobile
    Batman did a fart and paralysed the wheel
    the wheel wouldn't go
    the engine wouldn't start
    all because of Batman and his supersonic fart.

3. I went to the Chinese restaurant
    to buy a loaf of bread bread bread
    I saw a Chinese lady
    and this is what she said said said
    My name is elli elli
    Chickali chickali
    Chinese chopsticks
    Willy willa whisky (*or* Rom pom pooli – *Lucy's version*)
    Pow Pow Pow

4.   We break up, we break down
     We don't care if the school falls down
     No more English, no more French
     No more sitting on the old school bench
     If your teacher interferes
     Turn her up and box her ears
     If that does not serve her right
     blow her up with dynamite

     Teacher, teacher, we don't care
     We can see your underwear
     Is it black or is it white
     Oh my god it's dynamite.

5.   My mummy is a baker
     My daddy is a dustman
     Yum yummy pooey, ticker tacker tooey

     My sister is a show off
     My brother is a cowboy
     Yum yummy pooey, ticker tacker tooey
     Turn around and pow.

6.   I'm a little Dutch girl Dutch girl Dutch girl
     I'm a little Dutch girl from over the sea.

     Please will you marry me marry me marry me
     Please will you marry me from over the sea.

     No I won't marry you marry you marry you
     No I won't marry you from over the sea.

     Why won't you marry me marry me marry me
     Why won't you marry me? from over the sea.

     Because you stole my necklace necklace necklace
     Because you stole my necklace from over the sea.

     Here is your necklace necklace necklace
     Here is your necklace from over the sea.

     Now will you marry me marry me marry me
     Now will you marry me? from over the sea.

     No I won't marry you marry you marry you
     No I won't marry you from over the sea.

     Why won't you marry me marry me marry me
     Why won't you marry me? from over the sea.

     Because you stole my bracelet bracelet bracelet
     Because you stole my bracelet from over the sea.

     Here is your bracelet bracelet bracelet
     Here is your bracelet from over the sea.

     Now will you marry me marry me marry me
     Now will you marry me? from over the sea.

     No I won't marry you marry you marry you
     No I won't marry you from over the sea.

Why won't you marry me marry me marry me
Why won't you marry me? from over the sea.

Because you stole my ring ring ring
Because you stole my ring from over the sea.

Here is your ring your ring your ring
Here is your ring from over the sea.

Now will you marry me marry me marry me
Now will you marry me? from over the sea.

Yes I will marry you marry you marry you
Yes I will marry you from over the sea.

Now we're getting married married married
Now we're getting married from over the sea.

(*Repeat this format with each of the following lines:*)

Now we've got a baby, from over the sea
Now we're getting older
Now we're dying
Now we're dead
Now we're witches
Now we're ghosts
Now we're dust
Now we're nothing
Now we're in heaven heaven heaven.

7.   1 2 3 together
      Up together
      Down together
      Backs together
      Fronts together
      Up, down, in, out
      Sides together
      Bums together

8.   My boyfriend's name is Tony
      He comes from Macaroni
      With a pickle on his nose
      and ten fat toes
      and this is how my story goes
      One day as I went walking
      I heard my boyfriend talking
      with two little girls and two black curls
      and this is what she said
      she said I L-O-V-E love you
      I K-I-S-S kiss you
      I jumped in the lake and I swallowed a snake
      and came up with a belly ache.

9.   I'm Popeye the sailor man
      Full stop
      I live in a caravan
      Full stop
      When I go swimming

I kiss all the women
I'm Popeye the sailor man,
Full stop
Comma comma dash dash.

10.   When Susie was a baby
she went goo, goo, goo, goo, goo

When Susie was a sister
she went scribble scribble
scribble scribble scribble

When Susie was a schoolgirl
She went
Miss Miss
I can't do this

When Susie was a teenager
she went help help
I've lost my bra in my boyfriend's car

When Susie was a mummy
she went, cook cook cook cook cook

When Susie was a granny
she went knit knit knit knit knit
I've lost my stitch.

Jessica had not played any of these games before she started school, but quickly picked them up in play with older girls. All these games have been recorded elsewhere by collectors of children's folklore. The Opie and Opie (1985) collection confirms that the same songs were to be found in other parts of the UK at the time Jessica was singing them in Bedford, and that many of them had been around for a long time. 'I'm a little Dutch girl' and 'When Suzie was a baby' have their origins in the eighteenth and nineteenth centuries, and are two of a genre which the Opies call 'mimicry' since they mimic and rehearse a little girl's expectations of life. Popeye rhymes have their origins in the 1930s film culture, whilst Batman is a more recent TV import. The 'Chinese restaurant' can be traced to a 1920s version about a Chinese laundry where the laundry man wraps the loaf in a table cloth (Opie and Opie 1985: 465).

None of Jessica's versions is definitive, all took place in existential contexts, and all depended on the circumstances of the moment in which they occurred. Taped when she was just five, they are often immature versions, only partially understood. One, which entailed spelling the word 'love', had seemed like a secret code known only to her friends and herself. The singing games that little girls play are an evolving dynamic form; adaptable and innovative, whilst maintaining an amazing continuity.

This continuity was further illustrated when I returned to the same playground seven and eight years later, and was able to collect many of the familiar songs in slightly different versions, as well as some that I had never heard before in that playground.

1.   A ship sailed from Bombay
      Sailed in the old fashioned way
      And there sat Sharon with tears in her eyes
      And out popped Richard
      from out of the skies
      Singing darling I love you I do
      I'll always be faithful and true
      He bent down to kiss her
      But wow did he miss her
      Singing darling I love you I do

2.   My boyfriend gave me an apple
      My boyfriend gave me a pear
      My boyfriend gave me a kiss on the lips
      And threw me down the stairs
      I gave him back the apple
      I gave him back the pear
      I gave him back the kiss on the lips
      And threw him down the stairs
      I took him to a scxy film
      to watch a sexy film
      And when I wasn't looking
      he kissed a sexy girl

3.   (*Chorus: Chinese Restaurant*)
      And this is what she said
      My name is Elvis Presley
      Girls are sexy
      Sitting in the corner
      Drinking pepsi . . . ooh oh
      I'm an uptown wally
      Still be living in a Tesco trolley
      All she wants is an A team van
      And she's going out with action man

4.   When Suzie was a baby
      She went a ga ga ga
      When Susie was a toddler
      She went scribble, scribble
      When Susie was a schoolgirl
      She went miss, miss, I don't know
      where my pencil is
      When Susie was a teenager, she went
      oh ah I lost my bra
      I left my knickers in my boyfriend's car
      When Suzie was a mummy
      She went, go and shut that door
      When Suzie was a granny,

> She went knit, knit you silly old twit
> When Suzie was a skelington
> She went click clack, click, clack, click
> When Suzie was an angel
> She went go and start again

5. My mummy is a baker, yum yummy
    My sister is a show off, curly, curly
    My daddy is a dustman poo pooey
    My brother is a cowboy
    turn around and bang.

The 1986 version of 'When Suzie was a baby' seems sharper and more knowing than the earlier one, but the singers are a year and a half to two years older and more confident than Jessica was when I recorded her original version in 1979. There was also a polished performance of 'My mummy is a baker', with its elaborate dramatic actions. In addition there were two action songs which were new to me; 'A ship sailed from Bombay' – which is derived from the 1916 song 'Bless 'em all' (Opie 1986) – and 'She's an uptown wally' – which parodies a 1983 pop song. The roots of both these songs indicate that they, too, have continuity with the songs of previous generations.

A brief return to the school reassured me that all these songs continue to flourish, and that even those which we might have expected to fade away had not. For instance, despite the Opies' prediction that it would soon disappear because of its structured form, 'I'm a little Dutch girl' was still popular. The players had speeded things up by omitting the ring and bracelet episodes, and by having the couple *divorce* two verses before they die. This created a more manageable text which could still be elaborated in any way the players wished if they had time. And the 1987 version of the 'Chinese restaurant' had also become distinctly innovative. The Chinese lady no longer sang 'My name is elli, elli; chickali, chickali; Chinese chopsticks' but, with a change of tune and tempo, and with dancing to match, she proclaimed:

> My name is Dorothy
> I'm a movie star
> I've got a cute, cute figure
> And a lovely guitar
> I've got hips, walla, walla, walla
> And lips, kiss kiss kiss
> And if you want to marry me
> Just jump in my car.

The oral transmission that takes place on the playground is out of the hands of adults; it is child initiated and mediated. All we can know for a fact is that it takes place between the ages of five and nine (Opie and Opie 1985: 2) The games are well documented by collectors of children's folklore (Opie and Opie 1985; Sutton-Smith and Havedon 1959; Knapp and Knapp 1976; Webb 1985), and yet their continued existence in the face of all the other distractions of the modern world remains a wonder and a mystery. There seems to have been up till now no satisfactory explanation of the role these rhymes play in the development of children's (and especially girls') social competence.

Girls' oral culture as a means of empowerment

My first collection of singing games played by a five-year-old in her first weeks at school offers evidence of the existence of a thriving oral tradition and of a particular *girls'* culture. Jessica's songs are typical of those which accompany clapping, skipping, and ball-bouncing games wherever young girls are gathered together. I want now to examine them more closely to see what they reveal about what it is like to be young and female and growing up in a society which still, despite some significant reforms, favours males. To do this, it helps to group the songs, as I have done below.

Rude or subversive	*Clapping games and nonsense*	*Women's life experience*
My friend Billy.	I went to the Chinese restaurant.	I'm a little Dutch girl.
Batman and Robin in the Batmobile.	Hands together.	When Suzie was a baby.
I'm Popeye the sailor-man.		My mummy is a baker.
We break up, we break down.		My boyfriend's name is Tony.

The first group contains songs which Jessica and Lucy in a recent conversation considered 'really rude' and which made them feel 'really hard' when they played them. Jessica found even hearing them quite embarrassing to begin with and denied remembering Batman and Robin, 'about his supersonic . . . whatever . . .'. The word 'fart' is clearly too vulgar to use on a recording when you are eleven, but Lucy is less delicate and claims that 'everybody used to sing that'.

It is difficult to account for the transmission of these games and rhymes, and the existence of this flourishing oral culture among very young children. Transmission takes place when most of the participants are just about to 'enter into literacy' (Cook-Gumperz and Cook-Gumperz 1981) and are, it could be argued, in a state of 'residual orality' (Levine 1986). At this stage in their lives they seem particularly receptive to the highly structured and rule-governed oral activity of these highly textured rhymes which play with language in formulaic ways. All the games are emotionally charged involving elaborate dramatic routines in which the text controls the players.

I want to argue that the games are far more than interesting historical phenomena, relics of a past when there was less TV, traffic and other diversions, but are powerful agents for socialisation, enculturation and resistance. The games both transmit the social order and cultural information – particularly about gender – and provide a means to challenge it.

An interesting feature of children's folklore and oral tradition is that it is not kept alive by public performance or adult intervention. It is intensely private and there may be a danger in attempting to capture or exploit it. On the whole, most adults, parents and teachers, seem unaware of its existence: 'Oh, I don't think that sort of thing goes on any more. Isn't it supposed to be dying out?' a deputy head said recently. Their games are most successfully a secret domain.

> *Jess:*   We used to go and sort of hide away in that little dip past the, um . . .
> *Lucy:*   canteen
> *Jess:*   and we used to play in there and sing those songs and do all the clapping games.

Lucy and Jessica had their own ideas about who did and did not know about their singing games.

> *Jess:*   I reckon teachers sort of walking through the playground would have heard them and things like that but I don't, they never took much notice of them or anything, they didn't . . .
> *Lucy:*   But they weren't really in the playground much were they, I mean we thought they were all too rude.

Boys, too, were excluded. Jessica and Lucy admit that some boys joined them in singing some of the ruder songs but they comment on the absence of the boys. Their explanation is the gender specificity of the songs:

> *Lucy:*   Because no, most of them were about girls though, weren't they?
> *Jess:*   Yeah, I mean
> *Lucy:*   I mean it was, I mean you'd never catch the boys singing the one about, um, 'please will you marry me?'
> *Jess:*   No
> *Lucy:*   It's too
> *Jess:*   I mean that was just sissy, wasn't it?
> *Lucy:*   Yeah, the boys would never have been seen dead doing that.
> *Jess:*   I don't, I can't think where the boys must have been . . . I didn't even notice what the boys were doing when we were playing our games.

This emphasis suggests that there was a flourishing girls' culture on their playground. My recent visits, eight years later, confirm that this continues to be the case.

The clapping games helped Jessica in her first weeks at school; she was able to participate in non-threatening group interaction, to play with language, to rehearse adult roles, to investigate and challenge social and sexual aspects of the world and to become involved in peer-group relationships; the gender specificity of the games introduced her to a girls' culture.

The games can also be seen as discursive practices in which children can become powerful (Walkerdine 1981). The five-year-old girl is particularly aware of her physical weakness and powerlessness in the face of older children and of boys in particular. Rhymes like 'My friend Billy', provide ammunition for resistance to the relations of power in the playground and are the means by which they may seize power in discourse. Such rhymes can render boys powerless and vulnerable: 'I gave him back the kiss on the lips and threw him down the stairs'. Taboo rhymes are not childish acts of rebellion but tools for resistance and criticism. In Jessica's repertoire of ten songs, three enable her to seize power by making boys, teachers and the school the powerless objects of their discourse.

This kind of play is also a vital means to socialisation. The potentially traumatic situation of arriving at school without friends can be alleviated by finding a friend with whom it is possible to build a system of shared meanings and understanding, so that the world becomes a more predictable place (Davies 1982).

Stewart (1978) suggests that from a very early age rhymes and games of this kind give children access to the means to challenge particular forms of discourse. In singing these songs, little girls are not simply acquiescing in the stereotypes but learning to challenge and question them. To use a Hallidayan metaphor (Halliday 1978: 186) the playground can be seen as the environmental determinant of the texts which have taken place on it and these texts or linguistic structures are a realisation of the social structure, capable not only of transmitting the social order but also of maintaining and even modifying it.

Shaping text to shape experience

At a period in their lives when most of them can neither read nor write, children on the playground are playing with literary forms and highly textured oral discourse. The language of the games is not language to get things done but language which seems to have no purpose outside itself, dominating the situation which it creates and shapes.

To begin to understand what is going on here, it helps to look at some of the formal features of the texts which seem to control the players so effectively. The co-occurrence of so many items which seem to echo and repeat each other is typical of what Halliday calls 'collocational cohesion'; items from the everyday world rub shoulders with deeper psychic fantasy, snakes, witches and ghosts alongside bakers, dustmen, schools and knitting. Long cohesive chains are built up out of lexical relations of different kinds; these do not have to depend on anything more than their association with each other. More complex semantic structures are the formulaic ones of narrative, 'and this is what she said', 'and this is how my story goes'. A quick look at 'Batman and Robin' illustrates the amount of lexical cohesion even in a short text.

'*Batman and Robin* in the *bat*mobile': Batman and Robin are cohesive because of their proximity in the discourse, and their partnership in the fiction beyond the text itself, *bat*mobile echoes *Bat*man, the reiteration of Batman (three times) *fart* (twice), *go* and *start* as near synonyms, *start* rhyming with *fart*, *wheel and engine* relating both by anaphoric reference and collocation to the batmobile and *go* and *start*, all combine to give this rhyme its particular quality of text, its particular 'texture'. Compare this with 'Jennifer Went to School' (McCullagh 1983). This was the complete text of one of the readers Jessica's class was using in summer 1979 and the class I recorded in 1986 were also using. It seems to have less cohesion and a much less complex texture than any of the singing games in Jessica's collection:

Jennifer got up
Jennifer went out
Jennifer got on the bus
Jennifer in school
Jennifer went home on the bus
Jennifer and John
Grandmother and
Grandfather
Jennifer went to bed.

In Jessica's repertoire there are a large number of linked items; one collocational chain concerns gender differences. The role relationships they portray are those of school and family. The most prominent cohesive element, accounting for the largest number of lexical items, derives from a constant testing and questioning of sexuality and the challenging of sex roles; this results in an impressive chain of collocational cohesion: willy, snake, curls, belly ache, show-off, boyfriend, underwear, fart, love, kiss, ring, necklace, bracelet, marriage, teenager, women, baby.

This list is reminiscent of Sylvia Ashton-Warner's (1980: 33) 'key vocabulary' and her belief that we should introduce children to the written word using the children's own words, what she calls 'the captions of dynamic life, words that are already part of the child's being'. The strongest cohesive links in the text of the singing games fall into this category, 'love', 'kiss', 'mummy', 'daddy', 'granny', 'brother', 'sister', 'baby', 'witches', 'ghost', 'snakes', 'dying', 'heaven', 'nothing', 'dust', 'fart', 'willy', 'underwear', 'supersonic', 'dynamite', 'wheel', 'engine', 'serve her right', 'blow her up', 'show-off', 'fall down', 'paralysed', 'don't care', 'jumped', 'swallowed', 'interfere', 'box her ears', these are *all* 'captions of dynamic life' and most of them not the adult-mediated vocabulary of the early reading texts children will be meeting in the classroom.

Speech play as a specialised genre has been neglected despite the fact that it is, as Hymes (1968) has shown, normal everyday interaction in all societies. Sanches and Kirshenblatt-Gimblett (1976) trace the development of children's speech play from the well-documented interest in playing with sounds (Weir 1962; Bruner 1975; and Halliday 1975), to playing with meaning. They are critical of the absence of theoretical attention to this area of children's language: 'The analysis of speech play could benefit from the notion of play as a means of enculturation, of games as buffered models of power within which the child can acquire some of the basic performances required by the adult culture.' Looking at children's verbal play in relation to their developing language, they find that children's speech-play forms are different from adult verbal art. There are major formal differences, the first being that children's syntagmatic development is less advanced – they rely on short-term memory and phonological structures. The five to seven age group characteristically uses phonologically determined features, like 'ping, pang, pong', 'eli eli chickali chickali', 'ticker tacker tooey' and 'rom pom pooli', whereas older children drop this morphophonological patterning of sequences which have no grammatical function and lexemes with no semantic reference but which are highly rhythmic, for more syntactically and semantically complex play with social roles. Jessica's rhymes have characteristically short simple verses, often of less than five lines and seventy words. They share common features: a four stress metrical unit, frequent use of rhyming couplets, simple stanzaic structure, use of internal rhyme and the use of devices like repetition and concatenation which enable the players to extend the production, as in 'I'm a little Dutch girl', way beyond their normal syntagmatic span. Formulaic devices like, 'and this is what she said' or 'turn around and pow' typically enable them to continue or to stop at will.

Children's ordinary discourse does not display the same degree of disciplined, formal patterning, control of rhythm, metre, rhyme, stanzaic forms, metaphor, simile, syntactic repetition and morphophonological patterns. These are, however, all features of effective adult oral discourse and writing, and children's speech play would therefore seem to be vital to the acquisition of literacy.

The language of resistance and protest

Garvey (1977: 7) suggests that this kind of speech play is ritualisation. Her definition of ritualistic play accounts for some of the striking and inexplicable features of the singing games. When play is performed in a ritualised manner, it involves controlled rhythmic repetition, and is characterised by a precise regulation of behaviour which involves intonation, verbal rhymes, extreme regularity of exchange and split-second timing: all features of the hand-clapping games. This kind of ritual is not only characteristic of children's play but of particular kinds of adult behaviour; it constitutes a formative principle in magical incantations and spells, religious chants, cheers for football teams, political rallies, riots, in fact in many events where members of a group must be synchronised to express solidarity.

The language generated by ritual play could also be classified as 'antilanguage', the language a subculture uses to set itself apart from the established society by creating an alternative reality (Halliday 1978: 177). It can be the language of literature and at the same time the language of social resistance and protest. The singing game can be explained as verbal art, as highly textured discourse, as antilanguage, as a language of resistance, as constitutive of a subculture and as language which transmits the beliefs of society in particular ways.

Orality to literacy

But none of this, on its own, accounts for the continued existence of these games as an oral tradition. Another perspective might see them as part of children's transition from a predominantly oral to a written culture. It is easy to overlook or underrate that period in children's lives, when they are not fully literate and thus operate more in an oral than a literate environment. Walter Ong's (1982) study of the oral character of language and the primacy of oral speech even in our high-technology, literate Western culture, throws light on a period of transition which all children have to negotiate, as they move from the purely oral experience of very early childhood into the literate society outside the home.

Up to the point at which they start school most children rely heavily on oral signals for making sense of their experience; school introduces an element of discontinuity with the practices of their everyday life. 'The *oral* language experience of children is looked upon as a preparation rather than a separate stage of experience, and we do not always give it sufficient thought, nor recognition of experience and its processing that is necessary for the child to enter into literacy' (Cook-Gumperz and Cook-Gumperz 1981: 98).

At this stage for Jessica and her friends all their words were primarily oral, they had no texts for their rhymes but relied entirely on memory; on the playground they were firmly in an oral culture, or in what Levine (1986) would call a state of 'residual orality'. Orality requires a different cognitive organisation of experience from literacy (Ong 1982; Luria 1978). If there are no written texts then the material must be organised for easy recall, 'In a primary oral culture, you have to do your thinking in mnemonic patterns, shaped for ready oral recurrence' (Ong 1982). Thus thought relies on rhythm and pattern, repetition and antithesis, alliteration and assonance in material which is 'patterned for retention and ready recall' (Ong 1982: 34). All these are features of the speech play of children on the playground. One aspect of this residual orality which may well be overlooked or underestimated is the verbal memory skill which it entails. Jessica's repertoire is impressive for the sheer number and range of items she has committed to memory.

As important as the mnemonic devices, though, are 'the existential contexts which surround oral discourse'. On the playground, groups of familiar friends generate and support performance, which itself relies heavily on gestures, vocal inflection and facial expression. Oral memory depends on a high somatic component; hand and body activity characteristically accompany it. The oral lore of the playground is performance and it is inseparable from the movement which both accompanies and responds to it: hand clapping, skipping, dancing. All Jessica's rhymes entailed action of varying degrees of complexity, 'we used to do a sort of dance'. The oral word does not exist in a simply verbal context, as the written word does, but is part of an existential situation which engages the body.

Orality cannot be a permanent state in any culture but there is a complex and variable interpenetration of orality and literacy. Oral transmission is not a remnant of the past, a series of isolated survivals but, as we can see on the playground, a powerful reminder of 'the resilience of distinctively oral modes in the heart of societies with centuries of familiarity with paper and print' (Levine 1986: 189). Children entering school at five, particularly those from different cultural backgrounds (Scollon and Scollon 1981) will often be affected by a residual orality, a particular mindset which will predispose them to adopt oral rather than literate strategies in the classroom. On the playground, with their peers, socialisation will continue to be dominated by an oral tradition which is likely to be a continuation of the orality of their homes; there may be a marked discontinuity with the demands of the school.

References

Ashton-Warner, Sylvia (1980). *Teacher*, London, Virago.

Brice-Heath, Shirley (1983) *Ways with Words: Language, Life and Work in Communities and Classrooms*, Cambridge, Cambridge University Press.

Bruner, J. S. (1975). 'The Ontogenesis of Speech Acts', *Journal of Child Language*, vol. 2, pp. 1–19.

Cook-Gumperz, Jenny and Cook-Gumperz, John (1981) 'From Oral to Written Culture: The Transition to Literacy' in Marcia Farr Whiteman (ed.), *Writing: the Nature, Development and Teaching of Written Communication. Vol. 1: Variation in Writing*, Hillsdale, NJ, Erlbaum.

Davies, Bronwyn (1982). *Life in the Classroom and Playground. The Accounts of Primary School Children*, London, Routledge and Kegan Paul.

Garvey, Catherine (1977) *Play*, London, Fontana.

Grugeon, E. A. (1986). 'The Singing Game: a Five-year-old's Preliterate and Preliterary Competence', unpublished MA dissertation, London University Institute of Education.

Halliday, M. A. K. (1978). *Language as a Social Semiotic*, London, Edward Arnold.

Halliday, M. A. K. (1975). *Learning How to Mean: Explorations in the Development of Language*, London, Edward Arnold.

Hymes, D. (1968). 'Linguistic Problems in Defining the Concept of One Tribe' in J. Helm (ed.), *Proceedings of the 1967 Spring Meeting of the American Ethnological Society*, Washington, University of Washington Press.

Knapp, Mary and Knapp, Herbert (1976) *One Potato, Two Potato: The Folklore of American Children*, New York, Norton.

Levine, Kenneth (1986). *The Social Context of Literacy*, London, Routledge and Kegan Paul.

Luria, A. R. (1978). *The Selected Writings of A. R. Luria*, New York, M. E. Sharpe.

McCullagh, S. (1983). 'Jennifer went to school', Book 12 in *One Two Three and Away*, London, Collins.

Ong, W. (1982) *Orality and Literacy: the Technologizing of the Word*, London, Methuen.

Opie, I. (1986). Private communication.

Opie, I. and Opie, P. (1985). *The Singing Game*, Oxford, Oxford University Press.

Sanches, M. & Kirshenblatt-Gimblett, B. (1976). 'Children's Traditional Speech Play and Child Language' in Barbara Kirshenblatt-Gimblett (ed.), *Speech Play: Research and Resources for the Study of Linguistic Creativity*, Pennsylvania, University of Pennsylvania Press, pp. 65–110.

Scollon, Ron and Scollon, Suzanne, B. K. (1981). *Narrative, Literacy and Face in Interethnic Communication*, Norwood, NJ, Ablex.

Stewart, Susan (1978). *Nonsense. Aspects of Intertextuality in Folklore and Literature*, Baltimore, Md, Johns Hopkins University Press.

Sutton-Smith, B. and Havedon, E. (1959). *The Games of New Zealand Children*, Chichester, Wiley.

Walkerdine, V. (1981). 'Sex, power and pedagogy', *Screen Education*, no. 38.

Webb, Father Damian (1985). *Children's Singing Games*, Saydisc Records.

Weir, Ruth (1962). *Language in the Crib*, The Hague, Mouton.

14 Counting out: form and function of children's counting-out rhymes

WILLIE VAN PEER

The emergence of separate oral cultures for adults and children

Since the eighteenth century the oral cultures of adults and children have been different. Up to that time children shared with adults the same games, the same toys, and the same stories. When a child knew a rhyme, it would almost certainly have heard it from an adult, in the company of other adults, and its meaning would have been located in the realm of the adult world. With the dawn of the Age of Enlightenment, however, the old unity between the adult's and the child's oral cultures was gradually broken down, and an oral culture which genuinely belonged to the child alone began to emerge. The present-day effects of this evolution are apparent enough; we think twice about exposing children to explicit conversations on certain taboo topics, and adults may not engage in skipping or counting-out rhymes, or in the fantasy games that most children spontaneously become involved in, without feeling a degree of self-consciousness. The changing view of childhood, which has led to the development of major differences between the child's and the adult's oral culture, is more complicated than it at first seems, simply because it is not possible to *completely* insulate the two cultures from each other. Patterns of domestic life and of child-rearing make it impossible to maintain an absolute compartmentalisation of either the adult's or of the child's oral world. What we have instead is a *dialectic of interaction*, in which two cultural worlds exist apart from each other, but simultaneously sustain one another. The dialectical relations between the two cultures establish the concrete forms of oracy that both groups may become involved in. In this chapter, the indirect interaction between the oral culture of the adult and that of the child will be studied with reference to one text type, the 'counting-out' rhyme.

The counting-out rhyme as a game in its own right

As the name suggests, counting-out rhymes (or dipping rhymes, as they are usually called by children themselves) display a relationship between the formal,

i.e. rhyming, and functional, i.e. counting, characteristics. The formal characteristics are immediately apparent; the rhymes are relatively short (usually not more
than about forty words), demonstrate rather strong versification, metrical pattern,
and end-rhymes, and often use alliteration and assonance. These 'literary'
devices occur in the rhymes in considerable variety and sophistication, witnessing
to the spontaneity and creativity of their inventors. The functional qualities reveal
themselves in the particular oral interactions in which they are embedded,
interactions in which both the verbal and the non-verbal components are highly
standardised. Indeed a dipping rhyme will be declared invalid by the other
children if the 'dipper' does not meet the *exact* requirements of the ritual and use
the *exact* wording of the text. Through such highly ritualised counting-out rhymes
children appoint a participant to a special role, a role which is sometimes desired
but which can also be disliked. Counting-out rhymes are used as a *decision
procedure*, and are therefore preliminary to a game.

The decision-making function of the counting-out rhyme will be described in
some detail below, but before moving on to that description, I must say something
about the other major function of the rhyme. To assume that the *sole* function of
the rhymes is a decision-making one is to suppose that an unwieldy procedure has
been universally adopted for getting done something socially important, and that
would not fit with what we know about the way language functions for other
transactional purposes. Children engage in the same dipping rhyme over and
over again, without any apparent sign of becoming bored – they may, on the
contrary, be seen to enjoy the performance; we can be pretty certain, therefore,
that they take part in the ritual for the pure delight of doing so. Dipping rhymes
may thus be said to form a kind of *game* in themselves. Their dual quality, as a
decision procedure and as a game to be enjoyed for its own sake, lies at the heart
of the way in which they function in children's oral culture.

In so far as dipping represents a game in its own right, the central feeling that it
allows children to experience is 'delight'. The word 'delight' is something of a
blanket term, however, used to include various forms of participation that enter
consciousness as pleasurable, agreeable, or gratifying experiences. I will, therefore, consider briefly what constitutes delight in this case. First, there is the highly
patterned structure of the text and the ritualised procedure of execution. As
with certain 'literary' constructs which give delight, rhyme, rhythm and metre
all contribute to the *musical qualities* of the text and may be enjoyed for
their own sake. (For a full account of the underlying psychological mechanisms of
these forms of delight, see Davies 1978). Second, there is an element of *suspense*
and potential *relief* involved. Each child participating realises that something is at
stake, that he or she will be allocated either a desired or a disliked role in the game
that is to follow. He or she knows that to be facing some kind of 'danger',
although while also being aware that there is a possibility of escaping the 'danger'.
This element of *contest* lies at the heart of play is a cultural phenomenon
(Huizinga 1955). And in this case, unlike many others in which the powerful are
able to minimise the effects upon themselves at the expense of the less powerful,

all participants face an equal amount of potential danger. Because the 'danger' is equally distributed, each child is able to face bravely the prospect of being counted out (or not, as the case may be). At the same time, the suspense remains high enough for some feelings of anxiety to be retained beneath the brave face, so that when a child is eventually counted out he or she experiences either relief or disappointment, according to the rules of the ritual.

Dipping rhymes and social power

The provision of delight, anchored in the musical qualities of the language, the ritual nature of the procedure, and the suspense and relief experienced, is not the only function of the dipping rhyme. As I mentioned earlier, counting-out rhymes also have an important social function because of their potential for organising power relations within the group. The essential function of the dipping rhyme is the division of roles, more specifically the assignment of one (dis)preferred role in a game to be played instantly. At first sight there appear to be more compelling ways of assigning roles within a group; a child may dominate by exerting physical force, for instance. Interestingly, however, physical force is used relatively rarely in assigning roles within a group. This is not to say that physical force is not in some cases resorted to when peers are making decisions about who should do what; the significant thing is that physical force is not the only means of reaching decisions, nor even the most common. Game-like approaches are far more commonly adopted: approaches in which alertness, skill, deception, and other forms of wit play a prominent role. And there are good reasons why counting-out rhymes are *regularly* employed for this purpose. The continual and undiscriminating use of physical domination or of ordeals which rely upon mental or bodily agility would be counter-productive, resulting in the same children – the younger, less-skilled, less-alert ones – always being appointed to the disliked roles. Two further serious problems would arise if this was to happen. First, since these children are the ones endowed with less physical strength, it is unlikely that they will outsmart the other children in any game dependent upon physical prowess. Consequently, any challenge inherent in the game will be somewhat diminished, and the game might deteriorate to a point where it was no longer worth playing. Second, since games are voluntarily engaged in, children might decline to take part if they found that they were having to play the disliked role all the time, which would leave the others either unable to start the game at all or having to adopt the disliked roles themselves.

The social problem which arises when a group has to choose someone to take on an unpleasant role is easy enough to formulate: how to appoint someone to the role in such a way that the ensuing game can be played without hurting anyone's feelings. It is my contention that counting-out rhymes present one solution, and apparently a rather successful one. The solution to how to organise the forthcoming game presents itself in the form of a prior game, one which is dependent upon the use of a formulaic oral text presented in a ritualistic manner – the counting-out rhyme. More particularly, the efficiency of the counting-out rhyme as a social organising device may be ascribed to the fact that it introduces something which other possible procedures do not offer, namely the element of *chance*. The outcome of a counting ritual is dependent upon a number of *ad hoc* factors; among them, the point in the circle at which counting starts, the length of the rhyme, and the ratio of counts versus syllables. This means that the 'dipper' is not in a position to predict on whom the count may eventually fall.

Most children are quick to realise, however, that if they carry out some swift calculations before using a short rhyme, they can turn the count to their own advantage. The shorter the rhyme is, the easier it becomes to manipulate its outcome by working out at which person in the circle one has to begin counting in order to arrive at a given point. Two rhymes, one Flemish and the other French are of this kind:

> Olleke bolleke
> Riebesolleke
> Olleke bolleke
> Knol

> Une, mine, mane, mo
> Une, fine, fane, fo
> Maticaire et matico
> Mets ta main derrière
> ton dos

If all dipping rhymes were as open to manipulation as the two just quoted, the credibility of the dipping rhyme as a fair procedure would be seriously undermined. Hence, severe precautions bearing on the structure of the text and its interactive use are taken. A great number of rhymes, for instance, provide an additional element of chance.

> Old Mother Ink
> Fell down the sink
> How many miles did she fall?
> – *Three* –
> One, two, three.

> Charlie Chaplin
> Sat on a pin
> How many inches did it go in?
> – *Four* –
> One, two, three, four.

> Dic-dic-tation
> Corporation,
> How many buses
> Are in the station?
> – *Five* –
> One, two, three, four, five.

Here the outcome is dependent upon the answer given by one of the participants to a question posed by the dipper, who is therefore not able to manipulate the outcome. However, in this situation the opposite 'danger' becomes operative; the participant providing the answer is now able to manipulate the outcome of the counting out. The next examples show how further measures are introduced to prevent this from happening.

> As I went down the Icky Picky Lane,
> I met some Icky Picky people.
> What colour were they dressed in,
> Red, white, or blue?
> – Red –
> R-E-D spells red.
> And that's as fair as fair can be
> That you are not to be 'it'.

> My mother and your mother
> Were hanging out the clothes.
> My mother gave your mother
> A punch upon the nose.
> What colour was the blood?
> Shut your eyes and think.
> – Blue –
> B-L-U-E spells blue
> And out you go
> With a jolly good clout
> Upon your big nose.

> Eachie, peachie, pear, plum,
> When does your birthday come?
> – Fourteenth of December –
> 1,2,3,4,5,6,7,8,9,10,11,12,13,14,
> D-E-C-E-M-B-E-R. You are out.

In these rhymes, before proceeding with the count the dipper spells out the letters of the number or word offered by another participant. This means that in many cases the passage between the answer and the end of the rhyme is as long as some other rhymes are by themselves. The last example reveals just how far such precautions against manipulation can go; nobody could reasonably dispute the fairness of the outcome in such a case.

The amount of work done to build in precautions is even more evident if we consider the problem who will do the counting out itself. Observation of children reveals that there is no fixed procedure. Occasionally one may see children resorting to counting out to see who is to do the 'real' counting out, but this is not standard practice. Usually it is quite simply the elder or the more dominant children in the group who automatically take on the role of dipper. At that stage, before the 'serious' business takes place, alertness, cunning, and physical strength are clearly accepted means of achieving a decision. (Although I have on one or two occasions observed that a younger child has been given a turn to do the counting out, for what appear to be 'diplomatic' reasons, e.g., to stop him or her crying. Such reasonable forms of turn-allocation are clear exceptions to the pattern, however, and seem to belong in the realm of immediate *tactics* rather than overall *strategies*.)

Children's oral culture and socialisation

Returning now to the *general* issue of the role played by counting-out rhymes in children's oral culture, the main points may be summarised as follows. The particular form of the counting-out text, and the interactive pattern in which it is embedded, provide the participants in the ritual both with feelings of delight and of social solidarity. Their *basic* function is of an altogether different nature, though. They primarily serve the purpose of role assignment preceding a game. Since the role concerned has specific (dis)advantages attached to it, it may be either sought or avoided. The game situation does not allow, however, for a straightforward settling of any dispute by means of physical domination or threat; instead the rhymes employ the element of chance as a way of avoiding conflict. This solution is not perfect, in that it still allows some degree of manipulation by the quicker-witted. Further precautions of all sorts have to be incorporated in order to ensure that 'pure' chance may operate. Even this does not entirely prevent some children from attempting to use either their physical or their mental superiority in an attempt to bring about an outcome more satisfactory to them than to the others, however, so can we really say that the counting-out 'game' successfully resolves the power struggle? To answer that question we must reconsider the relationship between children's oral culture and that of society at large, which we mentioned briefly at the beginning of this chapter.

It was suggested earlier that the discourse children engage in is in a number of key ways isolated from adult discourse, whilst this does not prevent these discourses from interpenetrating in a dialectical way. In the application of counting-out rhymes it would appear that children have developed their own solutions without any help from adults and in a way that must be acknowledged as undoubtedly creative. At this juncture it should be pointed out that the solutions children work out creatively are to some extent dependent on structural aspects of society at large. For instance, in a society where it is common for people to recognise the legitimacy of power achieved through luck, children may develop games in which chance plays such an important part. In addition, in modern democratic societies power resides in highly complex institutions whose concerns may or may not coincide with individuals' personal interests, but which in any case *present* themselves *as if* they were detached from the interests of those individuals. This is exactly what we find in the counting-out rituals; power is rejected unless it is operating irrespective of the interests of the person who distributes its consequences. The third way in which children's culture is related to the adults' grows out of the second, for at the same time as particular problems of power distribution are solved by the ritual working-out of asymmetry in a given interaction, the general asymmetries which attach to individuals because of, say, their superior physical strength persist outside of the particular situation. In this sense the child's world differs little from the adult's, where even though one situation of inequality may be solved through ritual interaction, social institutions in general remain open to manipulation by those who possess some form of fortuitous power.

Conclusion

The apparent independence of children's oral culture from the world in which grown-ups live would seem to be an illusion. In a very indirect and complex way, basic structural characteristics of society are incorporated in it, albeit in a transformed way. Children's oral culture, even in what may be viewed as trivial genres such as counting-out rhymes, reproduces power relations and the prevailing methods of coping with these. In this sense it possesses a strong ideological undercurrent in the sense indicated by Thompson (1984: 130–1). Note that this characteristic of children's games as a potential for cultural indoctrination has been observed before in cultures of a different kind (see Fortes 1976).

This analysis may – if it is correct – throw light on other problem areas as well. First of all, it answers the question why such forms thrive in children's culture – apparently because they are part and parcel of the structural elements of society *in general*, from which even a Rousseau-like isolation within a specialised children's oral culture cannot save them. That says something also about the fundamental relationships between the concepts of childhood and the structural conditions of society as a whole. While pedagogues would like to believe there to be an area of childhood dissociated in some way or other from the everyday concerns of the adult world, the present analysis would seem to demonstrate the unlikeliness of a total separation of the two realms of discourse. Their dialectical relationship should therefore not be denied but analysed critically, and the concrete forms of interpenetration to which this relationship gives rise should be studied. Finally, since counting-out rhymes are a *literary* type of text, the analysis says something about the relationship between literature and society. The literary texts children employ in this case allow possibilities for dealing with forms of social power, for learning about structural modes of membership allocation to either dominant or subordinate positions, i.e. mechanisms of exclusion, while at the same time enhancing group cohesion and offering the possibility of experiencing delight. It thus emerges from the present analysis that the forms and functions of children's oral culture are far from trivial. They are a powerful means both to explore and to constitute a cultural world which, although partly separated from adult society, nevertheless cannot but transform its structural characteristics and, hence, act as a socialisation device invented, paradoxically enough, by children themselves. As such, children's experiences in *their* world form the basis on which the reproduction of knowledge and feeling, of ideology and of power relations, is founded.

Methodological note

Other, more sophisticated methods, such as accurate transcriptions made from video-taped recordings would yield data which are more detailed and methodologically more reliable. However, for our present purposes, natural observations, matched to those of other observers, e.g., the verbatim descriptions provided by Opie and Opie (1957; 1959; 1969) allow for sufficient analytical scope and do not invalidate generalisations.

References

Davies, J. B. (1978). *The Psychology of Music*, London, Hutchinson.

Fortes, M. (1976). 'Social and Psychological Aspects of Education in Taleland' in J. S. Bruner *et al.*, *Play. Its Role in Development and Evolution*, Harmondsworth, Penguin, pp. 474–483.

Huizinga, J. (1955). *Homo Ludens: A Study of the Play Element in Culture*, Boston, The Beacon Press.

Opie, I. and Opie, P. (1957). 'Nursery Rhymes' in W. Targ (ed.), *Bibliophile in the Nursery*, Cleveland, The World Publishing Company.

Opie, I. and Opie, P. (1959). *The Lore and Language of Schoolchildren*, Oxford, Oxford University Press.

Opie, I. and Opie, P. (1969). *Children's Games in Street and Playground*, Oxford, Oxford University Press.

Thompson, J. B. (1984). *Studies in the Theory of Ideology*, Cambridge, Polity Press.

Name index

Oracy Matters

Oracy concerns competence in talking and listening. But it concerns far more than that, for it is a condition of learning, a state of being in which the whole school should operate. This recognition of the wider role of oracy means that there is now a new tide flowing, not just in an individual subject area, but throughout the curriculum, recognized by the establishment of the National Oracy Project.

The International Convention at the University of East Anglia in 1987 was the first major conference to take oracy as its theme, and the papers selected from it which are included in the book include the latest work of some of the leading scholars and teachers in the field. It is edited by three members of the UEA School of Education which is recognized as the foremost centre for oracy studies in the UK.

The Editors

Margaret MacLure is Lecturer in Education at UEA, with experience of working on major language projects such as the Bristol longitudinal study and the APU tests of oracy. Dr MacLure is currently working with Terry Phillips on the 'Becoming Argumentative' project at UEA. She is a Steering Committee member of the National Oracy Project.

Terry Phillips is Lecturer in Education at UEA. He is particularly concerned with the oracy and literacy of learners in the middle years of schooling upon which he has published. He is currently working with Margaret MacLure on the 'Becoming Argumentative' project at UEA.

Andrew Wilkinson is Professor of Education at UEA. He directed the team which originally produced the concept and term of oracy. He is currently Chairman of the National Oracy Project.

The Contributors

Douglas Barnes, Deborah Berrill, Gen Ling Chang, Jacqui Cousins, John Dixon, Derek Edwards, Roger Fowler, Graham Frater, Elizabeth Grugeon, David Halligan, Martin Hughes, Margaret MacLure, Janet Maybin, Neil Mercer, Stephen Parker, Willi van Peer, Terry Phillips, Harold Rosen, Gordon Wells, Andrew Wilkinson.

Open University Press

ISBN 0 335 15855 2